Dance Spaces:

Practices of Movement

Dance Spaces:

Practices of Movement

UNIVERSITY PRESS OF SOUTHERN DENMARK · 2012

Dance Spaces:
Practices of Movement
© The authors and University Press of Southern Denmark 2012
Printed by Narayana Press
Cover Design by Donald Jensen
ISBN 978 87 7674 689 6

Printed with grantly support from:

Nordic Culture Fund

The Ministry of Culture
Committee on Sports Research

University Press of Southern Denmark
Campusvej 55
DK-5230 Odense M
Phone: +45 6615 7999
Fax: +45 6615 8126
www.universitypress.dk

Distribution in the United States and Canada:
International Specialized Book Services
5804 NE Hassalo Street
Portland, OR 97213-3644 USA
www.isbs.com

Distribution in the United Kingdom:
Gazelle
White Cross Mills
Hightown
Lancaster
LA1 4 XS
U.K.
www.gazellebooks.co.uk

CONTENTS

SPACE AND ARTISTIC PRACTICE

SPACE AND EMBODIED COMPETENCE

ACKNOWLEDGMENTS

The initiative to publish this book originated in the contributions to the 10th conference of the Nordic Forum of Dance research (NOFOD), which focused on space as a theme in dance research. However, in many ways the initiative for the book is also grounded in our work in the NOFOD board, which we began about eight years ago. In this sense, the theme of the book and, not least, our editorial collaboration, is based on the interesting discussions, exchanges of ideas and mutual reflections on the challenges of describing and analyzing different practices of dance, which we have shared formally and informally during the NOFOD board meetings. As the very first thing, we therefore thank the NOFOD board, its members and close collaborators.

We are especially thankful to all the authors who have contributed to this publication for helping to make the editorial process run smooth. We are also very grateful to the twelve reviewers who provided the volume with academic rigor through their constructive and critical commentary during the processes of the double blind review.

We would also like to thank the research unit and institutions we are part of in our daily work, 'Movement, Sport and Society' at The Institute of Sports Science and Biomechanics, University of Southern Denmark; and the Performing Arts Research Centre of the Theatre Academy, Helsinki. They have supported our work in NOFOD as well as our editorial work related to this anthology.

Finally, we wish to acknowledge the financial support from 'The Nordic Culture Fund' and 'The Ministry of Culture Committee on Sports Research' for making this publication possible.

Susanne and Leena

INTRODUCTION

Susanne Ravn and Leena Rouhiainen

The articles presented in the anthology *Dance Spaces: Practices of Movement* originate from selected and extensively revised contributions for the 10th international NOFOD conference proceedings. Like the conference titled Spacing Dance(s) – Dancing Space(s), the anthology is strongly motivated by the fact that space continues to be explored and debated within dance practices and studies as well as the human sciences more generally. Yet, there are still only few writings offering a contemporary view on how the relation between movement and space can be tied to the descriptions and analyses of actual movement practice. *Dance Spaces: Practices of Movement* takes as its point of departure diverse conventions of and perspectives on practices and discourses in dance. Already owing to its embodied nature, dance is essentially spatial. It both forms, produces, and takes place in space. Following influential feminist philosopher and cultural theorist Elizabeth Grosz, many researchers agree that "space does not become space by its being the space of movement; rather, it becomes space through movement, and as such, it acquires specific properties from the subject's constitutive functioning in it" (Grosz 1995, 92). This anthology aims to link conceptual descriptions that concern space *as* process and *in* process to the undertakings of specific movement practices in dance. In the following paragraphs, we would like to offer a few salient analytical points on the manner in which space can be understood to be involved in and to impact the practices of dance.

Philosopher Henri Lefebvre identifies three constitutive elements of social space: spatial practice or perceived space, representations of space or conceived space and representational or lived space. The first relates to the somewhat cohesive interactional environments individuals and communities operate in. The second is about the conceived meanings and understandings through which developers and designers produce space. The third in turn is connected to the experience with related images and symbols. It is associated with how space is challenged, reinforced and changed through its use by subjects (Lefebvre 1974/1991, 38-40). While the interrelationships of these elements are complex, Lefebvre points out that all the different kinds of spaces involve each other. Thus, spatial localisations cannot be taken for granted. He writes: "The heart as *lived* is strangely different from the heart as *thought* and *perceived*" (Lefebvre 1974/1991, 40).The quotation depicts the complex location that the bodily organ of the heart, like any other subject matter, can assume. Nonetheless, Lefebvre underlines that spatial practice cannot be understood without the use of the body and that different spatial aspects should be interconnected in such a manner that a subject may move from one to another without confusion (Lefebvre 1974/1991, 40). At the same time, one needs to be aware, as Friedman and van Ingen (2011, 89) emphaise that the way different social practices interlock these elements is important to "the process of forming and transforming the social relations of power". Indeed, despite implying that spatial analysis is necessary for understanding how the body impacts and is impacted by the environment, neither Lefebvre nor Friedman and van Ingen exemplify how the three constitutive elements pervade each other in the actual movement practices of subjects and communities. As we point out below, in dance studies a step in this direction has already been taken. Additionally, by addressing the intricacies of the spatial nature of dance performance, the articles presented in this anthology continue to address this problem and offer some further avenues to solving it.

Geographers Mike Crang and Nigel Thrift point out that generally across the academic disciplines "space is a representational strategy" (Crang and Thrift 2000, 1). In the descriptions of bodily practices that relate to self and other, they indicate that the concept of space often becomes bound up with "binaries of inside versus outside and present versus absent" (ibid., 7). In her book *Dance, Space and Subjectivity* (2001), dance scholar Valerie Briginshaw demonstrates how different (video-graphed) dance pieces actively confront and question such binaries. Her analyses highlight that the presented dance pieces both co-constitute the subject and space through movement and reveal the nature of this constitution. Briginshaw's book is a field opening one in that it concretely addresses how space is produced by the environmentally embedded and embodied performance of the selected dance pieces. In so doing, Briginshaw not only forefronts how dance as a site-specific event can unravel our experiences of given places but successfully opens new dimensions in the sociological and philosophical discussion of the constitutive processes of spatial practices. Following Briginshaw's initiative, this anthology offers views on the emergence of space by analysing dance practice through active participation and contextual perspectives as well by focusing on different time frames and eras. Thus, the articles in the anthology move from the intimate sense of being present in dancing to the wider perspective of historical discourses on dance.

In many ways feminist geographer Doreen Massey's (2005) conceptions on the social construction of space resonate throughout the analyses, theories and conclusions presented in the articles. Her politically-oriented work centrally emphasises that "if time is the dimension of succession then space it the dimension of the simultaneous existence of more-than-one" (Massey 2011, 37). In this sense, space is about a simultaneity of stories-so-far. Consequently, the space which we might conceive of as external to us "is the dimension of an infinity of stories other than our own" (ibid., 37). Massey thereby underlines that the ability to structure space is a source of considerable social power. Power is both "embodied and embedded within the relations that structure spatiality" (ibid., 38). This means that one form of power is (most often) intricately interwoven with other forms of power. Since space is produced and structured through relations and practices "not just the shapes produced but also the qualities embedded in those relations" are political (ibid., 38). Utilising Massey's conceptions of space in the analysis of dance performance and practice, means to rephrase the challenge of understanding the body as both a material reality and socio-cultural construction. It can likewise help highlight the political significance of the processes through which space becomes embodied and subjects become spatialised in dance.

The articles in the anthology address how historical and geopolitical influences impact our understanding and practice of dance art. In them, the kinds of spaces and interrelationships, which different forms of dancing generate, are considered. Aspects of embodied space that dancing relies upon are likewise discussed. Through a few case examples, some of the articles take a closer look on how recent artistic practice in dance utilises given environments and constructs space.

As an introduction into dance related conceptions on space, the first article by Sarah Rubidge addresses choreographic space by appreciating the diverse settings and environments in which contemporary dance is performed and dialoguing with topical philosophers and theorists on space. The article gives a short overview of previous understanding of space within modern dance. From there the text moves on to delineate a more updated view on choreography that extends the realm of both concert dance and proscenium stage. The article takes a relational view on space and argues that choreographed space interlaces its dynamic and material features.

Lena Hammergren's article addresses the geopolitical region of the Nordic countries and discusses examples in which the local banner of democracy has acted as a means of including and excluding dance, people and genres. Her insights highlight ideologies related to class, ethnicity, artistic authority and ownership and their ramifications on the kinds of spaces of encounter dance has offered beginning from the 1960s in the North. Paying attention to an earlier period in time, Hanna Järvinen addresses the representations of modern dance in photographs from 1900 to the 1930s. Simultaneously focusing on the political and ideological implications they convey of modern space, she argues that the images were imbued with nostalgia that still influences the manner in which we construct dance history today. Among other things, she points out that the images are based on ideas of nature with a moral and political outlook that, while complementing modern dance, acted as an ideology of exclusion for other forms of dance.

Whilst exemplifying that space is constantly both created and re-established in characteristic ways in diverse dance genres, Diane Oatley describes and discusses how liminal spaces become established in the flamenco dance. Oatley unfolds the complexities of the habitus of flamenco and argues that it is both formed by the actual dancing subject as well as formative of the same subject. That is, the two formative aspects of the space created by the flamenco dancer are formed by the actual embodied practices and the related narrative constructions of the dancing. As they interlink, a liminal space is produced that fosters an embodied transformation.

By observing how theoretical concepts offer insight into practical experience of improvised tango dancing, Susanne Ravn offers a detailed discussion on how interaction takes shape in this form of dancing. She indicates that the differences in the actual practice of forms of Argentinean tango both question and inform philosophical concepts and descriptions. In the philosophical explorations of the interactional process of dancing, Ravn emphasises that philosophers and dance scholars need to keep focus on these differences so that the not-yet-thought-of is taken heed of in the theoretical descriptions on how space comes into being.

Centered round her in-practice experiences, Camilla Damkjaer examines the specific spatial characteristics of the circus discipline vertical rope. In her writing, she reflects upon the verticality of space by interlinking her experiences with different kinds of textual spaces. She accomplishes an understanding of how the complex web of practice, thinking and expertise establishes experienced space. The article communicates the space of movement of the vertical rope and a relation between movement and text — the spatiality and temporality of written words.

Paula Kramer's article introduces a practice-as-research project involving outdoor dance in what she terms nature space. Her understanding and conceptualisation derive to a large degree from experience with diverse somatic and improvisational practices. She argues that in the environments of nature space dancers become decentralised and that this influences the manner in which they act and share both a human and non-human world in a vibrant co-existence. She informatively describes the premises of her artistic work and introduces her specific approach of disseminating the investigative work in the form of research installations.

Leena Rouhiainen's contribution presents the process of constructing a performative installation environment. More specifically it describes how the bodily awareness work with which the performing artists were engaged influenced the setting-up of a spatial dramaturgy that invited audience participants to explore their own embodiment. While introducing a distinct collaborative artistic project, the text offers insight into how artistic settings foster observational bodily interaction with the environment and produce forms of emplacement.

In her article, Charlotte Svendler Nielsen focuses on the lived and embodied dimension of both experiences and spaces in artistic-educational teaching and learning in a primary school setting. By taking a closer look on what happens in a dance project working with creative dance in the second grade, Svendler Nielsen indicates how the teacher might create an open atmosphere by showing that she dares put herself in vulnerable situations. By embracing vulnerability as well as by wondering both with and about the children's experiences, the teacher manages to open the 'normal' situational space of learning anew.

Shantel Ehrenberg presents an in-depth exploration of how the look and feel of the dancing body is co-constructed. She relates this look and the feel to what the dancer experiences as external and internal embodied spaces. On the basis of interview material constructed with one professional dancer, Ehrenberg's phenomenological analysis challenges the sharp spatial distinction between the internal and external in embodied experience. She argues that these dimensions are intertwined in the actual daily practices of the dancer.

Spatial processes are complex. As just exemplified in this brief overview of the articles, exploring space and dance can range from discussing ideological and political spaces of inclusion and exclusion to the spaces of intimate interaction of bodies with other bodies and environments in the moment of dancing. All the articles point to the fact that there is no simple and neutral space that movement would fill, but rather that space is created and reestablished through the moments and materials in which dance happens and is discoursed upon. However, we think that the articles also contribute in diverse ways to describing and understanding space *as* process and *in* process. This they do not least in how these processes are demonstrated to include a moving body — ... dancing.

REFERENCES

Briginshaw, Valerie. 2001. *Dance, Space and Subjectivity.* Hampshire & New York:
Palgrave

Crang, Mike and Thrift, Nigel. 2000. *Thinking Space.* London & New York: Routledge

Friedman, Michael Todd and van Ingen, Cathy. 2011. Bodies in Space: Spatializing Physical Cultural Studies. *Sociology of Sport Journal,* 28(1), 85-105.

Grosz, Elizabeth. 1995. *Space, Time and Perversion.* New York & London: Routledge

Lefebvre, Henri. 1974/1991. *The Production of Space.* Translated by Donald Nicholson-
Smith. Malden MA: Blackwell Publishing.

Massey, Doreen. 2005. *For Space.* London: Sage

Massey, Doreen. 2011. "For Space: Reflections on an Engagement with Dance." In *Proceedings from the 10th International NOFOD Conference, Spacing Dance(s) – Dancing
Spaces. Odense 2011,* edited by Susanne Rvan, 35-44. University of Southern Denmark.

CHOREOGRAPHED
DANCE SPACES

ON CHOREOGRAPHIC SPACE

Sarah Rubidge

Abstract

In this article the notion of choreographic space is viewed through understandings of space forwarded by thinkers such as Gilles Deleuze and Félix Guattari, Brian Massumi, Manuel deLanda and Susanne Langer, theorists such as Michel de Certeau and Henri Lefebvre, and geographers Doreen Massey, Nigel Thrift and Paul Rodaway. In the context of the increasing use of new spaces for choreography (urban buildings and streets) and new modalities of choreographic practice such as the generation of choreographic installation spaces and screendance, the article proposes that these theorists offer a rich resource for a discussion of choreographic space. It is argued that the everyday notion of space as a container for action (extensive space) is increasingly being challenged by the notion that space is *produced* by movement, that is by relational activities which generate an affective, or qualitative, space (intensive space). In this article the notion of choreographic space is predicated on the conception of space as a dynamic, relational concept. It suggests that choreographic space is constituted as intensive space, a transient spatiotemporal network of forces, vectors and tensions, processual rather than stable and, crucially, experiential, and goes beyond the dance. Additionally, the article proposes that extensive and intensive space are by no means oppositional forms of experiencing space, rather they are co-present in any experience of choreographic space whether that experience is of participant, performer or audience. As such, the article argues that choreographic space is an in/extensive space, one that interlaces the dynamic textures of qualitative space and the stable features of material space within a process of reconfigurations of the latter's affective contours.

Introduction

In this article the notion of choreographic space is extended beyond the dance, and viewed through the prism of understandings of space forwarded by philosophers such as Gilles Deleuze and Félix Guattari (1987), Brian Massumi (2002, 2010), Manuel deLanda (2002) and Susanne Langer (1953); theorists such as Michel de Certeau (1991) and Henri Lefebvre (1994); and geographers such as Doreen Massey (2005), Nigel Thrift (2007), Allan Pred (1977), and Paul Rodaway (1994). These thinkers have been instrumental in changing the way in which we understand space. In the context of the increasing use of new spaces for choreography (for example, urban buildings and streets), of new modalities of choreographic practice such as the generation of choreographic installations and videodance works, and the escalating use of choreography as a metaphor in disciplines such as geography, science, and urbanism, these theorists offer a rich resource for a discussion of choreographic space, both within and outside of the dance. As such the focus of this article is on choreographic *space* not on choreographing movement *per se*. Bodily movement is not its primary choreographic concern, rather, more general spatial aspects of choreographic practice, such as composition of the relational play between individual entities in motion, are. As a result, the position is taken here that, whilst dance might be synonymous with choreography, as Susan Foster (2011) notes, the notion of the choreographic is no longer confined to dance.

With respect to choreographic space, the everyday notion of space as a container for action, an external space within which we move (extensive space), is increasingly being challenged across the disciplines by the notion that space is *produced* by movement, that is, by relational activities which generate an affective, or qualitative, space (intensive space). Using the immersive choreographic installation as an example of choreographically generated spaces that are consciously predicated on the notion of space as a dynamic, relational, experiential concept, the suggestion is made here that 'choreographic' spaces (whether or not created by a choreographer) are constituted as transient spatiotemporal networks of forces, vectors and tensions that are processual rather than stable and, crucially, experiential. Although the concept of choreographic space is open-ended, and clearly now extends beyond dance practice, in general parlance it often refers simply to the spaces within which choreography takes place (theatre spaces, installation spaces,[1] urban space, domestic spaces, the 'natural' space of rural landscapes). Nevertheless, as will be seen, it can also refer to the altogether more liminal dynamic spatiotemporal space that is inherent in any choreographic design and is generated by the activity of dancers as they perform a choreographic work, and, importantly, by people as they engage in everyday movement in public spaces. Here a choreographic interplay, or emerging relation, between performers or individuals actively shapes (or produces) the space in which they move by creating a dynamic, interweaving network of vectors, tensions and transient forms. It is suggested that this dynamic form shifts within the material space, and that this can modulate our visual and felt perception of the material space that we move within.

Early Challenges to Choreographic Space

From a dance perspective choreographers have been actively engaged in an interrogation of accepted notions of what constitutes 'choreographic' space since at least the 1950s, when Merce Cunningham first began to decentralise theatrical space through his reconfiguration of the stage space. Abandoning the conventions attendant on the frontal focus of theatrical space in his stage performances he facilitated a perception of choreographic space that was multi-directional in focus, with none of the 'strong' or 'weak' areas that were taken as given by a previous generation of choreographers (e.g. Humphrey 1959). In addition, the intricate configurations of relations between dancers that his choreographic methods generated challenged further the conventions of spatial organisation in choreography practiced by his chorographic predecessors, and the theories of space, including those referred to as 'space harmony', developed by movement theorist Rudolph Laban in the first half of the twentieth century (Laban 1966[2]). However, Cunningham went beyond even this, opening the way for an extended understanding of choreographic space, for in the early 1960s he began to use public spaces for performances of his choreographic work. These performances constituted composite presentations of moments taken from a number of Cunningham's pre-existing choreographic works and reconfigured into a fresh choreographic structure. He called these 'events', the first taking place in Vienna in 1964.

Other choreographers of that period, influenced by developments in theatre such as Alan Kaprow's 'Happenings', also began to move out of the theatres and crucially to explore a broader conception of the choreographic. These included, amongst others, choreographers from New York's Judson Church Dance Theater (many of whom had previously danced with Cunningham or taken compositional classes at the Cunningham Studios) who mounted an even greater challenge than Cunningham to the primacy of the theatrical space in choreographic practice by dropping their "usual motives for movement and action" and letting themselves "be drawn by the attractions of the terrain and the encounters they find there" (Debord 1995). In this they were implicitly following the principles of the *dérive* propounded by the Situationists. By taking their choreography out of the studio into the city the Judson Church choreographers radically extended notions of viable spaces for choreography. Similarly, the adoption of everyday movement as a primary choreographic content extended the movement vocabulary of dance, and opened the way for seeing everyday behaviour as choreographic. Lucinda Childs's *Street Dance* (1964) and Trisha Brown's *Man Walking Down the Side of a Building* (1970) and *Roof Pieces* (1971) are examples of this new practice. These challenges to the conventions of 'choreographic' space continued throughout the 1980s and 1990s, with choreographers who specialise in site-specific dance siting their choreographic practices in public, or at the very least non-theatre, spaces. Site-specific dance continues to thrive as an established genre of choreographic practice in the twenty-first century.[3]

However, it is notable that what is increasingly described as 'choreographic' events in public spaces is not always generated by choreographers and dancers, for they can be generated unintentionally by the collective motion of people in a street, a station concourse or an airport, although (with the exception of Flashmobs) as choreographic events these are generally more to do with the un-intentional collective spatiotemporal configuration of individuals moving within an environment than they are about the deliberate composition and organisation of movement and/or movement images within that space. Nevertheless, it can be argued that, in the spirit of 1960s' choreographic experiments with non-dancers, the composite movement of members of a crowd can temporarily transform what Marc Augé describes as 'non-places' (Augé 1995) into choreographic spaces.

Other significant challenges to conventional notions of spaces for choreography have been advanced by videodance, or screendance, artists. The work of these artists has continued Maya Deren's early experiments with choreography and film, and in doing so explicitly extended the location of choreographic space to include the 'virtual' space of the television screen.[4] (Indeed, videodance artist Douglas Rosenberg (2000) argues explicitly that 'videospace' is a site for choreography). Installation artists who worked with digital media, video and film have extended these initiatives still further by creating installation works using single and mul-tiple projection screens for example, works by Bill Viola such as *Catherine's Room* (2001), *Going Forth By Day* (2007), (Sam Taylor Wood's *Killing Time* (1994), Julian Isaacs's *Ten Thousand Waves (2010)*, and others.) These, sometimes inadvertently, generate choreographic environments through the interplay between the content that was displayed on the screens, the spatiotemporal interconnections between the imagery on the screens, and/or the relational interplay between the screens and the motion of performers or spectators as they interact with or view the works.

Dance artists turned their attention to multiscreen installations in the mid-1990s, many using digital technologies.[5] One result of this was that the choreographic nature of multiscreen installation environments became deliberate rather than contingent. Many of these digitally augmented audiovisual installation spaces, for example, multiuser immersive installations such as *trajets [V2]* (Susan Kozel and Gretchen Schiller 2004-2007) and *Sensuous Geographies* (Sarah Rubidge and Alistair MacDonald 2003) became explicitly choreographic *spaces* in their own right, for they simultaneously constituted a new material space and a three-dimensional 'felt' sense of space that drew attention to the embodied experience of the participant (Birringer 1998). Additionally, through the detail of the computer programming that drove the behaviours of the installations, they created the conditions for the generation by participants of informal choreographic events within and with the installations.[6] These installation works thus deliberately generated not only a material space that could be perceived visually (which I will align later with extensive space), but also an intensive, *felt* space, generated through the relational forces, vectors and tensions that permeate the installation space when it is in action. Both, I will suggest, are central features of choreographic space.

The result of the practices that challenged the conventions of the choreographic space from within dance is that the notion of choreographic space as an extended concept has become ripe for debate. As will be noted, two implications of the term 'choreographic space' can be identified in the above. The first is simply that it is a space for choreography. The second is that action within a space can render it 'choreographic'; that is, shift attention away from any overriding functional purposes of the space to the movement taking place in the space, movement that transforms the material space into an active, dynamic flow of relational forces, vectors and tensions: space choreographed.

Although space as a dance concept had been analysed formally in the early to mid-twentieth century by theorists such as Laban, and extended in the latter part of that century (Preston Dunlop 1981; Longstaff 1996), the implications of the notion of space itself as being choreographic, as being *produced*, with all that that implies, was not theorised in depth in dance studies until the beginning of the twenty-first century when dance scholars such as Valerie Briginshaw (2001) grasped this somewhat neglected nettle. It was evident that the depth of her analyses, which like those of many dance scholars at that time were permeated with a political sensibility, was made possible by the work of theorists and phi-losophers, scientists and mathematicians, social scientists and physicists who had been engaged in a re-visioning of the concept of space in the twentieth century. They conceived of space as a dynamic processual event rather than a fixed entity. Briginshaw, like geographers Doreen Massey (2005) and Nigel Thrift (2007), drew extensively on discussions on space initiated by such thinkers, in particular the work of social theorists such as Michel de Certeau (1984), Henri Lefebvre (1991), and philosophers such as Gilles Deleuze and Félix Guattari (1987). In turn, the understandings of space mooted by all these writers have proved to be very pro-ductive in the exploration of choreographic space undertaken in this article.

Intensive and Extensive Space

It is notable that, although theoretically the notion of choreographic space has begun to incorporate a number of the understandings of space that have been developing across disciplines during the twentieth and twenty-first centuries, in everyday practice common-sense understandings of space (which conceive of it as being something that has stable contours and is external to us) still tend to perme-ate our understanding. Crucially there has been a tendency to adopt the position that we perceive space optically.[7] (In everyday terms, choreographic space may implicitly be considered *something* that is danced *in*, that is, space is thought as a container for choreographic action.) It is these common-sense notions of space that were challenged by the writers and thinkers mentioned above through the development of the concept of space-time in physics, of Riemannian geometry and topological space in mathematics, the introduction of notions of smooth/striated space and intensive and extensive space by Deleuze and Guattari (1987). This was coupled with a growing understanding of the import of the insights of J.J. Gibson (1966; 1979) that all modes of perception, including the visual, are multi-modal and relational. This has led to an increasing realisation that what we *see* is no longer sufficient as the basis for understanding the world/s we inhabit.[8]

In philosophical terms what I am calling common-sense understandings of space identify what is known as 'extensive' space, often referred to as Euclidean or Cartesian space. This space has boundaries, is static, and is divisible and measur-able, and external to us. A Cartesian space is composed of points through which we are able to plot the positions occupied by objects at a given time, and through which we are able to measure dimensions and distances between entities. Exten-sive space is space 'in a state of arrest' (Massumi 2002, 7). During the twentieth century, the new conceptions of space developed in mathematics, science and philosophy opened the way to understandings of space that conceive of space as being transient, dynamic, relational, in process rather than fixed. This space is qualitative rather than quantitative. Textured, fluid, its contours malleable, its presence is 'felt' (Manning 2009). This is space in flux, space characterised not by consistency and stability but by variation, space that is *achieved* through a continuous interplay between vectors, directions, elements, and shifting volumes and textures. Multidimensional rather than metrical, topological rather than topographical, this is 'intensive', or dynamic, space. Crucially it is experienced haptically, kinaesthetically, experientially, rather than optically.[9] In contrast to extensive space, intensive space does not operate through visual points of reference, but through shifting qualities and potentials, or "zones of intensity" (de Landa, 2005, 50). These emerge as we move, act, experience. Intensive space is thus *produced* rather than given, and produced, it is argued, specifically by movement (Massey 2005; Thrift 2007; McCormack 2008).

These notions are particularly valuable in developing an understanding of choreographic space that extends beyond the space in which we move into the 'virtual' spaces that are generated by 'choreographic' events.[10] De Certeau, for example, notes that the movement of people in a space generates a space "composed of intersections of mobile elements...actuated by the ensemble of movements deployed within it, [which] only exists when one takes into consideration vectors of direction, velocities and line variables" (de Certeau 1984, 112). It is the latter, along with the assemblage of movements that are generated by the ensemble of individuals that imbue an extensive space with a qualitative dimension, and transform it into intensive space. Lefebvre both echoes and extends this notion by arguing that "every social process is the outcome of a process with many aspects and contributing currents, signifying and non-signifying, perceived and directly experienced, practical and theoretical" (Lefebvre 1991, 110). This composite of currents produces intensive spaces and generates variable perceptions of extensive spaces, perceptions that, by virtue of the continuous play of vectorial and spatiotemporal tensions are permeated with what Deleuze and Guattari (1987) call *affect*.[11]

Thus the space that is produced by movement is not material space, but the tenor of a space, the affective atmosphere that suffuses and surrounds the movement quality (Massumi 2011, 112). Crucially, this kind of affective space is produced by *all* types of movement taking place within a material space, not only by dance movement. Additionally, because the tenor of the space is experienced, the sense of the external 'space' might be transformed as the light changes with the movement of the sun, or in accord to the amount, type, kind or purpose of the activity taking place within the space,[12] or even with the state of mind or mood of the individual who experiences it. At an experiential level these conditions are coupled with individual experiences of a material space that are generated by personal histories, prior experiences, memories, associations and socio-cultural perspectives to create a (temporary) but a highly personalised affective space (Massey 2005), one which coexists with any number of other personal affective spaces, all of which are permeated by different ideas, conditions and understandings. The generated space is thus not only personal, but shared, and as such can also have political implications.[13] These, however, are only one part of what Massumi (2011, 65) calls its "affective tonality".

If, as Lefebvre (1991) and de Certeau (1984) suggest, the everyday flows of movement in a space generate a very particular relational, dynamic space then we are also moving towards a notion of choreographic space that embodies the thinking of these and other writers such as Susanne Langer (1953), Gilles Deleuze and Félix Guattari (1987), Brian Massumi (2002; 2011) and Manuel de Landa (2005). At the same time the notion of choreographic space is being extended beyond the world of dance. In the choreographic spaces produced by the immersive installation works mentioned earlier the spatiotemporal interplay between participants not only echo the social and spatial interplays that take place in public spaces, but also deliberately generate the 'zones of intensity' of intensive space. Just as in public space, that interplay creates spatiotemporal vectors of energy and tension between participants, and between participants and the material features and dimensions of the space within which they move. However, the installation spaces are composed specifically to generate a felt space for both participant and 'viewer' (the two modes of engagement are interchangeable for any individual participating in these installations). As such they deliberately invoke within the installations Massumi's "double capture of separate dimensions of experience" (Massumi 2011, 79-80), albeit privileging the proprioceptive/kinaesthetic experience. This is, in part, what gives such choreographic spaces their expressive force.

This dual experience of space was particularly evident in *Sensuous Geographies* (Rubidge and MacDonald 2003). *Sensuous Geographies* was a large-scale interactive installation, the material features of which were made up of a number of screens which hung from the ceiling and surrounded a central (empty) area some 10 metres in diameter. The screens, however, were of significance only because as an architectural feature they defined the 'inner' space noted above. The significant area of the installation was the central (inner) area, for this was the interactive space in which the 'audience' who engaged actively with the installation generated and spatialised sounds in real time, and thus created the sonic environment in which they moved.[14] This created an audible, yet kinaesthetically experienced web of sound and sensation, which was generated and modulated in real time by the ebb and flow of participants and sonic environment. This sensation was accessible to the 'viewers', who were also immersed in the sonic space, inasmuch as it extended beyond the active space in the centre of the installation.[15]

Although it invoked different technical and perceptual principles, the dual experience of space was also evident in Schiller and Kozel's installation *trajets [V2]*. This installation privileged video projections rather than sound, albeit projections that were designed to be felt, rather than seen, for in the video projections, which were distributed across a number of long, narrow screens hanging down into, and filling, the installation space, "clear lines or the borders of a body may not be distinguish[able]…the information is comprehended on a visceral level. Bodies are ever present but not represented, never sharply defined" (Schiller online no date).[16] Intended to invoke a 'kinetic sense…of sensual data…of perceptual states and…physiological responses" (ibid.), at the same time this installation invited participants to navigate a space that responded to its behaviour, for the screens on which the video imagery was projected responded to the movement trajectories of participants as they moved through the installation, the screens turning this way and that in response to the participants' motion as the latter's trajectories moved towards, moved away from or passed by the screens.

Sensuous Geographies and *trajets [V2]* challenged conventional notions of choreography, of choreographic space, and of performer and viewer, in that they were deliberately created as spaces for choreographic activity that was *both* seen and felt by all who engaged with the installations. As art-driven examples of what Massumi and Erin Manning (Murphie 2008) call research-creation[17] (in which art and philosophy, theory and practice lie on the same creative plane, productively resonating with each other *as* the research process is enacted), both constituted speculative research endeavours into the notion of choreography itself. Both were interactive installations that responded to the behaviour of the participants in such a way that the material installation environment was augmented in some way to generate an intensive space.

Further, in each installation, both those who were actively engaging with the interactive interface of the installation and those who were standing outside the active space looking in (the two roles were interchangeable for all participants) were to a greater or lesser extent embedded within the material choreographic space.[18] In *Sensuous Geographies* the movement of the active participants ('performers'), via the responses of the interactive environment, generated a spatially mobile soundworld of ever-changing sonic trajectories and dynamics, which they were simultaneously hearing and experiencing haptically. However, if *viewing* the activity taking place in *Sensuous Geographies* from outside the (inter)active installation space, by virtue of seeing the motion of the participants and *feeling* the movement of the sound, the sonic environment was experienced not only visually and aurally, but also kinaesthetically, that is extensively *and* intensively.[19] Here participants could simultaneously observe the materiality of the choreographic activity taking place in the installation in terms of the spatiotemporal interplays between participants and their environment, *and* kinaesthetically experience the flow of sonic textures that were being generated and modulated by the choreographic actions that swirled around them.[20] In *trajets,* by contrast, the relation between material forms that comprised the architecture of the installation and the participants were reconfigured as participants moved among the screens. This caused the screens to turn to face this way and then that, and then that, and then… and then… As such, not only was the material form of the installation space continually reconfigured, the screens also seemed to 'perform' with the participants to create a composite choreographic event from an intricate assemblage of humans and screens.

Both *trajets* and *Sensuous Geographies* could therefore be seen as artistic manifestations of the notion that choreographic space is a composite of extensive and intensive space. In the context of this paper what is of particular interest is that these installations are *designed* to be experienced simultaneously intensively and extensively.[21] They implicitly take on Lefebvre's notion that human beings in general do not relate to space as a picture, rather "they know that they *have* a space, and that they *are* in this space…." (Lefebvre 1991, 94, my italics). Just as we situate ourselves in a space as active participants when we are *in* public/domestic/work spaces, rather than simply contemplating the space as something to be viewed, so too do participants in immersive installations and audience members in site-specific works become situated as *active* participants in an implicitly choreographic event. Further, I would suggest that when they are active participants, and experiencing the space intensively, contra Grosz (2001, xv) who argues that immersion does not afford distance, they are simultaneously aware at some level of space as some*thing* outside of themselves, something that has boundaries, something that they are inhabiting.

Conversely, even when viewing a dance work as a 'picture' taking place in the material space of the stage the *experienced* as well as visual texture of the space we see as audience seems to change. As we perceive the streams of energy that are generated by the motion of its inhabitants, their interrelations and changing spatiotemporal rhythms and velocities flow this way and that. The intensivities produced permeate the space, modulating our felt experience of the performance space. Neuroscientists (for example, Gallese 2005) suggest that, even as we perceive, we vicariously experience through embodied simulation the sensations of the rhythms and velocities as they "in all their multiplicity interpenetrate one another…forever crossing and recrossing, superimposing themselves on each other" (Lefebvre 1991, 205). As will be seen, this is in accord not only with Massumi, but also with Susanne Langer's much earlier experiential analysis of choreographic activity (Langer 1953). I would argue that the interweaving *rhythms and velocities* create an experiential dynamic, choreographic space, and with it, by virtue of the relational dynamics that obtain between bodies in motion and the space within which it they move, a new dynamics of the 'fixed' material space. This creates a newly perceived material space, which results directly from choreographic activity. This space does not, indeed could not, exist prior to that activity, for material space always presents itself as "a pulsed array of possibilities to be pursued" (Gins and Arakawa 2002, 42), an array that choreographers of whatever persuasion grasp and transform into a newly formed experiential, or intensive, space.

Langer's 1953 discussion of vectorial space, formulated directly in relation to choreographic events, is particularly illuminating in this last context, for it offers new perspectives on, yet resonates with, those forwarded by Lefebvre and de Certeau in their discussions of everyday space, with Deleuze and Guattari's discussions of intensive space, and with Massumi who explicitly addresses the resonances he finds between Langer's thought and his own (Massumi 2011). Langer acknowledges the vectorial nature of choreographic space, but identifies that space as a space of virtual powers or forces, analogous, I would suggest, to Deleuze and Guattari's term 'intensive' space. Langer argues explicitly that the relations between the dancers is more than a spatial one, it is a relation of forces, and that the forces that they exercise, they seem to be as physical as those which orient the compass needle toward its pole, really do not exist physically (Langer 1953, 175-176). Dancers, she suggests, do not merely create physical movements, they create virtual gestures, which extend beyond the materiality of their bodies. The virtual gestures become an extended actualisation of the intricate interplay of the trajectories and tensions that permeate the interrelations between dancers and the space within, through and with which they dance.[22] It is this last that is of interest in the article, rather than the bodily movement of the dancers. Indeed, Langer suggests that this virtual movement pervades one's perception of the activity of a dancing group or ensemble, for "…one does not see people running around; one sees the dance driving this way, drawn that way, gathering there — fleeing, resting, rising and so forth..." (Langer 1953, 175). She goes on to argue that the prototype of the 'forces' that generate this dynamic choreographic space is not the 'field of forces' associated with physics, but "the *subjective experience* of volition and free agency" (ibid. my emphasis). Specifically she argues that "the sense of vital power, even of the power to receive impressions, apprehend the environment *and* meet its changes, is our most immediate self-consciousness...the play of felt energies is as different from any system of physical forces as psychological time is from the space of geometry (Langer 1953, 176). As Langer notes, this is as true of the viewer as it is of the dancer.

The parallels between Langer's mid-twentieth century thought and late twentieth century perceptions of space such as those discussed by Brian Massumi (2002; 2011), along with the newly discovered role of embodiment in understanding space, are evident. Massumi describes the experience of the dance as one of "non-local linkages, not the individual movements taken separately or in aggregate" (Massumi 2011, 140), a "Universe of Dance … in which bodily vitality affects are kinaesthetically thought-felt to merge and diverge, repeat and vary, folding in and out of each other in their own manner" (ibid.). This description resonates with Langer's ideas and with the ideas explored in this article. Nevertheless, Massumi's focus on the body, and on bodily movement in this discussion of dance to some extent detracts from the arguments regarding choreographic space being proposed here — that it is the qualitative dimension of trajectories of motion, whether or not created by dancing bodies, that generate a *choreographic* space, not only dancing *per se*. As such, it is proposed that the choreographic is not necessarily entwined with dance, although the dance might necessarily be choreographic. That said, Massumi's notion that "pure" dance "converts extra-dance factors into *dance forces*" (Massumi 2011, 144), and implicitly has the "compositional power to mutually include; to bring differentials of experience together across their disjunction, to unitary experiential effect: to effectively convert heterogeneous outside factors into immanent forces..." (ibid.) draws these ideas on dance closer to the notion of choreographic space discussed in this article. Nevertheless, it is his speculations on relational architecture (Massumi 2011, 80) and music (Massumi 2011, 145-146) that resonate more closely with the ideas being pursued here than his speculations on dance.

In/Extensive Space: Beyond Binaries

As has been implied above, intensive and extensive space are not mutually exclusive. In immersive installation works and many site-specific works that take place in public spaces, because the viewers are enveloped by both the material and the choreographic space, they find themselves simultaneously viewing the material space, and experiencing the space of active forces of which Langer and Massumi speak. Nevertheless, as Doreen Massey (2011, 43) notes, entities although malleable and in flux, are not without stability and substance, for "...they do exist. And they do persist".[23] Further, as Michael Mehaffy (2010) and Nikos Salingaros (2010) argue, the *design* of the material spaces with which we engage can affect both our behaviour within the space and the detail of *how* we see (and feel) when we see what we see, and thus gives rise to the 'vitality effect' of which Massumi (2011, 43-44) speaks. The design of material spaces, including the material architecture of immersive installations, is an example of "a technical staging of aesthetic events..., emanating a living quality that might resonate elsewhere to unpredictable affect and effect" (Massumi 2011, 80).

It is this interlacing of the material and dynamic, of the bounded and vectorial, of the intensive and extensive in choreographic space that emerges as of particular interest in this discussion, as over the last two decades the oppositions implied by the formulation of the features above as binary distinctions have been challenged. Rather than being considered mutually exclusive, it is acknowledged that they overlap, interweave, co-exist. For example, Lefebvre (1991, 110) noted that space is both "perceived and directly experienced", and Deleuze and Guattari (1987) that intensive, or smooth space is always interrupted by temporary crystallisations of the flows of intensive forces that create the relations between and variations of its multiple lines of direction, and between its qualitative textures.[24] Correspondingly, as we know when viewing a dance performance, even when experienced optically, the material space in which the dance takes place is imbued by the movement of the dance with inherently variable qualitative dimensions and textures that can undermine the apparently stable identity of the space. Indeed if, as Paul Rodaway (1994, 55) argues, space is mapped haptically as well as visually, it is of necessity in/extensive, that is, simultaneously intensive and extensive. Manuel de Landa (2005) approaches this merging of the intensive and extensive from a different direction, suggesting that the qualitative dimension of intensive space is implicated in the very production of extensive space, for it is "in this processual zone [that we] can witness the birth of extensity and its identity forming frontiers" (de Landa 2005, 83).

Perhaps, then, the two concepts (extensive space and intensive space), rather than being seen as different in kind should be seen as implying different modes of perceiving (or experiencing) space.[25] Elizabeth Grosz (2001) addresses the difficulties inherent in making a distinction between the two modes of experiencing space explicitly. She takes steps to resolve the conundrum of the apparent gap between being immersed in a space, and thus in a subjective *state* at the mercy of "the immediacy of immersion that affords no distance" (Grosz 2001, xv), and being an 'objective' observer of a space/event, and thus never able to occupy the outside fully "for it is always other, different, at a distance from where one is" (ibid.). However, she does this by positing a further space, one that is neither inside nor outside, neither intensive nor extensive, but one that lies between the two. This she calls the 'space of the in between'. The latter she argues is 'space of open-ness and of undoing'. It is a space that 'disrupts the operations' of 'inside' and 'outside' (Grosz 2001, 93). Further, rather than being a space of fixed identities, the 'space of the in between' is a space of becoming, a space of transformation. This notwithstanding, implicitly the 'space of the in between' constitutes a *third* space, albeit one with unstable, permeable margins. I would argue that being immersed in a space does not necessarily entail being unaware of the material space one occupies, nor that to perceive extensive space necessarily denies the experiential, inasmuch as post-Gibson theories of perception argue that *any* perception, even visual perception, constitutes a composite of several perceptual modes, including the haptic (Nöe 2004; Thompson 2008). Thus an optical perception of extensive space can simultaneously be somatic and experiential, particularly when what is perceived visually entails motion, whether actual or virtual.

Massumi (2002) avoids the dilemma confronted by Grosz by resolving the conundrum in a different way. Rather than positing another space, he argues that the different forms of space, the vectorial/bounded, intensive/extensive, smooth/striated are *coextensive*. Thus Euclidean and non-Euclidean space, material space and dynamic space, extensive and intensive space co-exist, interweave, are co-present in any experience of a space. The built space within which movement takes place does not change its shape or dimensions physically (or if it does not in a way that is perceptually discernible), however, it does change in terms of the form it takes in our perceptual experience.[26] As viewers, even though viewing optically from 'outside', as Langer notes we *experience* the ebb and flow, the expansion and contraction of the dynamic space created by the performers/participants as they move. As a result, by virtue of the dynamic spaces that are being generated within the material space by their movement, the perceived spatial characteristics of the environment are modulated perceptually. Thus, as the solo dancer, trio, duet or ensemble of dancers moves this way and that in the space of the performance, or, as a composite unit extends and contracts as the spatial relations between dancers change, the spatiotemporal vectors that characterised the dynamics of the material space before the movement began dissolve and are re-formed. First one, then another feature of the material space is linked, now with one feature then with another, the features getting closer or moving further away by virtue of the motion of the perceiver. The network of vectors and tensions are almost made visible when features are foregrounded then backgrounded as the relations between the mobile and 'static' features of the space change.[27] This alters the perceived dimensions of the space for the viewer, giving rise to a different experience of the environment that s/he is occupying. In Massumi's terms 'the dynamic form of the event is *perceptually felt*, not so much *in* vision as *with* vision or *through* vision...' (Massumi 2011, 17).

Similarly, even when immersing oneself in a space, as does the participant in an immersive installation, even though immersed in the *sense* of the space one is always aware, at some level, of one's relation to the material environment, the space in which one is immersed. Consequently, as participants/dancers, even whilst immersed in the haptic/kinaesthetic experience of the intensive space we generate in and through our movement/activity, we are simultaneously able to discern (albeit not always consciously) the boundaries of the space in which we move and its material features (the latter including other participants/performers and the audience). In this way, in Langer's terms, we are able to "apprehend the environment and *meet its changes* [in] our most immediate self-consciousness" (Langer 1953, 176, my emphasis). Thus, as dancers and participants in installation environments and/or in choreographic works that take place in urban or natural spaces, we experience the installation space and/or the space in which the performance takes place coextensively; the choreography *in* the space transforming the latter into a felt choreographic space. The same can be true of the experience of space for people in their everyday experience, for as Albert Michotte notes, "felt-perceptions of movement quality [continue] behind, across, and through objective encounters" (Michotte 1963, quoted in Massumi 2011, 109). Even though they normally go unrecognised, these "felt perceptions are operative in all circumstances" (ibid.). The works of Trisha Brown and Lucinda Childs, events such as Flashmobs, and projects such as *(in)visible dances* (2010), created by choreographer Luca Silvestrini for the International Dance Festival Birmingham, can serve to bring these felt perceptions to the forefront of our attention in everyday situations.

Conclusion

It has been interesting to note during my research for this paper the difference in tenor of the descriptions of dynamic space offered by Langer in 1953 (as a choreographic concept), and those of Lefebvre and de Certeau some thirty to forty years later. Although writing from the perspective of the viewer, Langer writes as if from the 'inside' in phrases such as, "It is the feeling of power, and the play of such felt energies..." (Langer 1953, 176). Lefebvre (1991) and de Certeau (1984), conversely, although sympathetic to the intensities and dynamics generated in the everyday spaces they describe, and clearly making an attempt to immerse themselves within them, write of those intensities as if experiencing them extensively. Nevertheless, Langer's perspective is of significance when considering the possibility that not only dancers, but also audience members can feel the difference in qualities in de Landa's 'zones of intensity' that are generated by a particular choreographic space, even one that they are not immersed in intensively.[28] This implies that we can experience the sensation of actions vicariously through generating an embodied simulation from an optical experience of the movement of others (Gallese 2005). Thus, when taking the role of audience in a dance performance, we are able to embody to a greater or lesser degree, the intensities of the interplay of forces that the dancers generate and that we perceive on the stage, particularly those generated when engaging in ensemble or group activity.[29] As such, just as the dancer on the stage or a participant in an immersive installation participates in the event through an embodied engagement in the ebb and flow of energy, so too can the audience.

These psychophysical, or intensive, results of the relations between the movement of individuals and entities (either alone or as part of an ensemble), and the space they move within, are, it is argued, central to the generation of choreographic space. It is this that generates what we might call a 'felt' space, the space of being and of feeling, and of becoming. As such, as is implicitly suggested by the theorists discussed above, intensive space becomes implicated in the extensive (material) space in which any choreographic event, formal or informal, takes place. This interplay between the mutual influences of movement and the material environment on the generation of a choreographic space gives support to the notion proposed in this article that choreographic space is an in/extensive space, one that incorporates both the dynamic and the stable, and reconfigures the perceived contours and textures of material space through the movement activity that has constituted it. That this is as true of the space that is created by everyday movement in everyday environments as it is of the choreographic space that is actively created by choreographers indicates that choreographic space, although of the dance, goes beyond the dance.

BIBLIOGRAPHY

Auge, Marc. 1995. *Non-Places: Introduction to an Anthropology of Supermodernity.* London and New York: Verso Books.

Birringer, Johannes. 1998. *Media and Performance: Along the Border.* Baltimore: The Johns Hopkins University Press.

Briginshaw, Valerie. 2001. *Dance, Space and Subjectivity.* Manchester: Palgrave Macmillan.

Calvo-Merino, Beatriz; Julie Grèzes; Daniel E. Glaser; Richard E. Passingham and Patrick Haggard. 2005. "Action Observation and Acquired Motor Skills: An fMRI Study with Expert Dancers." *Cerebral Cortex* 15 : 1243-48.

Damasio, Antonio. 1995. *Descartes' Error.* New York: G.P. Putman & Sons.

Damasio, Antonio. 1999. *The Feeling of What Happens: Body and Emotion in the Making of Consciousness.* New York: Harcourt Brace.

Deleuze, Gilles and Guattari, Félix. 1987. *A Thousand Plateaus: Capitalism and Schizophrenia.* Translated by Brian Massumi. Minneapolis: University of Minnesota Press.

Debord, Guy. 1955. "Introduction to a Critique of Urban Geography." *Les Lèvres Nues* #6, September. Translated by Ken Knabb. Accessed May 20, 2011. http://www.cddc.vt.edu/sionline/presitu/geography.html

de Certeau, Michel. 1984. *The Practice of Everyday Life.* Berkeley: University of California Press.

de Landa, Manuel. 2005. "Space: Extensive and Intensive, Actual and Virtual." In *Deleuze and Space,* edited by Ian Buchanan and Gregg Lambert, 80-88. Toronto: University of Toronto Press.

Foster, Susan. 2011. *Choreographing Empathy: Kinaesthesia in Performance.* Abingdon, UK: Routledge.

Gallese, Vittorio. 2005. "Embodied Simulation: From Neurons to Phenomenal Experience." *Phenomenology and the Cognitive Sciences* 4: 23-48.

Gibson, James J. 1966. *The Senses Considered as Perceptual Systems.* Boston: Houghton Mifflin.

Gibson, James J. 1979. *The Ecological Approach to Visual Perception.* Hillsdale, New Jersey: Lawrence Erlbaum Associates.

Gins, Madeline and Arakawa, Shusaku. 2002. *Architectural Body.* Tuscaloosa: University of Alabama Press.

Grosz, Elizabeth. 2001. *Architecture from the Outside.* Cambridge, Massachusetts: MIT Press.

Humphrey, Doris. 1959. *The Art of Making Dances.* Pennington, NJ: Princeton Books.

Knabb, Ken, ed. 1995. *Situationist International Anthology.* Berkley: Bureau of Public Secrets.

Laban, Rudolph. 1966. *Choreutics.* Edited by Lisa Ullman. London: Macdonald Evans.

Langer, Susanne. 1953. *Feeling and Form.* London, New York: Routledge Kegan Paul.

Lefebvre, Henri. 1991. *The Production of Space.* Translated by Donald Nicholson-Smith. Oxford: Blackwell Publishing.

Longstaff, Jeffrey. 1996. "Cognitive Structures of Kinaesthetic Space: Re-evaluating Rudolf Laban's Choreutics in the Context of Spatial Cognition and Motor Control." PhD thesis, London: City University, Laban Centre.

McCormack, Derek. 2008. "Geographies for Moving Bodies: Thinking, Dancing, Spaces" *Geography Compass* 2(6):1822-1836.

Manning, Erin. 2009. *Relationscapes: Movement, Art, Philosophy.* Cambridge, Massachusetts: MIT Press.

Massey, Doreen. 2005. *For Space.* Los Angeles, London: Sage Publications.

Massey, Doreen. 2011. "For Space: Reflections on an Engagement with Dance." In *Spacing Dance(s) — Dancing Space(s);* Proceedings of the 10th International NOFOD Conference, January 2011, edited by Susanne Ravn 35-43. Odense: NOFOD and University of Southern Denmark.

Massumi, Brian. 2002. *Parables for the Virtual: Movement, Affect, Sensation.* Durham, N.C.: Duke University Press.

Massumi, Brian. 2011. *Semblance and Event: Activist Philosophy and the Occurrent Arts.* Cambridge, MIT Press.

Mehaffy, Michael. 2010. "Quality of Life by Design: The Science of a Structuralist Revolution." *Athens Dialogues.* Accessed May 20th, 2011. http://athensdialogues.chs.harvard.edu/cgi-bin/WebObjects/athensdialogues.woa/1/wo/AXJBwXbGWJO5KktAZipHLo/4.0.0.55.1.5.15.1.1.1.1.1

Michotte, Albert. 1963. *The Perception of Causality.* London. Methuen.

Murphie, Andrew. 2008. "Clone Your Technics! Research Creation, Radical Empiricism and the Constraints of Models." *Inflexions: a journal for research-creation* 1/1. Accessed May 20th, 2012. http://www.senselab.ca/inflexions/htm/issue1.html

Noë, Alva. 2004. *Action in Perception.* Cambridge, Mass: MIT Press.

Page, Scott L. and Scott Hawley. 2003. "Chromosome Choreography: The Meiotic Ballet." *Science* 8/301: 785-789.

Pred, Allan. 1977. "The Choreography of Existence: Some Comments on Hägerstrand's Time-Geography and Its Effectiveness." *Economic Geography* 53: 207-21.

Preston Dunlop, Valerie. 1981. *The Nature of the Embodiment of Choreutic Units in Choreography.* PhD thesis. Manchester: U.M.I.

Rodaway, Paul. 1994. *Sensuous Geographies.* London: Routledge.

Rosenberg, Douglas. 2000. "Video Space: A Site for Choreography". *Leonardo* 33/4: 275-280.

Rubidge, Sarah. 2007. "Sensuous Geographies and other Installations: The Interface of Body and Technology." In *Performance and Technology: Practices of Virtual Embodiment and Interactivity.* Edited by Susan Broadhurst and Josephine Machon, 112-126. Basingstoke: Palgrave.

Salingaros, Nikos. 2010. "Life and the Geometry of the Environment." *Athens Dialogues.* Accessed May 20th, 2011.
http://athensdialogues.chs.harvard.edu/cgi-bin/WebObjects/athensdialogues.woa/1/wo/AXJBwXbGWJO5KktAZipHLo/2.0.0.55.1.5.15.1.0.1.3.1

Thompson, Evan. 2008. *The Mind in Life.* Cambridge, Mass.: Harvard University Press.

Thrift, Nigel. 2007. *Nonrepresentational Theory: Space, Politics and Affect.* London and New York: Routledge.

Waldheim, Charles, ed. 2006. *The Landscape Urbanism Reader.* New York: Princeton Architectural Press.

ARTWORKS REFERENCED

Brown, Trisha. *Man Walking Down the Side of a Building.* First Performed: Wooster Street, New York City, USA, 1970.

Brown, Trisha. *Roof Pieces.* First Performed: Wooster Street, New York City, USA, 1971.

Childs, Lucinda. *Street Dance.* First Performed: Manhattan, New York City, USA, 1964.

Isaacs, Julian. *Ten Thousand Waves.* First shown: Sydney Bienniale, Australia, 2010.

Kozel, Susan and Gretchen Schiller. *trajets [V2]* 2004-2007. First mounted: Bilbao, Spain 2007.

Rubidge, Sarah and Alistair MacDonald. *Sensuous Geographies.* First mounted: New Territories Festival, The Arches, Glasgow, 2003.

Rubidge, Sarah and Garry Hill, with Nye Parry and Tim Diggins. *Passing Phases.* 1994-99. First mounted: The Place, London 1994.

Silvistrini, Luca. *(in)visible dances.* High Street, Birmingham, UK, 2010.

Taylor Wood, Sam. *Killing Time.* Tate Collection, London, 1994.

Viola, Bill. *Catherine's Room.* Tate Collection, London, 2001.

Viola, Bill. *Going Forth By Day.* Guggenheim Collection, New York, 2002.

WEBSITES REFERENCED

www.gretchen-schiller.com. Accessed on June 20, 2012. http://www.gretchen-schiller.org/trajets.html

www.sensedigital.com=.uk Accessed on June 20, 2012 http://www.sensdigital.co.uk/sg1

www.forsythe.com. Accessed on June 20, 2012. http://www.sensedigital.co.uk/sg1.htm

http://www.williamforsythe.de/installations.html?&no_cache=1&detail=1&uid=30.

NOTES

1   It is said of Dana Caspersen and William Forsythe's White Bouncy Castle (1997) that it "creates a choreographic space where there are no spectators, only participants" (www.williamforsythe.de/installations.html?&no_cache=1&detail=1&uid=30).

2   This book (edited by Lisa Ullman) comprised a collection of Laban's theories on space, and was published several years after Laban's death in 1958.

3   Examples are: From UK: Rosemary Butcher's North East Passage 1976 and D1, D2, 3D 1989-90; Rosemary Lee's Moments Shorelines 1987, Haughmond Dances 1990 and The Banquet Dances 1999; Siobhan Davies's 13 Different Keys 1999; Seven Sisters' Salome 1999 and DoubleTake 2000; From Spain: La Ribot's Dip me in Water 1997 and Piezas Distinguidas 2000; From USA: Stephan Koplowitz's Kohler Korper [Coal Bodies] 1999 and A Walk between Two Worlds 2005; Willi Dorner's Bodies in Urban Spaces 2007; From Denmark: X-Act's Kitt Johnston — Transform Series 1994-99 and Mellemrum #1 (Zwischenraum #1) 2008.

4   Examples of this form of choreographic practice include: Liz Aggis's Motion Control (2000) and Anarchic Variations (2002); Rosemary Butcher's Undercurrent (2001) and The Return (2005); David Hinton's Dead Dreams of Monochrome Men [with DV8] (1989) and Birds [with Yolande Snaith] (2000).

5   Susan Kozel and Kirk Woolford (Contours 1999), Igloo (Winterspace 2001), my own Passing Phases [with Garry Hill and Tim Diggins] (1994-99) and Sensuous Geographies [with Alistair MacDonald] (2003), Nic Sandiland and Rosie Lee (Remote Dancing (2004), Woolford (Will o' the Wisp 2005), Kozel/ and Gretchen Schiller (trajets 2007), Ole Kristensen (Body Navigation 2008).

6   Further details of Sensuous Geographies and video documentation can be accessed on www.sensedigital.co.uk/choreogpraphy.html; further details and video documentation of trajets can be accessed on www.gretchen-schiller.org/trajets.html.

7   These conceptions are not incorrect, merely partial. Indeed just as Newton's laws rather than Einstein's laws are what we live by in our everyday lives, so an understanding of space as being external to us enables us to navigate the world around us successfully.

8   Gibson's research on perception has had a significant influence on current under-
    standings of perception, as evidenced in the work of Antonio Damasio (1994; 1999),
    Brian Massumi (2002; 2011), Alva Noë (2004) and Evan Thompson (2008), all of
    whom incorporate into their discussions of perception, alongside the more specific
    senses of sight, hearing and smell, what many refer to as haptic perception.

9   Paul Rodaway (1994, 55), suggests that "each space and place discerned, or mapped,
    haptically is in this sense our space and because of the reciprocal nature of touch we
    come to belong to that space."

10 Here 'choreographic' refers to the composition of any motion in space-time, whether
    actively composed or perceptually experienced as composed.

11 Brian Massumi, translator of Deleuze and Guattari's A Thousand Plateaus notes that
    'affect', a term coined by Spinoza, and adopted by Deleuze and Guattari, refers to
    "…a prepersonal intensity corresponding to the passage from one experiential state
    of the body to another" (Deleuze and Guattari 1987, xvi, my emphasis).

12 An extreme example would be that the activities in the football stadia of Rwanda
    during the genocide produced very different (intensive) spaces to those that had
    been produced in the same material space before the Rwandan civil war. A far more
    commonplace example would be that space might be experienced differently when it
    is, respectively, sharply defined in the light of the sun and diffused at dawn or dusk.

13 Although the political dimensions of space are inevitably implicated in the choreo-
    graphic space discussed here, they take a back seat in this paper. Nevertheless, it
    is worth noting that the Situationists (Debord 1955) and theorists such as Michael
    Mehaffy (2010) and Nikos Salingaros (2010) argue that the form of material or built
    space is ideologically and politically driven, leading to the generation of particular
    forms of intensive space that are imbued with ideological positions, and that these
    subtly direct human behaviour within public spaces. "[C]ities have a psychogeo-
    graphical relief, with constant currents, fixed points and vortexes which strongly
    discourage entry into or exit from certain zones" (Knabb 1995, page number).

14 For technical reasons the participants wore long red, blue, or yellow robes, which in
    visual terms created a performance-like ambience. This was necessitated because the
    interactive interface (which was an optical motion tracking system) was activated by
    specific colours, requiring participants to be costumed in these colours.

15 Speakers not only surrounded the 'inner', or central, space, but were also placed
    around the walls of the room in which the installations was mounted, thus surround-
    ing the 'outer' space.

16 http://www.gretchen-schiller.org/trajets.html

17 A term developed by Brian Massumi and Erin Manning, which found its voice in
    their Technologies of Lived Abstraction project. Research-creation sees all research,

not only art-making, as "an assemblage to produce the new", as a form of 'worlding' (Murphie 2008).

18   Both installations were mounted in darkened spaces, and were navigable by participants. Participants could choose to inhabit the installation from the inside, or view the activity taking place within it from outside its material boundaries (see www.sense-digital.co.uk/sg1.htm: http://www.gretchen-schiller.org/trajets.html respectively).

19   A clear idea of the material structure of the installation, and the installation in action can be found on www.sensedigital.co.uk/sg1.html.

20   Sound as a medium is not contained by spatial boundaries, and thus inevitably extends far beyond the material space in which its source lies.

21   Intensive space was experienced vicariously by those who were viewing the activity of those engaging with the installations, in part because, even though at that moment observing the activity of those in the 'interactive' space, they were part of the community that the installation had generated.

22   This notion that gesture extends into space was addressed by Valerie Preston Dunlop (1981) in the development of what she calls CHUMM analysis, (Choreutic Units and their Manner of Materialization) in which both the actual and virtual spatial forms of choreography are addressed.

23   I am indebted to Doreen Massey for the many insights I gained from my conversations and discussions with her during the course of the 2011 Dancing Space(s) — Spacing Dance(s) conference in Odense.

24   The notion of 'temporary' can encompass many temporal scales, for even mountains continue the movement that was started during the geological events that led to their creation, albeit moving extremely slowly.

25   Gibson (1966) makes a distinction between exteroceptive and interoceptive (or distanced and intimate) senses and incorporates the haptic sense (in which he includes the somatosensory and proprioception) into the perceptual manifold.

26   It is the latter that site-specific choreography seeks to change by generating within a material space, a dynamic choreographic space that redirects attention and thus perception of the extensive space.

27   Such a 'performance' can be formal or informal, intentional or unwitting.

28   That this is possible is evidenced in the work of neuroscientists such as Patrick Haggard (University College London) and his colleagues, who have been investigating the activity of Mirror Neuron systems specifically in relation to dance (Calvo-Merino et al. 2005).

29   Neuroscientists have observed that, although the strength of the experience of embodiment differs as it is affected by familiarity with the patterns of movement being perceived, there is a neuronal response even amongst those with less experience.

SPACES OF ENCOUNTER: DANCING DEMOCRACY IN THE NORDIC REGION

Lena Hammergren

Abstract

This article looks at how dance and democracy interact in the Nordic region. It investigates "spaces of encounter" articulating how this region has become a site for material as well as mental inclusions and exclusions of dance genres and people, under the banner of democracy. Three examples are analysed: 1) the creation of a national, democratic cultural policy — in which art is defined as a tool for improving self-understanding as a unitary collective, 2) the creation of a national canon of artworks — in which art is used for securing a social cohesion around a national identity and 3) the "open source movement" — performances opposing artistic authority and ownership, and thus forming a certain kind of critique of how democracy can be defined from an aesthetic and socio-political viewpoint. The examples move in time, from the 1960s until today, and they articulate the move from ideologies of class, through ideologies of ethnicities to something I call the ideologies of political immanence.

Introduction

This article is a case study of how dance and democracy interact in the Nordic region with examples mainly from Denmark, Norway and Sweden.[1] Given the history of this region, I would like to emphasise that it should best be perceived as a "mental geography", rather than a fixed geography. Political, national, international and regional strategies have defined and continue to define where the borders should be drawn. However, I will not focus on changing geographies, but rather use the concept space as in "spaces of encounter", articulating how the region has become a site for material as well as mental inclusions and exclusions of dance genres and people, under the banner of democracy. The concept of democracy is here broadly defined and understood to embrace "multiple and contradictory subjects, inhabitants of a diversity of communities /... / constructed by a variety of discourses" (Mouffe 2005, 20). With a more narrow focus, democracy is also connected to the so-called Nordic Model comprising a welfare-based cultural policy with emphasis on egalitarian goals "guaranteeing citizens equal access to the benefits of culture" (Duelund 2003, 18). There are important differences between the Nordic countries in terms of history, culture and politics, but in this study the focus is on the shared welfare-based ideas that appeared after World War II.

Let me initiate this analysis by first addressing a personal perspective. I have been brought up in Sweden, a country whose politics during the 20th century have been marked by a social-democratic ideology and practice that included a range of reform programmes and strategies for securing social welfare and social equality. In addition, my personal life history includes a mother born in Finland, who suffered two wars between Finland and the former Soviet Union, and whose father disappeared after having moved to the latter country in order to support the early communist regime. Thus, when my mother immigrated to Sweden during the 1940s she brought with her embodied tensions between communism, social-ism and democracy. She was of course not alone in experiencing this pressure. Sweden and its neighbouring countries Denmark, Finland, Iceland and Norway, have acted as a mediating space between ideological forces emanating from the USA on the one side and the former Soviet Union, today Russia, on the other. So, the tension between "East" and "West" has been active in forming the Nordic societies and politics. Moreover, during the second half of the 20th century, it has become increasingly visible that the region also experiences tensions between a "North — South" perspective/divide.

All these aspects have affected my research on dance cultures in the Nordic region, and in particular, in trying to make sense of a fairly progressive political climate and its problematic, often discursively hidden shortcomings. I have needed other analytic tools than those provided by, for example, the deconstructions of imperialism or colonialism.

In the foreword to Robert J.C. Young's *White Mythologies*, Homi K. Bhabha formulates a critical standpoint that has helped me address the oscillating move-ment between practices of inclusions and exclusions that I have discovered in my analyses of dances performed in the Nordic region (Bhabha as reported by Young 2004). Young writes about Marx, Sartre, Foucault, among others. According to Bhabha, while doing so, Young contests "the Eurocentrism of those writers famously affiliated with the materialist projects of independence and emancipation" (ibid., x).

Since my own scholarly position includes writing from within what I conceive of as a fairly progressive culture, but also within a whole set of Eurocentric traditions and mindscapes, I feel targeted by Young's and Bhabha's critique, and therefore I will try to take on Bhabha's challenge that a contemporary scholar should engage in moving between, what he calls the "'*yes-but*' movement of dialectical thought" (ibid.). These famous authors have written eloquently about emancipation, but they are still deeply affected by a Eurocentric perspective. Translated into my methodology; I live in a fairly progressive part of the world, but there are still socio-cultural practices, including dancing, that are affected by what has been labelled a "whiteness-perspective", thus promoting an oppressive ideology in which exclusions and inclusions occur. These practices are seldom explicitly stated. They exist more commonly in hidden or unconscious social figurations.

For this analysis I will discuss three sets of dance practices that articulate different spaces of encounter, which are based on (seemingly) egalitarian grounds:

1. The creation of a national, democratic cultural policy — in which art is defined as a tool for improving self-understanding as a unitary collective;
2. The creation of a national canon of artworks — in which art is used for securing social cohesion around a national identity;
3. The "open source movement" — performances opposing artistic authority and ownership, and thus forming a rethinking of how democracy can be defined from an aesthetic and socio-political viewpoint.

The three examples move in time, from the late 1960s till today, and in my interpretation they articulate the move from ideologies of class, through ideologies of ethnicities,[2] to something I will, for now, call the ideologies of political immanence.

Social Democracy — Equal Rights to Dance?

During the 1960s Swedish authorities experienced a need to rethink its views on culture, much as a reaction to changes in both the national and international social climates. In some parts of the Nordic region, different groups protested against the Vietnam War, against the space programmes in the USA and the Soviet Union, against environmental destruction, and the exploitation of the "third" worlds. This wave of protest extended to a questioning of the condition of the foundations of democracy at home. In Sweden, people realised that the nation was composed of various national and ethnic minorities instead of a homogenous population. At that time migration to Sweden came mainly from different European countries such as Spain, Yugoslavia, and Greece because of their political situations, and from countries in Latin America, again depending on the political contexts.

Hence, it was during the 1960s that the nation's cultural life began to be regarded as a state concern that demanded the formulation of a unified national cultural policy, which was formally decided on in 1974 (Larsson 2003, 207 and passim). The major part of the policy-making was inspired by a broad definition of the concept "culture". It was dedicated to dispersing culture throughout the country, counteracting the effects of commercialism and making culture available to previously marginalised groups, particularly children and youths, the differently-abled and the working class (*Kulturrådet: Ny kulturpolitik*, 1972). Equal Rights to culture, became the central concept of the new cultural perspective. There is no mentioning of ethnic identities in the policy documents from 1974. This is remarkable given the social context of the time with its large number of immigrants, and programs for refugees. I will return to this problem below.

Art and culture were now believed to be excellent tools for addressing marginalised groups, and for improving their sense of self-understanding and comprehension of a democratic and equal society. This view demanded that target groups needed to be defined and described. People were classified according to typical social class categories: low income, short education, single mothers, and isolated families. These descriptions seldom took notice of the individual's lived experience, and the image of passive and victimised groups became increasingly stronger. So-called experts started to develop ideas of how certain artistic forms could be used to solve the minority groups' social discrimination and thus enable them to participate more fully in the "democratic" society (Pripp 2007).

Concerning the arts, one of the more important factors to develop during this period was the organisation of artists into national centres. The Dance Centre was formed in 1971 in Stockholm, and its aim was to coordinate the administration of performances by independent dancers and choreographers, and to deepen the public's interest in dance. In addition, members of the organisation became involved in the outreach programmes to different minority groups sponsored by the state. In this way they used their dancing in tandem with the cultural policy's emphasis on art as a tool for self-improvement — art as a method for achieving everybody's participation in forming a democratic society.

The dance company Kari and Karin was among the first independent groups to work in this manner. It was formed in the mid-1970s by the dancers Kari Sylwan and Karin Thulin. They had a background from the Swedish Royal Opera Ballet and from the Cullberg Ballet. Some of their dances, for example *Where have you hidden your body?* (a workshop/performance dealing with modes of liberating your body) and *In the Ninth Month* (a performance on being pregnant) were toured all over Sweden, and the company became part of the early feminist movement. The overall intention of the company was to help audiences to better understand their own bodies, and thus to be able to connect to the society via a common bodily experience — creating a strong link between audience, artist and society (Sylwan and Thulin 1981). From a critical viewpoint it is interesting to reflect on the potential effects of the dancers' physical skills and virtuosity in relation to their aim of wanting to communicate via a kind of corporeal empathy. The dance company's choice

Kari Sylwan rehearsing her solo the life of the dying swan, from *Portrait*, 1982. Photographer: Beata Bergström. The Music and Theatre Library of Sweden.

of dance techniques, i.e. European ballet and modern dance, articulates particular Western aesthetics that not every viewer necessarily could relate to. The desire to create a common understanding of corporeal experiences might have failed, because the performances were built on an assumption on shared values between dancers and audience. This appears, for example, in a dance based on jumping and turning, in which everyday practices of these movements were seamlessly linked to the highly advanced versions that professional dancers perform.

This vision of wanting audiences to be able to connect strongly to different art or cultural forms and to relate their experience to the practice of living in a democracy was also expressed in another objective within the national cultural policy from 1974. The policy wanted to support the individual's participation in her/his own creation of culture. One of the results was a strengthening of different amateur-oriented organisations. However, during the decade that followed, this goal became problematic. In the 1980s, people involved in folk music and folk dancing started lobbying for a more fair treatment of these activities, including the demand for higher state subsidies. The background was that in tandem with the theatrical dancing that was developing a stronger status as an art form, the folk dance organisations and folklore companies had become excluded from state support on the grounds of not working with innovation and new productions — the national criteria for state funding.

When both folk musicians and folk dancers started to work with the aim of changing the cultural policy, one of their central arguments was a reference to the growing concern for the multicultural dimensions of the society. The organisations stressed that the local Swedish culture was unique, and that by preserving these forms of dance and music, Sweden would contribute to the global cultural multiplicity. In a policy document they argued for the need to support traditional folk music and dance:

> The people who deepen their knowledge of folk music and folk dance will make comparisons to music and dance from other countries. They will also acquire insights in how other social classes' and nations' cultures have affected the culture of the lower classes. /.../ Participating in folk music and folk dancing can therefore create understanding and respect for other cultures. (Farago 1985, PM, my translation)

But it was only "Swedish" folk dance and music that the lobbying organisation believed needed support by the state, even though many dance cultures were visibly present in the country. One explanation to this standpoint can be the manner in which the ideologies of class were at work. This ideology stresses values that encompass the whole socio-political arena, including justice and equality for all, and it seeks to diminish group differences rather than emphasise them (Lundberg, Malm and Ronström, 2003, 20-26 and passim). Consequently, it was not considered a problem to secure financial support only for traditional Swedish culture, since it could act as a liberating tool for everyone. The "many" were seen as one, in order to secure democracy for all.

Fighting Against Racism

The arguments developed by the Swedish folk organisations may seem very dated from a contemporary perspective, but almost the same arguments appeared again during the 1990s in Norway, when people from different interest organisations wrote a strategic plan for how Norwegian folk dance and music should be given a more prominent position in Norwegian cultural policy. One of the goals and arguments was that learning and knowing about "your own" (i.e. Norwegian) dance and musical heritage helped create a more solid identity and thus, helped fight racism (Bakka and Ranheim 1995, 24), an explicit egalitarian objective. The logic was based on a distinction between national values and nationalism, where nationalism was considered the negative result of a lack of identity that the former (i.e. strong national values) could help to secure. The Norwegian argumentation mirrored the Swedish statements from the 1980s, when it explained that: "When you meet other cultures in Norway or in other countries, it is empowering to know your own cultural background" (ibid., my translation). The problem was of course that the "other" cultures of immigrant groups of people were already integral parts of what constituted Norwegian and Swedish identitarian dimensions. They were not articulations of dance cultures outside of the nation.

It is often described how important it was for Norway to secure a uniting of the country and its inhabitants after World War II, because of having lived under Danish and Swedish rule and later the Nazi occupation (Bakke 2003, 147-179). Thus, the strategic plan for folk music and dance can partly be explained against this background. Sweden did not have the same social and political experience, but it seems to have acted along similar policy lines in striving to build a democratisation of culture by placing emphasis on cultural cohesion. Irrespective of the different historical backgrounds, I find it important to look critically at the ways in which a presumed ethnic homogeneity existed in the two welfare states that were both striving for egalitarian goals.

A National Cultural Canon

A more recent example of a similar kind of thinking that involves exclusionary practices, was the publication of The Danish Cultural Canon in 2006, initiated by the Danish Ministry of Culture. The overall aim behind the canon that consisted of different artworks (architecture, performances, design, music, etc.) was said to "stimulate public dialogue" by giving reference points of what is considered "special about Danes and Denmark".[3] From the government's point of view, it was considered of major importance "to stimulate and consolidate Danish monoculture as a medium counteracting cultural relativism and multiculturalism".[4] This can be considered a provocative statement, and it belies the will to stimulate a critical public dialogue concerning what could be considered special about Danes and Denmark. Many of the experts who were chosen to select the artworks defended the canon by stating that: "We live in a chaotic time, devoid of a sense of history", and we "notice the same tendency in all of us /.../ we experience a need to relate to values that reach further than our noses, but at the same time are more open than they have ever been" (my translation).[5] It is possible that the chaotic time, articulated in the citation, was a reaction stemming from the encounter with multiple ethnicities.

According to the canon criteria, the selected works should display national qualities in a manner that they could not be disregarded "if we want to define what is characteristic and distinctive about Danish culture".[6] At the same time, the "selected works should /.../ illustrate that Danish art and culture have come into being in interplay and interaction with European and international trends".[7]

There are only three dance works included in the performance art section of the canon, and one additional dance is part of the category of children's culture. There are no Danish folk dances. This is interesting since the selection of music to the canon includes both folk songs and other popular music. The dances selected in the performance art section are *Sylfiden* created by August Bournonville in 1836; *Etudes* by Harald Lander, choreographed in 1948, and *Enetime*, by Fleming Flindt, created in 1963 and based on Eugene Ionesco's play *The Lesson*.

In the presentational texts that accompany the canon in books, DVD and a website, there are no explicit definitions of the Danishness that prevails in these ballets, as one could expect, since for example *Sylfiden* is considered typical of the Danish classical ballet aesthetics. Instead, there are more criteria articulated in the texts, which seem to be valid for an international canon of ballets. The performing arts' committee has proclaimed that their collection is the result of interactions with performances all over the world. With regard to the choice of dances, the world is limited to Europe and a kind of transnational ballet aesthetics. These circumstances are particularly interesting because several of the canon committees describing the other art forms are quite explicit in highlighting national characteristics.

The fourth dance, included in the category of children's culture, is *The Nutcracker*, in a new version from 2003 by the Danish hip-hop choreographer Steen Koerner. It can be considered as a mixed-media performance and involves speech, rap as well as street dance, and classical ballet. This mix articulates the awareness of many dance cultures living side by side, but it is difficult to find a more explicit commentary in the presentational text that seeks to deconstruct the domination of one culture over the other. Instead, it is remarked that it is the "magical ballerina" who creates the happy ending,[8] and hence is put in opposition to the street dance styles, which are representing the "evil" forces.

At work in the choice of all four dances is an unresolved discursive tension between what is conceived of as particularly Danish and what is international, between a monoculture and a multiculture, to use the concepts that are part of the government's main objective behind creating the canon. I do not argue that there is an explicit racist or undemocratic voice here. Instead, I find that a Eurocentric attitude is embedded in the inability to perceive a potential domination by "white" European ballet values over dance styles from other parts of the world.

The creation of a national canon of different artworks were hotly debated in Denmark as well as in other Nordic countries, but no other country has decided to create one. Some refer to the awareness of many cultures existing side by side, which makes it impossible to think of *one* national canon. I consider both this reaction, and the political discourses that stand behind the Danish canon, as responses to an "ideology of ethnicity" that has slowly replaced the focus on social cohesion that existed in the Nordic region up till the 1990s. In this context, the ideology of ethnicity puts stress on the relative character of a society's values, a standpoint from which one can argue that justice and equality imply the right to be perceived as *different*, not the "same", and embrace potentially different cultural values. The Danish government did not seem to accept this ideology, but they were still influenced by it and tried out various strategies in order to counteract its effects.

Open Source Movement

My last example addresses new trends in choreography-making that have been emerging in several parts of Europe since the beginning of the 21st century, and that I here, for analytical reasons, label the open source movement.[9]

One of the first initiatives that can be related to this trend occurred during the so-called "MODE05 open-source conference" on education in choreography, dance and performance that took place in Potsdam, Germany, in 2005. The conference became a platform for artists in the performing arts, for theoreticians, and activists who were interested in exploring how "the economy of ownership and distribution" in the worlds of art could be reversed (Cvejić 2009). The concept of "open source principles" was important, and was said to deal with "questions about the status of work with respect to [the] learning process" (ibid.). According to the conference organisers, the principle of "open source" involved strategies of, for example:

※ revisiting earlier dance works
※ using sound and images from mass media, like cinema or You Tube, and transposing them into live performances
※ publishing dance scores on websites, making them free for anyone to use
※ creating work aimed at overproduction.

Overproduction is an artistic method and it can result in producing by-products to the dance; for example, video excerpts from discussions and parties. An example is a dinner party organised by MyChoreography.org and put on the internet as "MyChoreograhy.org does Dinner Party". Besides photos there are written descriptions of the dinner party:

> Everyone gets to know each other when MyChoreography.org is around. They hosted a shoulder rubbing dinner for the artists-in-residence and staff at the fabrik Potsdam. /.../ Conversations about choreography took place within this choreography.[10]

As is evident in the quotation, the collective considers a dinner party a kind of choreography — and as such an intervention into the more conventional ways in which we understand the concept "a performance". This is in line with the desire, within the whole open source movement, to make "small-scale achievements" rather than addressing major themes or problems with the dance works produced by the artists (Cvejić 2009).

Another strategy is called 'revisiting earlier dance works', and MyChoreography.org exemplifies the strategy in their version of *The Rite of Spring* to music by Stravinsky first danced in 2008. Their version does not seem to perform any explicit political or aesthetic argument that could explain why they have chosen to perform a new production of this canonical dance work. Their manner of performing it rather hints at a notion of treating the dance as an open source, a score that can be visited and danced by all. But, they do not perform only one score, instead the performance appears to be a construction of fragments of several "Rites". In one section a male and a female dancer run heads on and collide breast to breast. This is a reference to the French choreographer Maurice Béjart's *The Rite of Spring* and its male and female collectives. Another reference is made to a solo performance from 2007, when the French choreographer Xavier Le Roy performed his version in which he used a recording of Stravinsky's music conducted by Sir Simon Rattle. The performance consisted of Le Roy conducting the music from this recording, having initially studied Rattle's interpretation, and playing the music on tape. Hence, to Le Roy the act of conducting was choreography in its own right.[11]

It is obvious that the open source movement addresses issues concerning the distribution of copyrighted material without the permission of the copyright holder. It is probably not a coincidence that Sweden during this same period has experienced a highly publicised lawsuit and trial concerning authorship and copyright. The Pirate Bay was a website that indexed and tracked BitTorrent files, and it has been one of the world's largest facilitators of illegal downloading. The attitude among the MyChoreography.org choreographers echoes The Pirate Bay, albeit on a smaller scale. There is no explicit mentioning of copyright issues in their texts, but the choreographers question the norms of both aesthetics and dance skills, and "who is allowed to perform what and where".[12] The attitude is expressed in a different manner in the Open Source Theatre Manifest (sic) published on the website "everybodystoolbox" in 2007, in which the two authors of the manifesto remark the following under the title Code of Conduct: "We will reuse, reconstruct and recycle ideas, scenes and material from everywhere. But we will always admit and openly say from where we have our material, ideas and methods".[13]

One of the theoretical inspirations to the movement is the French philosopher Jacques Rancière, and his 1982-proposed model of teaching, from the book *The Ignorant Schoolmaster*. These ideas have later been developed also with regard to the relationship between performer and spectator. Rancière argues that teacher and student are equal and the student should accordingly be encouraged to explore his or her own individual qualities — in his words; the student should learn what the teacher doesn't know. Since knowledge is not transmitted in continuity between a master and a student, ownership of knowledge does not mean anything, and it has no intrinsic value (Rancière 2009, 14). Consequently, copyright is not important.

The open source movement is a strong political statement, and it is significant — in relation to my other examples — that it avoids applying identity politics. This choice is evident in a self-published book (thus no copyright) written by performers and art activists: "This [book] is a no to identity politics, it's no group, it is each and every one of us" (Anon 2009, 8). Both the ideology of class and the ideology of ethnicity being present in my earlier examples have disappeared. As I have argued above, identity politics were used during the 1980s and 1990s, as they described class and national characteristics within communities working with folk music and dance. The open source movement explicitly resists categories such as gender, ethnicity, and class as the key determinants of performance interpretations. They are resisted, not because they are unimportant, they argue, but because "they are categories that do not simply exist externally to the cultural artefacts they are called to explain" (Hewitt and Pristas 2009, 41). Instead, politics are conceived of as immanent in the aesthetics as praxis, and thus in dancing as doing. By doing something, you perform a political act. Andrew Hewitt, whose book *Social Choreography* has played a role as theoretical support, articulates this in more detail whilst arguing that in both "the practice of choreography and in the critical discourses it generated, such categories were themselves being rehearsed and refined" (Hewitt 2005, 4).

Concluding Remarks

It is certainly possible to write appreciatively about the examples I have analysed in this text, and highlight their empowering effects. Many of the dancers, choreographers and activists mentioned have addressed important aesthetic and/ or socio-political questions in their respective context. My objective has been different and, influenced by both Young and Bhabha, I have aimed at critically investigating viewpoints that a Eurocentric perspective might hide. As a result I point out some of the ways in which I think dance has failed to adhere to the democratic, egalitarian goals of the Nordic welfare state.

Some of the dances discussed have in common a rejection of the unique artist or the unique choreography; consequently they seem to address issues of antihierarchical nature and of equality. The dance company Kari and Karin worked from within the new Swedish social democratic cultural policy, in which dance and other art forms were considered excellent tools for the citizens' improved self-understanding. This individual improvement was then believed to help people to collectively engage in the creation of a democratic society. The two choreographers' highly technical movement vocabularies stemming from the West were tied together in a seemingly unproblematic manner, as if they had an equal foundation based on everyday movement shared by all people. Some of their televised dances were built on relating highly advanced dance steps to pedestrian versions of similar movements. This choice excluded other kinds of dancing and moving, and thus revealed a universal assumption about how danced expressions can be shared between artists and audiences. In Norway and Sweden, national folk dances were used in a similar manner to invoke the understanding of the "many" as one, of dancing the "same" dance as a means to create social cohesion and equality among different groups of people.

Karin Thulin rehearsing a solo with texts by Samuel Beckett, from *Portrait*, 1982. Photographer: Beata Bergström. The Music and Theatre Library of Sweden.

Anxiety about multiculturalism and how Western democratic societies can integrate people with different cultural background has been prevalent in many contexts within the Nordic region. It has also been remarked that national policies, disregarding the demographic changes occurring since the 1960s, has kept a hegemonic focus on strategies aimed at homogeneity and social coherence (Nilsson 2003, 482-83). One of its most explicit social figurations appeared in the objectives behind the Danish Cultural Canon published in 2006, when the government wanted to counteract cultural relativism. On the surface the art canon seems to reject any notion of universalism, when it speaks about creating a Danish monoculture and lists artworks that are supposed to define Danishness. But the dances included in the canon are to a large extent based on the aesthetics of classical ballet, and consequently they display a universal understanding and prioritising of the Western dance culture.

The Rite of Spring performed by the collective MyChoreography.org uses the open source movement in their effort to rethink dance as an art form, and they address "the canon" in a different manner than the Danish example. To choose a canonical dance, and treat it as any ordinary movement and music material accessible on the Internet, has an empowering potentiality. Everybody can dance his or her own version of the canonical dances. But on closer investigation, one cannot find any explicit linking to or commentary about the local Nordic and European context in which they are performing, and therefore it could be argued that there is a similar universal assumption underlying their critical strategy as in Kari and Karin's performances from the 1970s and 1980s even though their stress on virtuosic dance skills articulate a different agenda. Chantal Mouffe has defined social agents living in radical democracies as "constituted by an ensemble of 'subject positions' that can never be totally fixed in a closed system of differences" (Mouffe 2005, 77). She clearly disagrees with identity politics that rely on essentialist definitions, but she argues that there must exist partial fixations because democracy "calls for the constitution of collective identities around clearly differentiated positions" allowing us to choose between different alternatives (ibid., 4). According to her, some subject positions have to be stated in each context. On that account it is relevant to wonder what happens if the doing of dance disregards differentiated subject positions and the local contexts in which it is practised as well as takes for granted equal accessibility (for example of the canon and Internet) and equal representation? From this perspective the open source strategy, irrespective of its productive questioning of the ontology of choreography and ownership, might be interpreted as articulating an "abstract universalism /.../ and the myth of a unitary subject" (Mouffe 2005, 21).

If the dance examples in this text are compared to one another, it seems as if they have all failed to achieve the kind of democracy that Chantal Mouffe writes about, since they function with a sense of "universalism" in which different acts of inclusion and exclusion operate. Conversely, it can be argued that "all forms of consensus are by necessity based on acts of exclusion", but according to Mouffe we should still strive for a "democratic equivalence", which does not negate individual differences (ibid., 84-85). It is open to debate to what extent the spaces of encounter between different practices, practitioners and discourses of dance have managed to perform this kind of democratic dancing in the Nordic region.

BIBLIOGRAPHY

Bakke, Marit. 2003. "Cultural Policy in Norway." In *The Nordic Cultural Model: Nordic Cultural Policy in Transition*, edited by Peter Duelund, 147-179. Copenhagen: Nordic Cultural Institute.

Duelund, Peter. 2003. "Cultural Policy: An Overview." In *The Nordic Cultural Model: Nordic Cultural Policy in Transition*, edited by Peter Duelund, 13-30. Copenhagen: Nordic Cultural Institute.

Hewitt, Andrew. 2005. *Social Choreography: Ideology as Performance in Dance and Everyday Movement*. Durham and London: Duke University Press.

Kulturrådet: Ny kulturpolitik. Sammanfattning. 1972. SOU, Statens offentliga utredningar, 67.

Larsson, Tor. 2003. "Cultural Policy in Sweden." In *The Nordic Cultural Model: Nordic Cultural Policy in Transition*, edited by Peter Duelund, 181-251. Copenhagen: Nordic Cultural Institute.

Lepecki, André. 2006. *Exhausting Dance: Performance and the Politics of Movement*. New York and London: Routledge.

Lundberg, Dan; Malm, Krister and Ronström, Owe. 2003. *Music, Media, Multiculture: Changing Musicscapes*. Stockholm: Svenskt visarkiv.

Mouffe, Chantal. 2005. *The Return of the Political*. London and New York: Verso.

Nilsson, Sven. 2003. *Kulturens nya vägar: Kultur, kulturpolitik och kulturutveckling i Sverige*. Malmö: Polyvalent.

Pripp, Oscar. 2007. "Kulturens soppstenar." *Exempel och erfarenheter, analys av året och tidigare insatser*. SOU 50: 262-282.

Rancière, Jacques. 2009 *The Emancipated Spectator*. Translated by Gregory Elliot. London and New York: Verso.

Sylwan, Kari and Thulin, Karin. 1981. *Kari och Karin i rörelse. En bok om vårt arbete.* Stockholm: Entré/Riksteatern.

Young, Robert J.C. 2004. *White Mythologies.* London and New York: Routledge.

UNPUBLISHED

Anon. 2009. "Reversed Revolution." *The Swedish Dance History*: 5-8.

Bakka, Egil and Ranheim, Ingar, eds. 1995. "Handlingsplan for Folkemusikk og Folkedans."

Farago, Lars. 1985. PM, "Dags för en rättvis behandling av folkmusik och folkdans i samhällets kulturpolitik." *Rådet för folkmusik och folkdans*, March 15. Private archive.

Hewitt, Andrew and Pristas, Goran Sergej. 2009. "Choreography is a Way of Thinking About the Relationship of Aesthetics to Politics — An Interview." *The Swedish Dance History*: 30-43.

INTERNET

Cvejić, Bojana. 2009. "Learning by making." Accessed May 8, 2009. http://summit.kein.org/book/export/html/235

MyChoreography.org does Dinner Party. 2010. Accessed January 2, 2010. http://inpex.se/node/241,

in situ productions 2010. Accessed January 5, 2010. http://www.insituproductions.net/_eng/frameset.html

Cultural Policies and Trends in Europe. 2009. Accessed May 8, 2010. http://www.culturalpolicies.net/web/denmark.

Councilof Europe/ERICarts. 2009. "Compendium of Cultural Policies and Trends in Europe, 10th Edition" Denmark, chapter 4.2.3. Accessed May 8, 2009. http://www.culturalpolicies.net/web/denmark

Kulturministeriet Danmark. 2010a. Accessed January 2, 2010. http://www.kum.dk/sw33918.asp

Kulturministeriet Danmark. 2010b. Accessed January 5, 2010. http://www.kum.dk/sw37439.asp

www.kulturkanon.kum.dk/boernekultur/noeddeknaekkeren/Begrundelse_Noeddeknaekkeren/

Everybodys Toolbox open source in the performing arts. 2010. Accessed January 12, 2010. http://www.everybodystoolbox.net/?q=node

The Open Source Theatre Manifest. 2007. Accessed May 8 2009. http:// www.everybodystoolbox.net/?q=node/116

NOTES

1   This text is part of a larger, trans-Nordic research project Dance in Nordic Spaces: The Formation of Corporeal Identities.

2   It is mainly within research on music that the two concepts class and ethnicity have been used in order to relate analyses of art to changes in the Swedish society, see Lundberg, Malm and Ronström 2003.

3   Cultural Policies and Trends in Europe 2009.

4   Council of Europe/ERICarts 2009, Cultural Policies and Trends in Europe 2009.

5   Kulturministeriet Danmark 2010a.

6   Council of Europe/ERICarts2009.

7   Kulturministeriet Danmark 2010 b.

8   www.kulturkanon.kum.dk/boernekultur/ noeddeknaekkeren/ Begrundelse_Noeddeknaekkeren/

9   André Lepecki lists some of the artists I place in the open source movement, and remarks that there are no proper names attached to their modes of working, although he picks out the "interrogation of choreography's political ontology" as their common theme (Lepecki 2006, 45).

10 MyChoreography.org does Dinner Party 2010.

11 in situ production 2010.

12 Everybodys Toolbox open source in the performing arts 2010.

13 The Open Source Theatre Manifest 2007.

"DANCING BACK TO ARCADY"[1] — ON REPRESENTATIONS OF EARLY TWENTIETH-CENTURY MODERN DANCE

Hanna Järvinen

Abstract

In this paper, I discuss the role of spatial and temporal escapism in representations of dance, ca 1900-1930. In particular, I focus on photographs as rarely used sources on what made this dance 'modern'. I argue that by understanding nostalgia as a radical desire to change the status quo the disparity between our ideas of urban, industrialised modernity and this imagery of allegedly 'modern' dancers skipping in flowing tunics on sunny meadows can be overcome. Consequently, the actual legacy of these representations lies in how they can help us question the qualia we still use for evaluating (representations of) dance to construct the history of the art form.

Introduction

Alpine landscapes, green fields, or the Acropolis are not the first images we associate with industrialised and urban European modernity, yet these are the settings of modern dancers in the first decades of the twentieth century (see Image 1). In dance research, these kinds of pictures of dancers are usually discussed only through what kind of dancing is represented — or rather, through who is the principal dancer in the picture (here, Rudolf von Laban). Less attention is paid to less famous dancers, and almost none to the question that interests me: what makes this dancing 'modern'?

Following Michel de Certeau's (1988, 117) argument about space as "situated as the act of a present (or of a time), and modified by the transformations caused by successive contexts", I focus on the political and ideological implications of the 'modern' space produced in these images and argue that placing dance in what to us seem retrospective settings (as with the kind of re-evocation of past great civilisations, especially Ancient Greece — see Image 2 — or in nature (rather than in an urban environment such as a garden or a park), as in Image 3 carries a particular legacy for the history of the art form.

In particular, the hegemonic view of art dance these images have helped to construe rests on a contemporary pedagogy and ideology that genders dance as female and represents it as healthy and joyful exercise that can cure the ills of modernisation and even serve eugenic aims. As the works and authors thus discussed have become the foundation of our narrative about dance's past, the ideology of exclusion — of particular forms, individuals, affects and spaces — evident in these early representations can help us question the qualia we still use for evaluating (representations of) dance and perhaps allow us to construct a different kind of history for the art form.

Modernity

The first decades of the twentieth century are the years of the 'dance craze', the proliferation of dance forms on stage and off. This proliferation includes publications that were no longer principally manuals by dancing masters wishing to 'copyright' their dances and secure a reputation and an income. Rather, the 'self-improvement' of the presumed reader shifted towards spectatorship and connoisseurship.[4] Even when such books purportedly promote a new pedagogy of dance (as in Dunham 1918), they reveal an astonishing emphasis on the *spectator*: the reader is not assumed engaged in dance practice. Dancing does not seem to require any awareness of body in space, whether balance or more complex kinaesthetic awareness. Illustrations further stress this perspective as they are posed for the camera, depicting and legitimating a particular aesthetic that justifies the social role of the (artistic) dancer as a professional *performer*.

Any discussion on modern dance raises the question, what is meant by 'modern'. In dance history, the term 'modern dance' has been reserved for the theatrical or art dance of later figures such as Doris Humphrey and Martha Graham. However, 'modern dance' and 'modern dancers' appear in the title of several books from the 1910s (e.g. Flitch 1912; Urlin 1912), which seem to discuss almost every possible kind of dance as 'modern'. As nearly all of the examples given are of dancers still actively performing on stage at the time of writing we might substitute the term 'contemporary' for 'modern', but this is equally confusing as today, 'contemporary dance' is used in Europe to connote dance emerging after the Second World War. For the same reason, notions like 'free-form' or 'barefoot' dance are equally misrepresentative, as many of the dancers lauded in these texts come from specific, codified and definitely shoed forms like ballet and flamenco.

However, what actually belies such a simple substitution of 'contemporary' for 'modern' is the presence of definite evaluation of different forms of dance vis-à-vis the notion of *modernity*. Although virtually none of the books on modern dance published prior to the First World War distinguish between forms of social dance and theatrical dance, *all* distinguish between healthy dancing that is graceful and harmonious and unhealthy dancing that is feverish and decidedly urban, epitomised by the syncopated rhythms of ragtime and the chorus line of Tiller Girls.[5] In other words, qualities we associate with urban modernity and modernisation (the process of becoming modern), and themes associated with contemporary life (without exotic, mythological or retrospective setting) are attacked as *inartistic* if not outright dangerous to the physical and social health that art should illustrate. (See Järvinen 2009 for discussion on one such work.)

Nostalgia

Therefore, rethinking what was modern in the images of these modern dancers requires a redefinition of another term, nostalgia. Today, we tend to think that nostalgia is sentimental longing for things past, a gilding memories receive in the unerring light of hindsight. But originally, nostalgia was a specific form of melancholia, a disease caused by prolonged absence from one's home — what came to be called homesickness. It is only by the mid-nineteenth century that nostalgia came to mean regretful or wistful remembrance of a past time that often acquired idealised qualities, and even today, nostalgia connotes both temporally and spatially (Turner 1987). Thus, it is possible to think of nostalgia as a longing for a (utopian) place that exists in the personal past remembered by the individual — not as much a *recherche du temps perdu* as a memory of a past place that time has gilded. Stressing the spatial connotation of nostalgia, I claim that it is this past place that the representations of dance seek to create — not for the individual but for the art form.

In his excellent article, Peter Fritzsche (2001, np) has noted that "Nostalgia not only cherishes the past for the distinctive qualities that are no longer present but also acknowledges the permanence of their absence. It thus configures periods of the past as bounded in time and place and as inaccessible". As such, Fritzsche argues, nostalgia is bound to an understanding of history as change that only emerged in the nineteenth century. In the second half of the nineteenth century, nostalgic historiography was used to criticise present practices, namely the kind of teleological historiography that culminated in the Enlightenment but continued in the form of positivism and social Darwinism in the nineteenth century. Teleological historiography represented the past as a progress towards the present, a continuous development from simple and primitive to complex and modern.

To follow Reinhardt Koselleck's (2004, 255-275) argument on the relationship between the horizon of expectations and space of experience as defining historical time, it is possible to argue that instead of a utopian future, late nineteenth-century historiography imagined a utopian past: the past of the Antiquity, (Medieval) national past, pre-industrialised agrarian and/or pastoral past. This imagined past was a contrast to the contemporary urban, industrialised present, but interpreted in ways that reflect the concerns of that present about the possibilities of the future. Moreover, if exile and alienation are, as Raymond Williams (1989) has argued, essential conditions of industrialised modernity, then nostalgia could epitomise (positive) dissatisfaction with this condition: the example of the past lost home and of belonging becomes a criticism of present circumstance of not-home, not-belonging.[6] Thus, nostalgia could function as the *counterpoint* to alienation and exile in modernity (and modernism) rather than as its direct opposite.

Taking nostalgia as subversive, it is possible to rethink its role in (representations of) early-twentieth-century modern dance. Although the fantastic, exotic or retrospective settings of this dance seem conservative and even escapist today, at the time, they epitomised nostalgia that was both modern and radical because it aimed for social and aesthetic change rather than conservation of the status quo. What tends to confuse us is that we understand 'modernity' as what, in this earlier chain of thought, *was* the status quo: the hectic present of the late-nineteenth-century metropolis. The less hurried, more "harmonious", "graceful", and "natural" — to cite the preferred aesthetic qualities associated with this dance — Other to modernity was critical of present ideas about progress as a solely positive phenomenon. As such, early-twentieth-century dance was nostalgic in the positive political sense of using the past to change and *revitalise* contemporary modernity. Hence, the landscape of this nostalgic space was alike the mythic Arcadia: a pictoresque[7] and apparently atemporal or eternal countryside (as in Image 2).

Illustrating Arcadia

In representations of modern dancers, the quality that I have chosen to call 'Arcadian' results from cultural references to the Antiquity and/or to nature as something picturesque, a kind of timeless, boundless space.[8] In practical terms of photographic representation, the meadow or a cloudy sky behind the dancers allows them to stand out clearly in shades of black and white. But the background is only seemingly neutral in that there is nothing to distract the viewer from the main figure of the dancer. Just as studio photographs used landscapes or cloudy skies to create a sense of extensive horizons beyond the main figure (as in Image 4), outdoor dance photography extends the picture space to infinity. This associates the spatiality of the representation with the assumed eternal values of aesthetics of the dance represented, but it also fixes the space, turning it into what de Certeau (1988, 117) calls place.

Arcadia is also a specific place: since the Antiquity, it has been a landscape of rural bliss, a space without specific temporal references. The Arcadian quality of the dance images discussed here results in part from the absence of references to the twentieth-century present. Even when the horizon is relatively high in the picture space, or limited by trees or mountains, any signs of current human habitation (such as roads, modern buildings, or telegraph poles) are excluded from these images of dance. As a consequence, beyond the occasional 'Greek' ruin, there are hardly any right angles in the images: even trees act as wings of a stage (see Image 5). This staged quality recalls how the dance illustrated as performed in nature and, based on the skimpy costumes of the dancers, in the warmth of an eternal summer, was actually performed in the built environment of the theatre and the salon during the social season — winter. The texts that these images complement never address this paradox, which should caution any researcher from using these pictures as documents of actual dancing.[9]

Besides the fact that actual movement qualities of dance can only be implied from two-dimensional still photographs in shades of grey, well into the 1920s depicting dance was fraught with the technical restrictions of cameras that had trouble capturing rapid movement even outside in direct sunlight.[10] Consequently, most dancers were photographed in studio settings, posed so as to appear moving, and the resulting images were retouched to give a pose — such as one of a dancer standing in arabesque — the appearance of additional movement, usually a leap, or of hovering above the ground (as in Image 4).[11]

This means that almost none of the photographs reproduced as representing modern dance are snapshots of dancers in movement. Moreover, their composi-

1. Johann Adam Meisenbach. 1914. Rudolf von Laban and Dancers in Ascona. Courtesy of Kunsthaus Zürich, The Estate of Suzanne Perrottet.

2. Raymond Duncan. 1903. Isadora Duncan at the Parthenon theater. Courtesy of the Digital Gallery of New York Public Library.

3. Frédéric Boissonas. 1913. Dalcroze-Schule (Group of multiple dancers in a meadow). Courtesy of Agence Photographique de la Réunion des Musées Nationaux et du Grand Palais (Musée d'Orsay, Paris).

4. L. Roosen. 1934. Vaslav Nijinsky as prince Albert in the second act of Giselle. Courtesy of the Wellcome Trust.

5. Unknown photographer. S.a. A modern Aurora. From Dunham 1918, 100.

6. Unknown photographer. 1898. La Loïe Fuller. Cover of December issue of Théatre. Paris: Jean Boussod, Manzi, Joyant & Cie, Villanova University Digital Library, Source: World Periodicals.

tions are not accidental (as in snapshots) but carefully composed to represent particular aesthetic and/or ideological values. For example, although pedagogical images exaggerated poses to an extent to clarify what was required in a particular step or attitude, virtuosity was shunned: it is obvious that professional dancers could lift their feet higher or flex their bodies more than shown in these pictures, but to do so would go against aesthetic ideals through which "low" or "merely entertaining" forms of dance were gradually set apart from art dance.[12]

To compensate for the stillness of the two-dimensional picture and perhaps also to emphasise the apparently vast space in which the dancing took place, compositions favoured strong diagonals for the extremities of the body and the placement of the dancing figure in the forefront of the picture space. Particularly with solo dancers, this emphasises the three-dimensionality of the body. Serpentine curves (see Montague 1994, 101) are prominent in poses and in the antique draperies of many of the dancers. One particularly common pose was throwing one's head back with the upper body arched, particularly when skipping lightly or standing on the ball of one foot, arms extended to embrace the space around the dancer.[13] Usually, this signified joy (Carter 2011, 19), one of the primary affective attributes of dance.

Inaesthetic Dancing

As is often the case, what is not illustrated explains as much as what is included. Of staged dance, the spectacular and highly popular grands ballets of Luigi Manzotti that celebrated modernisation, electricity, and urban pastimes are notably absent, as are most positive references to music hall ballets.[14] However, contemporary ballet is lauded as exemplary, particularly in its recent Russian incarnations (e.g. Caffin and Caffin 1912, 140-145). Ballet's aesthetic is also visible in books on dance pedagogy (e.g. Rath 1914, esp. 9-13, and images facing 16, 34 and 40), and as Theresa Buckland (2003, 26-27) has shown, in contemporary discourse, the aesthetic qualities of social dancing and those of performed folk or theatrical dancing tend to get conflated, in part because dance pedagogy embraced both social and theatrical ('fancy dancing') forms (Buckland 2011, esp. 111-117, 150-159). This slippage between stage and ballroom is interesting because it is precisely this period that sees the establishment of a hierarchy between stage and ballroom that is at the heart of dance studies (ibid., 13-16).

Since most books used by these new dance authors focused on social dances, they figured prominently in the histories offered as introductions to contemporary artistic practice (e.g. Caffin and Caffin 1912, 2-43). But social dances also indicated the condition of society at a given time, and their evaluation is thus indicative of the author's view of the particular historical period or group of people (ibid., 229-243 on "Court Dances" cf. on "Eccentric Dancing" 255-279 cf. on "Folk Dancing" 280-301). In contrast to older social dances (such as quadrilles or the polonaise), most of the fashionable social or ballroom dances of the 1900s and 1910s, *particularly* ragtime dances, are represented as bastardised or degenerate forms. They are savage rather than primitive, originating amongst lower classes and races and associated with 'low' forms of theatre like cabarets. Except for few "sanitised" staged versions, no photographs of such 'unhealthy' dance are presented to the reader.[15] This is in marked contrast to arguments about 'proper' theatrical dance, whatever its actual social or national origin or the extent of sex or nudity displayed: it is admirable, laudable, moral, and ample illustrations accompany the text.

The true Other to modern dance is therefore not ballet, but the contemporary social fashion for ragtime dances — the cakewalk, the shimmy, the Grizzly Bear and the Turkey Trot. This kind of dance

> reeks of the fetid atmosphere of crowded slums from which the wholesomeness of nature's sunshine has long been excluded. Its emotions have nothing of the healthy colouring of natural instincts; they are the products of perverted instincts. [--] Every movement is constrained; every gesture stiff, angular and confined, as if bred from constant jostling with other bodies in a crowded narrowness. Corresponding to the crampness of the movements is the lack of fluency and continuity in their combinations, the tempo of the dance is jerky; with intervals of sluggishness and bursts of delirious speed; a very denial of rhythm, every movement seeming to be the result of a sudden impulse that disdains control. (Caffin and Caffin 1912, 271-272)[16]

Sunshine, open spaces, steady fluid rhythms — these are the characteristics of natural, healthy dancing. Cultural revitalisation lay in the past, in "the old graceful motions natural to man in a less artificial state" and "the old buoyant and even rhythms" that the urban metropolis had destroyed (Flitch 1912, 103-104). City life was not only crammed, it was both too easy, encouraging bad habits and physical inactivity, and too hectic, interspersed with spurts of action that resulted in nervous tensions and disease. Proper dance was the contrast to all this: it embodied the aesthetic qualities of nature, which Flitch, like many others, associated with clouds, water, wind and trees (ibid., 103-106, *passim*, see also fn 19 below.)

As Rachel Fensham (2011) has recently discussed, nature (or rather, Nature) justified dance as an art form. Already in 1906, Reginald St.-Johnston had used a strategy that was to remain a staple in dance literature for the next half a century: the appeal to the primitive origin of dance as indicating the art form held a truth that had been lost in the process of civilisation. Presaging Curt Sachs and John Martin, he claimed that this proved dance was the origin of all art.[17] Thus, the truth-claim of dance as art was linked once more with the idea of (nostalgic) nature — the transcendental truth of dance was the body's essentially primitive energy, a sort of physical manifestation of what Henri Bergson called 'élan vital', the mysterious essence of all living things.[18] In photographs, the eternal summer of the Arcadian field is the obvious choice for representing such ideals.

However, artistic dancing (including appropriate forms of social dance) did not aim to complement the nostalgic lifestyle, but rather substituted it: advocates of dance did not demand a flight from the comforts of modernisation or require audiences to come and watch dancing on meadows or forest glades. Although some prominent dance makers had residences where such performances would have been possible (such as Laban's at Monte Verità and Dalcroze's at Hellerau), performing outdoors usually still meant performing on a *stage*. But this staged dance exemplified how the contemporary body, burdened by modernity, could be relieved and cured through a new body culture.[19] The space of the dance images simply represents these values — its purpose is not to document, but to symbolise.

Aesthetics and Politics of the Modern Body

The rhetoric used of ragtime dances points to the political alliance this discourse formed with such contemporary sciences of the body as eugenics and (the misleadingly named) Social Darwinism. This reveals the class-specificity of the dance books — their authors and presumed readers. Only the bourgeoisie had the secure income and significant amount of leisure to indulge in reading about their pastimes and also degeneration was primarily the fear of the middle classes.[20] However, there is a deeper connection between the nostalgia of modern dance and eugenics: eugenics, too, was a form of resistance to modernity, a dynamic solution to the profound changes that contemporary society was undergoing in the wake of modernisation.

Amidst contemporary fears of nervous shocks caused by life in the metropolis, the flowing movements of the proper kind of dance — on stage or off — were imbued with moral principles, with ideas of what was healthy for the body, and through the body, the spirit, the individual, the class, and the nation.[21] Conversely, any breach of the acceptable aesthetic of grace indicated lack of discipline, a victory for the unruly, thrill-seeking, uncivilised, primordial physical body. Much of the contemporary interest in health, sports (for boys) and dancing (for girls) stemmed from a need to regulate the body of the individual as a means to regulate the mind and behaviour of the individual. The physical body was important because biology was destiny and because the individual stood for the sex, the class, and the race.[22] Few voices in the wilderness contested the racist and misogynist premises of contemporary discourse on culture,[23] but the overwhelming majority took recourse to what they had been taught was scientific fact — that 'we' were naturally better than 'them'.

As an art of the body, dance was at a focal point of a search for a cure to modernisation (e.g. Britan 1904, 51; Caffin and Caffin 1912, 229). The discourse naturalised the idea that dance was nature re-learned, a return to an ideal condition preceding civilisation. Some proponents of dance even argued it could directly benefit eugenics by showing the physical fitness of the individual to her and his potential partners (Robinson 1914; similarly Jaques-Dalcroze 1930, v; and Ellis 1923/1933, 58-60). In the eugenic context, the health of the body was, after all, measured with fundamentally aesthetic qualia: notions of symmetry, harmony, line, and (racial) appropriateness dominated the analyses.

This discourse tied dance to a rather limited set of aesthetic principles and presumptions about appropriate audience responses: grace, nature, flow, and racial vitality produced pleasure, joy, and an optimistic sense of harmony. Beauty was supposedly not only universal and unchanging, but a moral statement. Hence, it is problematic that well into the 1980s, dance research taught us that the early free-form dance of the "Great American Pioneers" was 'abstract', that it *did not* preach a message.[24] Although religious arguments for and against dancing were a particularly American phenomenon (e.g. Hubbert 1901), as Linda Tomko (1999, esp. 36-70) has shown, all the American dance pioneers shared a background in movements of moral reform, which directly contributed to the emphasis they placed on dancing as a moral exercise.

In an equally misleading manner, the dress reform movement of which Isadora Duncan's tunics and Léon Bakst's Orientalist designs for the Ballets Russes are presented as prime examples gets represented as a dramatic movement for women's emancipation (e.g. Hanna 1988, esp. 132-133). Dancers in flimsy draperies become linked with progressive social forces, their sinuous curved movement with the (inevitable) historical momentum towards our present ideals of political equality. Yet, the actual space of political reform was precisely that of the modern city shunned in the dance discourse. As Valerie Steele (2001, 76) has noted: "Attacks on the corset were often linked to ideological campaigns in favor of motherhood, reflecting fears that if women broke away from their domestic sphere, the entire social order would be threatened."[25] Few suffragettes were interested in the dress reform: contemporary images and advertisements in suffragette magazines reveal a concern with the latest fashions and with the image of the charming young demonstrator taking to the streets for her cause (Burt 2010).

In the early twentieth-century representations of women dancing in the Arcadian field, the woman dancing became one with 'nature', inseparable from the background in which she danced. When the rhetoric of a 'natural body' and of dance as a 'natural' form of exercise was used to justify the moral and spiritual superiority of the 'new woman' (e.g. Malnig 1999), it tied her to instinct rather than intellect. As Elizabeth Grosz (1994, esp. 3-5, 14-16) has pointed out, this was a dangerous rhetorical trap that enabled a conservative, essentially patriarchal discourse, where woman was nature, the excess of civilisation. It also silenced the dancer in the discourse: the dance books under scrutiny here rarely addressed what the dancers actually did — beyond evocations of waves and other nature metaphors, analysis of the movement qualities, step sequences, gestures or how emotional or narrative effects were created for the spectator are suspiciously absent. Dance became something so natural it escaped rationality and analysis, like the dancing of the woman: inexplicable, silent and fixed on the picture plane.

Conclusions

I have argued that nostalgia functioned as criticism of contemporary modernity in the discourse of early twentieth-century modern dance but that this nostalgia was critical of contemporary modernity and modernisation. As such, this discourse tied staged art dance to a certain set of affective responses and aesthetic forms that produced a particular kind of 'modern' body. Eugenics and other contemporary sciences of the body and of society spoke of harmony, grace and flowing movement in a manner strikingly reminiscent of the definitions of this 'appropriate' dance in dance literature. Conversely, the rhetoric used of dance subscribed to an organic view of history, where cultures rise, flourish and wither like plants; and where the body of the individual represents the body of the class, the society, and of the race.

The legacy of early-twentieth-century evaluations about the value of particular dance styles lies in the naturalisation of this political agenda. The choices made as to which dance makers are canonised and researched, for example, still reflect these century-old texts. All too often variety entertainment and ragtime dances, like 'old-fashioned' grands ballets celebrating modernisation, are relegated to the role of the Other to the real art of dancing — taught in passing as interesting examples of contemporary culture and of the 'dance craze' of the tens and teens, but not subjected to the same detailed investigation as the (select) figureheads of staged art dance. Certainly, much of the focus on "the Great American Pioneers" in research on dance rests on their canonisation in early twentieth-century books on modern dance discussed here.

Because of the conflation of modernism in dance with particular pioneer figures and their ideas of nature as a moral (and political) stance, the anti-modernisation of this cultural moment and its problematic relationship to modernism in other art forms has passed almost unobserved. The visual heterodoxy of the early — twentieth — century modern dance — anything from Orientalist creations and billowing clouds of silk to dirndls and pseudo-Greek tunics — distracts from their shared need to look for the perfect aesthetic somewhere else, somewhere conceptually Other to the present. This search was not politically innocent or neutral: whereas popular ragtime dances were admonished as a sign of urban degeneration, the great artists of dance could turn the movements of the primitive Others into real art that promised a great and healthy future — for those who heeded their call.[26] As such, dance was of supreme importance as a sign of the state of contemporary society and should also be focal in any study of that society.

Understanding how both nostalgia and eugenics were projects aiming for the improvement of humankind and its future is imperative for any explanation of the unholy union of modern dance and movements for racial hygiene that were well on their way prior to the First World War, although they only culminated in the mass spectacles and extermination camps of the Third Reich. In the discourse of healthy and unhealthy bodies — of individuals, societies and races — the body was evaluated with aesthetic criteria such as grace, symmetry and harmony identical to evaluations of contemporary dance. Like contemporary dance, it was also placed in a seemingly ahistorical, 'natural' space that emphasised its alleged universality. Perhaps for this reason, the nostalgic space of early-twentieth-century dance resonates with the reassertion of the lost power of the white imperialist (Briginshaw 2001/2009, 36-37) while the specificities of how this dance created space (indicated in e.g. Louppe 2010, esp. 130, 135, 138) have yet to be properly analysed, in part because what remains of past dance is, as I hope to have shown, fraught with questions about 'proper' representation and interpretation.

BIBLIOGRAPHY

PRIMARY SOURCES:

— 1911. "The Russian Ballet as a Vehicle of Artistic Ideas." *Current Literature* August, 195-197.

Allan, Maud. [1908]. *My Life and Dancing*. London: Everett & Co.

Applin, Arthur. [1911]. *The Stories of the Russian Ballet*. London: Everett & Co.

Bergson, Henri. 1996. *Matter and Memory*. Translated by Paul S. Palmer. New York: Zone Books (from 5th French ed., 1908).

Bie, Oskar. 1923. *Der Tanz*. 3rd ed. Berlin: Julius Bard.

Britan, Halbert H. 1904. "Music and Morality." *International Journal of Ethics* 15 (1): 48-63.

Caffin, Caroline and Caffin, Charles H. 1912. *Dancing and Dancers of Today: The Modern Revival of Dancing as an Art*. New York: Dodd, Mead And Company.

Dunham, Curtis, ed. 1918. *Dancing with Helen Moller: Her Own Statement of Her Philosophy and Practice and Teaching Formed upon the Classic Greek Model, and Adapted to Meet the Aesthetic and Hygienic Needs of To-Day*. New York and London: John Lane Company, The Bodley Head.

Ellis, Havelock. 1923/1933. *The Dance of Life*. London: Constable & Co.

Flitch, J.E. Crawford 1912. *Modern Dancing and Dancers*. Philadelphia and London: J.B. Lippincott Co. and Grant Richards Ltd.

Fuller, Loïe. 1913. *Fifteen Years of a Dancer's Life*. Boston: Small, Maynard & Co.

Hubbert, J.M. 1901. *Dancers and Dancing: A Calm and Rational View of the Dancing Question*. Nashville, TN: Cumberland Presbyterian Publishing House.

Jaques-Dalcroze, E[mile]. 1930. *Eurhythmics Art and Education*. Translated by Frederick Rothwell, edited by Cynthia Cox. London: Chatto & Windus.

Kinney, Troy and Kinney, Margaret West. 1914/1936. *The Dance: Its Place in Art and Life*. 3rd, rev. ed. New York: F.A. Stokes Company (rev. ed. 1924).

Nordau, Max. 1993. *Degeneration*. Translated by George L. Mosse. Lincoln and London: University of Nebraska Press (German 1892).

Perugini, Mark E. 1915. *The Art of Ballet*. London: Martin Secker.

Rath, Emil. 1914. *Æsthetic Dancing*. New York: The A.S. Barnes Company.

Robinson, Louis, Dr. 1914. "The Natural History of Dancing." *The Nineteenth Century and After*, February.

St.-Johnston, Reginald. 1906. *A History of Dancing*. London: Simpkin, Marshall, Hamilton, Kent, & Co.

Thomas, William I. 1907. "The Mind of Woman and the Lower Races." *The American Journal of Sociology*, 12 (4): 435-469.

Urlin, Ethel L. 1912. *Dancing Ancient and Modern*. New York: D. Appleton Company.

SECONDARY SOURCES:

Au, Susan. 1988/1993. *Ballet & Modern Dance*. London: Thames and Hudson.

Brewster, Ben and Jacobs, Lea. 1997. *Theatre to Cinema: Stage Pictorialism and the Early Feature Film*. Oxford and New York: Oxford University Press.

Briginshaw, Valerie A. 2001/2009. *Dance, Space and Subjectivity*. London: Palgrave Macmillan.

Buckland, Theresa Jill. 2003. "Edward Scott: The Last of the English Dancing Masters." *Dance Research: The Journal of the Society for Dance Research* 21 (2): 3-35.

Buckland, Theresa Jill. 2011. *Society Dancing: Fashionable Bodies in England, 1870-1920*. Basingstoke and New York: Palgrave Macmillan.

Bunnell, Peter C. 1998. "Towards New Photography. Renewals of Pictorialism." In *A New History of Photography*, edited by Michel Frizot, translated by Susan Bennett, Liz Clegg, John Crook, and Caroline Higgitt, 310-333. Köln: Könemann (French 1994).

Burt, Ramsay. 2010. "The Politics of Embodied Freedom in Early Modern Dance and Suffragette Protest." Part 1 of professorial lecture 27.5.2010. Accessed June 1, 2010. url: http://vimeo.com/12171776.

Carter, Alexandra. 2011. "Constructing and Contesting the Natural in British Theatre Dance." In *Dancing Naturally: Nature, Neo-Classicism and Modernity in Early Twentieth-Century Dance*, edited by Alexandra Carter and Rachel Fensham, 16-30. Basingstoke and New York: Palgrave Macmillan.

Ciplijauskaité, Birutė. 1976. "Nationalization of Arcadia in Exile Poetry." *Books Abroad* 50 (2): 295-302.

Daly, Ann. 1995/2002. *Done into Dance: Isadora Duncan in America*. Middletown, CT: Wesleyan University Press.

de Certeau, Michel. 1988. *The Practice of Everyday Life*. Translated by Steven Rendall. Berkeley, Los Angeles, London: University of California Press (1984).

Eichberg, Henning. 1990. "Forward Race and the Laughter of Pygmies: On Olympic Sport." In *Fin de Siècle and Its Legacy*, edited by Mikuláš Teich and Roy Porter, 115-131. Cambridge and New York: Cambridge University Press.

Erenberg, Lewis A. 1975. "Everybody's Doin' It: The Pre-World War I Dance Craze, the Castles, and the Modern American Girl." *Feminist Studies*, 3 (1-2): 155-170.

Fensham, Rachel. 2011. "Nature, Force and Variation." In *Dancing Naturally: Nature, Neo-Classicism and Modernity in Early Twentieth-Century Dance*, edited by Alexandra Carter and Rachel Fensham, 1-15. Basingstoke and New York: Palgrave Macmillan.

Fritzsche, Peter. 2001. "Specters of History: On Nostalgia, Exile, and Modernity." *The American Historical Review* 106 (5). Accessed December 16, 2009. url: http://www.historycooperative.org/journals/ahr/106.5/ah0501001587.html

Frizot, Michel. 1998a. "Speed of Photography: Movement and Duration." In *A New History of Photography*, edited by Michel Frizot, translated by Susan Bennett, Liz Clegg, John Crook, and Caroline Higgitt, 242-257. Köln: Könemann (French 1994).

Frizot, Michel. 1998b. "A Natural Strangeness: The Hypothesis of Color." In *A New History of Photography*, edited by Michel Frizot, translated by Susan Bennett, Liz Clegg, John Crook, and Caroline Higgitt, 410-429. Köln: Könemann (French 1994).

Gallagher, Catherine. 1987. "The Body Versus the Social Body in the Works of Thomas Malthus and Henry Mayhew." In *The Making of the Modern Body: Sexuality and Society in the Nineteenth Century*, edited by Catherine Gallagher and Thomas Laqueur, 83-106. Berkeley and Los Angeles: University of California Press.

Goering, Laura. 2003. "'Russian Nervousness': Neurasthenia and National Identity in Nineteenth-Century Russia." *Medical History* 47: 23-46.

Gould, Stephen Jay. 1981/1984. *The Mismeasure of Man.* London, New York, et al.: Penguin Books.

Grosz, Elizabeth. 1994. *Volatile Bodies: Toward a Corporeal Feminism.* Bloomington and Indianapolis: Indiana University Press.

Guest, Ivor Forbes. 1992. *Ballet in Leicester Square: The Alhambra and the Empire, 1860-1915.* London: Dance Books.

Hanna, Judith Lynne. 1988. *Dance, Sex and Gender: Signs of Identity, Dominance, Defiance, and Desire.* Chicago and London: University of Chigaco Press.

Hatt, Michael. 1999. "Physical Culture: The Male Nude and Sculpture in Late Victorian Britain." In *After the Pre-Raphaelites: Art and Aestheticism in Victorian England*, edited by Elizabeth Prettejohn, 240-255. New Brunswick, NJ: Rutgers University Press.

Järvinen, Hanna. 2003. *The Myth of Genius in Movement: Historical Deconstruction of the Nijinsky Legend.* Turku: University of Turku.

Järvinen, Hanna. 2009. "Critical Silence: The Unseemly Games of Love in *Jeux* (1913)." *Dance Research* 27 (2): 199-220.

Kealiinohomoku, Joann. 2001. "An Anthropologist Looks at Ballet as a Form of Ethnic Dance." In *Moving History/Dancing Cultures: A Dance History Reader,* edited by Ann Dils, Ann Cooper Albright, 33-43. Middletown, CT: Wesleyan University Press (orig. 1969/1970).

Koselleck, Reinhardt. 2004. *Futures Past: On the Semantics of Historical Time.* Translated by Keith Tribe. New York: Columbia University Press (German 1979).

Louppe, Laurence. 2010. *Poetics of Contemporary Dance.* Translated by Sally Gardner. Alton: Dance Books (French 1997).

Malnig, Julie. 1999. "Athena Meets Venus: Visions of Women in Social Dance in the Teens and Early 1920s." *Dance Research Journal* 31 (2): 34-62.

Medvedev, Sergei. 1999. "A General Theory of Russian Space: A Gay Science and a Rigorous Science." In *Beyond the Limits: The Concept of Space in Russian History and Culture*, edited by Jeremy Smith, 15-47. Helsinki: SHS.

Montague, Ken. 1994. "The Aesthetics of Hygiene: Aesthetic Dress, Modernity, and the Body as Sign." *Journal of Design History* 7:2, 91-112.

Olsson, Cecilia. 1999. "Rena kroppar — smutsiga rörelser." In *Forskning i rörelse: Tio texter om dans*, edited by E[rna]. Grönlund, L[ena]. Hammergren, C[ecilia]. Olsson and A[nne]. Wigert, 154-172. Carlssons: Stockholm.

Segel, Harold B. 1998. *The Body Ascendant: Modernism and the Physical Imperative*. Baltimore, ML: The Johns Hopkins University Press.

Steele, Valerie. 2001. *The Corset: A Cultural History*. New Haven, CT: Yale University Press.

Thomas, Helen. 1995. *Dance, Modernity and Culture: Explorations in the Sociology of Dance*. London and New York: Routledge.

Toepfer, Karl. 1997. *Empires of Ecstasy: Nudity and Movement in German Body Culture, 1910-1935*. Berkeley, Los Angeles and London: University of California Press.

Tomko, Linda J. 1999. *Dancing Class: Gender, Ethnicity, and Social Divides in American Dance, 1890-1920*. Bloomington: Indiana University Press.

Turner, Bryan S. 1987. "A Note on Nostalgia." *Theory Culture & Society* 4: 147-156.

Wagner, Ann. 1997. *Adversaries of Dance: From the Puritans to the Present*. Urbana and Chicago: University of Illinois Press.

Williams, Raymond. 1989. *The Politics of Modernism: Against the New Conformists*. London: Verso.

Woodcock, Sarah. 2010. "Wardrobe." In *Diaghilev and the Golden Age of the Ballets Russes, 1909-1929*, edited by Jane Pritchard, 129-163, 214. London: Victoria and Albert Museum.

Zerner, Henri. 2005. "Le regard des artistes." In *Histoire du Corps. Vol. 2: De la Révolution à la Grande Guerre*, edited by Alain Corbin, 85-117. Paris: Editions Seuil.

NOTES

1   The title of Chapter 6 in Dunham 1918, 101.

2   For different representations of Antiquity, see also e.g. Caffin and Caffin 1912, 297; Allan [1908], following 72.

3   Sometimes both, as in Caffin and Caffin 1912, 297.

4   The selection in the bibliography is by no means comprehensive, but I have tried to quote the most influential examples from the Anglo-American discourse. Elsewhere in Europe, similar discourses have been illustrated e.g. by Olsson 1999.

5   See e.g. Caffin and Caffin 1912, esp. 255-279 the chapter on "Eccentric Dancing",
    incl. 259-261 on cake-walk as "a comedy lifted from the child-age of humanity, not-
    withstanding that it is costumed in a travesty of modern fashion" danced by "primi-
    tive child-man" and 271-279 on the horrible, perverted urban variety dances of the
    "underworld" of cabarets. In the 1920s, opinions begin to change — thus, Bie 1923,
    363-365 is far less negative towards these new society dances ('Neue Gesellschafts-
    tänze') and praises the tango as their highest form. On opponents of dance, see Wag-
    ner 1997, 236-291, 363-397; Malnig 1999 on the rhetoric used to justify new social
    dance as healthy; also Buckland 2003, 19-20, 23-24 and 33n72.

6   See e.g. Ciplijauskaité 1976 on the lost homeland as Arcadia in twentieth century
    poetry; Turner 1987, esp. 150-152 on the spatiality and temporality of the nostalgic
    paradigm.

7   I am quite aware that this also associates dance with the beautiful rather than the
    sublime — a discourse I have briefly addressed in Järvinen 2003, esp. 178-180.

8   I have borrowed these terms from Sergei Medvedev's (1999) discussion on Russian
    space.

9   Yet, e.g. Toepfer 1997 uses the wonderful pictures he has unearthed as *documents* of
    performance practice — see note 12 below.

10 Until the 1930s, direct sunlight was necessary because shutter speeds and film reso-
    lution were too slow for artistic photography of rapid movement, so that the flutter
    of cloth in wind or the expression of a leaping dancer would end up blurred in the fi-
    nal print (Frizot 1998a). Although colour was available (Frizot 1998b, 411- 417), it was
    even slower and more expensive, so most images of dancers were in black and white.
    These were sometimes manually coloured-in for the more lavish publications such as
    Le Théatre (as in Image 6). The absence of colour affects how we experience images
    of dancers of the period, and how we (intuitively) understand their dancing. This is
    particularly true with Fuller's work, which depended on stage lighting effects — and
    colour — that could not be produced out of doors.

11 Retouching seems crude to us, because the photographic print fades over time, mak-
    ing retouching more apparent. E.g. Gould 1984, 171. Today, we can quite clearly see
    added shadows and corrected (unbent) slipper tips in images of, for example, Nijin-
    sky of whom few images were taken in actual movement, as in Image 4.

12 E.g. St.-Johnston 1906, [7] argues that "'cake-walks,' high-kicking, and other extrava-
    gant forms" were a sign of the decay of contemporary dance. See Hatt 1999; Zerner
    2005, 90-96 on aesthetics of images of the body; on the importance of the nude in
    body culture see, e.g. Segel 1998 and Toepfer 1997, although the latter exaggerates
    the extent to which dancers *performed* nude — despite photographic representations,

dancers used silk leotards to give the appearance of nudity on stage. Woodcock 2010, esp. 143.

13 Variations of such pose is seen in one of the images of *Isadora Duncan at the Theater of Dionysus* in 1903 (New York Public Library Jerome Robbins Dance Division, id: ps_dan_cd3_38. Accessed 5. January 2012. url: http://legacy.www.nypl.org/permissions/imagesref.cfm?id=94&catid=9) (on the ball of the right foot, left back from the knee at c. 45°; body in serpentine curve; arms extended horizontally front and back); in Caffin and Caffin 1912, 297 depicting the students of a Miss Beegle (four dancers standing on the flat of the right foot, left back from the knee at c. 45°; arms up; holding hands with other dancers; head at diagonal backwards tilt); in some of the images of Dalcroze dancers by Frédéric Boissonas (such as Image 2 or *Dalcroze-Schule (Four Dancers in Flight)*. Accessed 27. November 2011. url: http://photoseed.com/collection/single/dalcroze-schule-four-dancers-in-flight/, depicting four dancers leaping, right legs extended down, left horizontally back from the knee; arms raised;)" holding hands with other dancers; head thrown back), also depicted similarly in *Hellerau: Bewegungsstudie* in Bie 1923, following 376 (four dancers skipping in line, with arms extended back at downwards angle of c. 45°). See also the cover of *Dancing Naturally: Nature, Neo-Classicism and Modernity in Early Twentieth-Century Dance*, edited by Alexandra Carter and Rachel Fensham, 1-15. Basingstoke and New York: Palgrave Macmillan; Daly 1995/2002, esp. 102.

14 Notably, in ballet histories Manzotti's works like *Excelsior* (1881) and *Sport* (1897) *still* get represented as examples of ballet in its worst decline.

15 Even with older social dance forms, the illustrations tend to depict ballet dancers in obviously staged versions of these forms. The most famous exhibition performers of 'sanitised' contemporary dances were Irene and Vernon Castle. E.g. Erenberg 1975, 159-166; Malnig 1999; Tomko 1999, esp. 28-29; Wagner 1997, 255-257.

16 Caffin and Caffin 1912, 271-272. Similar examples also in Guest 1992, 108, 124, 137. See also Nordau 1993, 34-37 on poisoning of the body causing degeneration, and 37-44 on nervous fatigue.

17 St.-Johnston 1906, 10-11, 14-15; similarly, Caffin and Caffin 1912, *passim*, e.g. 8-13; Urlin 1912, esp. ix; Applin [1911], 11; Perugini 1915, 27-28; Ellis 1923/1933, 33-34. For a good analysis of the appeal of 'primitive' dance to Western scholars, see Kealiinohomoku 2001, esp. 34.

18 In his 1896 book *Matière et mémoire* (*Matter and Memory*, Bergson 1996) Bergson attached perception to material reality. According to Bergson, since we are our bodies, the movement of our bodies is the means for us to both learn of and analyse our being. The capacity for motion defines our level of consciousness. Plants are less conscious than we are because they are not as capable of movement as we are. This

is because capacity for movement defines our capacity for action. By this, Bergson means a specific kind of acting: action is always conscious, it is opposed to habit, and it always produces a reaction that changes our consciousness, our being. Therefore, most of the things we do are not actions in this sense — they are habitual, and although habits may be conscious, they do not change anything in our being.

19 In view of how nervous diseases were seen as typical to modern, urban life, this made perfect sense. Gallagher 1987, 83-90 on body as an indicator of society; Goering 2003, 28-34 on the link between nervous disease and social theories, esp. 29 on how nervousness was believed to be a condition only of contemporary civilisation. Also Malnig 1999, esp. 40, 43, 48 for a discussion on the link between new dance and ideas of a healthy, 'natural' body.

20 Gould 1984; Eichberg 1990.

21 The view that "beauty without morality is impossible" (Nordau 1993, 327) was also common in dance writings, e.g. St.-Johnston 1906, 15; Fuller 1913, 168-72; Duncan quoted in Flitch 1912, 107. As Daly 1995/2002, 112 notes, "Duncan's construction of a 'Natural' body did indeed imply a race and class hierarchy."

22 Gallagher 1987, 83-90 on Malthus and how the health of the body became the indicator of the condition of the society; Wagner 1997, esp. 252-254 on dance and changes in the American physical education system.

23 See Thomas 1907 for a remarkable exception. The author disproves e.g. Spencer's theories regarding the lower mental capacities of lower races and women by pointing out how individuals' mental capacities are products of their upbringing and the society in which they live.

24 This attitude is particularly evident in textbooks, such as Au 1988/1993, and in how dance is discussed outside dance studies, as in Segel 1998, 80-91.

25 See also ibid., 59-85, 137-158. Malnig 1999 has similarly shown how, in women's magazines, social dance was represented as a consumer good through which women could aspire to conservative, *domestic* stability.

26 Even in works that extensively discuss folk dancing, Western dancers, especially Ruth St.Denis, are placed on equal footing, even lauded as experts of dances from both the Middle and Far East. See e.g. Kinney and Kinney 1914/1936, 196-227.

SPACE AND DANCE GENRES

THE WOUND THAT NEVER HEALS: FLAMENCO DANCE AS TRANSFORMATION IN LIMINAL SPACE

Diane Oatley

Abstract

The article explores some of the features of the embodied and shared spatiality produced by the flamenco dancing body, specifically in terms of the transformation that occurs in the dance through the establishment of liminal space. Through an analysis of a performance of the flamenco dance *soleá*, employing Victor Turner's analysis of liminal space and ritual, and Federico García Lorca's treatment of the concept of *duende*, the article demonstrates how through the dance the body's materiality is reiterated and established as a habitus comprising a diversity of cultural influences. This is then related to the concept of flamenco as a manner of being in the world, a claim that is both prevalent within flamenco and a source of controversy. Exploring this controversy reveals some of the difficulties traditional flamenco scholarship would appear to have in finding expression for flamenco's hybridity, and further, how such hybridity is related to the liminal space produced by the dance. The state of yearning embodied by the flamenco dancing subject in the production of liminal space thus proves to contain a dense complexity. Further analysis of the structure of the *soleá* discloses a lyrical dimension augmenting spatiality. As such, while the *soleá's* linear narrative of crisis negotiation and resolution in liminal space is shown to be a key feature of the dance's habitus, it is the very embodiment of the space of yearning particular to that crisis that is held to be flamenco's primary distinguishing feature.

Flamenco is the embodiment of yearning, impassioned struggle, and transformation, here by dancer Patricia Ibañez from Jerez de la Frontera. Photographer: Pablo Leoni.

Introduction

> … the *duende* wounds, and in trying to heal that wound that never heals, lies the strangeness, the inventiveness of a man's work. (García Lorca, 1933/2004)

The above quote goes to the heart of the thematic focus of this article: the flamenco dancing body in relation to an embodied and shared spatiality. I will in the following explore some of the features of such spatiality, specifically in terms of the embodied transformation that occurs in flamenco dance within the establishment of liminal space. The path of this exploration has uprooted along the way a number of questions regarding the origins and evolution of flamenco as an art form — as a folkloric practice and a dance for the stage — and disclosed some of the apparent difficulties involved in finding expression for flamenco's hybridity.[1] As will be demonstrated here, hybridity contributes to producing the very 'wound' that I hold to be a defining feature of flamenco, a wound that flamenco studies seem to a large extent to be intent on healing.

Flamenco's history remains fraught with contention, but I will begin here with a brief presentation of some generally accepted facts. The art form of flamenco is the result of a process of transculturation; the merger of the musical culture of the gitano[2] population that immigrated to Andalucía around 1425, with the musical and folk traditions of that region (Leblon 2003, 47).[3] Written evidence exists of *gitano baile* (Romani dance) from as early as the 1700s (Navarro and Pablo 2005), but it was in the course of what is referred to as the *edad de oro* ("the golden age") in the period 1869-1910 that flamenco acquired the form that is recognised today (ibid.).

Flamenco as a dance form presents, develops and transmits a specific manner of being in the world through the reiteration of a form of embodied subjectivity. This has been made possible in part through flamenco dance's capacity to embody and invoke a particular difference as habitus,[4] or "those embodied rituals of everydayness by which a given culture produces and sustains belief in its own 'obviousness'" (Butler 1997, 152). It is my contention that one of the means by which this habitus functions in flamenco is through the dance, as a means of reasserting, reconstructing and reclaiming itself, its obviousness. One key aspect of such habitus in terms of flamenco is that of *reciprocality*. To cite feminist philosopher Judith Butler: "In this sense the habitus is formed, but it is also formative; it is in this sense that the bodily habitus constitutes a tacit form of performativity, a citational chain lived and believed at the level of the body" (Butler 1997, 155). In the context of flamenco, the habitus as defined by Butler here emerges through a form of reciprocality, in the sense that it is both *formed* by the dancing subject and is *formative* for that same dancing subject.

Habitus and Compás

The habitus of flamenco dance is discernible as a form of embodied presence in both the movement itself and in the tradition as a whole. With respect to this embodied presence, the concept of *compás,* meaning literally compass, but in terms of flamenco music and dance, rhythm, is a key and defining feature. Having *compás* in flamenco implies being able at any given time to navigate the rhythmic landscape of flamenco music.[5] In practice, *compás* entails a profoundly embodied understanding of the music, and of flamenco as a cultural tradition and art form. The competency represented by having *compás* is then an example of the *habitus* of flamenco: it entails sedimented knowledge in the body, which is fundamental. It is a matter of dancing a particularly embodied subjectivity where the focus is on the movement in and for itself — within the confines of a strictly defined movement language. A movement quality is produced through the dance creating a specific experiential horizon. The *compás* as habitus represents in my mind one of the means by which flamenco, however much it is also a dance for the stage, remains securely grounded in its parallel evolution as a folk tradition, where the dance is practiced and performed in the context of collective rituals and celebrations.

As a means of illustrating some of these points I will use examples from a flamenco dance performance of the branch of flamenco *soleá* performed by the dancer Farruquito (Juan Manuel Fernández Montoya). Farruquito is from the Farruco dynasty of Seville, one of the more well-known and indeed significant flamenco families. It could be said that he and his family, in particular his now deceased grandfather Farruco, represent flamenco *puro*, or traditional flamenco. The *soleá* piece in question begins with 5 minutes of music alone, during which Farruquito, the dancer, enters and waits, clapping in the *soleá compás*, before beginning to dance. The mood is sombre, meditative. The dancer's initial movements are slow, in keeping with this state, expressive of the emotions which the music instills and evokes. The dancer does classical marking steps in the rhythm of the *soleá*, inhabiting and cultivating this landscape for three verses, slowly, pensively, in movement combinations that are introverted and intimate, elegant and strong, and expressive of grief. This establishes a visceral plane of being, which in general terms can be said to represent a particular loss borne in solitude — the death of a loved one, unrequited love, etc. Through the course of the *soleá*, the dancing protagonist will embody this loss, beginning in the state of its mourning, to be gradually resurrected, like a phoenix from the ashes. As such, the *soleá* stages a transformation.

Liminal Space

The theme of transformation brings us to liminality. Anthropologist Victor Turner in *The Anthropology of Performance* defines liminality as "a betwixt-and-between condition often involving seclusion from the everyday scene" (Turner 1988, 101). He connects such liminality to rituals associated with passage from one status or life condition to another, either collectively or individually. Passage in this sense can be exemplified by the thematic focus of flamenco on key life crises or thresholds — such as marriage, birth, and baptism in the context of collective celebrations, and otherwise in the form of an individual artist's existential reflections about death, unrequited love, poverty, suffering, etc. The *soleá* in question here, danced as the embodiment and surmounting of pain, illustrates such a passage from one life condition to another. A second feature of liminality as defined by Turner is that of the subjunctive mode, which is characterised by a state of wishing, desiring, yearning, rather than about an established statement of fact. Again, the *soleá*, in that it expresses the pain of bereavement, or existential anguish, and the subsequent transcendence of that pain, certainly corresponds with this. On the whole, it can be said that the predominant mood of flamenco in general is that of the subjunctive mode: of a profoundly felt yearning.

Particular to this mode in the context of liminality and ritual is the aspect of reflexivity: the act of an individual or culture reflecting upon itself and/or its existence, as a subject and as a tradition, through what Turner terms metacommunication, "the generation of a new language verbal or nonverbal, which enables them to talk about what they normally talk" (Turner 1988, 103). Dance can certainly be understood as a non-verbal language enabling such metacommunication, offering the possibility for an embodied reflection. Turner expands on this further, stating that metacommunication is a matter of "a man in his wholeness wholly attending" (ibid., 103). The latter would be that which we in the dance world refer to as embodied presence.

Liminality in Performance

Is liminality as defined here visible then in the performance in question? The choreography of the *soleá* gradually evolves into a series of complex *zapateado* or footwork sequences producing rhythmic climaxes within the otherwise meditative, virtually hypnotic state generated and maintained in the first 5 minutes of the piece, from which the dancer then instigates a break involving a shift in tempo. This change then builds and intensifies to the end of the piece, through a series of *subidas*, or movement crescendos that climax and subside, like waves advancing and retreating, but with each climax raising the visceral energy to another plane, until he reaches the bridge of the *escobilla,* a segment of the *soleá* composed of footwork, during which the dancer improvises around a repeated rhythmic phrase. This bridge leads into the *bulerias* which concludes the *soleá*.

An experiential space is created through physical ruptures — the body seems to be twisted and pushed to or even beyond the edges of its physical limitations, as if sensation is being wrung out of it. The dancer appears at this point to be 'in his wholeness wholly attending' or exceedingly present; inhabiting a space that is intimate and private — Farruquito commits repeatedly what in dance is traditionally speaking a faux pas: he looks down at the floor, or at his feet, focused, introverted, as if he is dancing for himself alone, something which enunciates both his solitude, and the aspect of embodied reflection referred to above. And then he lifts his head, at times he cries out, and returns to us. The embodied subject that emerges again and again, each time with renewed strength, with greater insistence, is both vulnerable and increasingly triumphant and proud, both private and public. The overall atmosphere is one of a subjunctive mode: of desire and a deeply felt yearning. This in itself sets the stage for a transformation.

The transformation that occurs in this particular performance can be seen superficially in the initial removal of his jacket, the subsequent freeing of his shirttails, the unbuttoning of that same shirt, until his *panuela* hangs like a noose around his bare neck, reminiscent of the encounter with death and mourning that informs the atmosphere of this piece. He pares off the inessentials, stripping down to the bare bones of his grief. In the final section we see Farruquito dancing with his brothers in triumph. The aspect of ritual is underscored here by the connectedness of the dancers, four brothers, this is a family affair. The dancers are working within a tradition that has been passed down orally for generations. Beyond this, it is clear that Farruquito has travelled to another existential plane; when one sees the four of them dancing together, he is clearly running the show, and the sense is of his having blazed a trail through anguish, cleared out a space which they may now enter and take part in upholding. There is a technical virtuosity to all of the dancers, but they are not in any sense transmitting the same thing, Farruquito is inhabiting a space and emanating a visceral presence that they are not.

Duende

Federico García Lorca (1933/2004), the Andalucian poet and dramatist, might say that Farruquito is channeling *duende* here, or the spirit of evocation that he — and in fact many — held to be a defining characteristic of flamenco. I introduce the word *duende* here because it is helpful in explaining this visceral presence further, and in connecting some of the dots between the disparate concepts I am trying to unite here and further relating them to flamenco. García Lorca was the first to develop the aesthetics of this term, and in doing so he connected it to flamenco as an art form. It must be said that his lecture *Theory and Play of the Duende* (1993) can appear initially to further mystify rather than clarify *duende* as a cultural metaphor. However, when the essay is read against the concepts I have introduced here, interesting resonances are produced.

García Lorca states: "All that has dark sounds has *duende*. And there's no deeper truth than that. Those dark sounds are the mystery, the roots that cling to the mire that we all know, that we all ignore, but from which comes the very substance of art"(1933/2004, 3). *Duende* is, "A mysterious force that everyone feels and no philosopher has explained" (ibid.). One's initial reaction to the latter statement might be that it is not particularly helpful; reading this through Butler, however, allows an interpretation of this as a reference to unarticulated knowledge. Everyone feels it, but even philosophers are unable to explain it. It is, 'the mire that we all know, that we all ignore' or again, with Butler, the body's materiality, exceeding interpellation,[6] "from which comes the very substance of art" (ibid.).

Further, "The *duende* is not in the throat: the *duende* surges up, inside, from the soles of the feet. Meaning, it's not a question of skill, but of a style that's truly alive: meaning, it's in the veins: meaning, it's of the most ancient culture of *immediate creation*" (ibid., my emphasis). *Duende* is something that is produced with an immediacy, implying a collapse of the distance between the body as subject and object, in what Turner describes as a 'flow' arising in the 'play frame of liminality': "this particular union of primary processes [...] where action and awareness are one and there is a loss of the sense of the ego" (Turner 1988, 107). In the clip in question, Farruquito the dancer has moved through an act of immediate and embodied reflection or metacommunication within the play frame of liminal space to produce such a flow enabling transformation.

And finally, García Lorca states "The arrival of the *duende* presupposes a radical change to all the old kinds of form, brings totally unknown and fresh sensations" (García Lorca 1933/2004, 6). Such a "radical change" would imply a process of transformation, in which the practitioners have to "rob (themselves) of skill and safety"... or move out of the realm of the known, of received notions, so ..."[their] duende might come and deign to struggle with them at close quarters" (ibid.). Through the transformation 'totally unknown and fresh sensations' or something new is then born, unarticulated knowledge finds expression, which is in effect the performative gesture. Through the improvisational mode which is also a defining feature of traditional flamenco, the dancer moves out of the realm of the 'known'; the struggle García Lorca refers to is clearly evident in the agonistic structure of the *soleá*, as the dancer retreats into himself, again and again, to pause, confront his pain, reflect, and then emerge with renewed force and power, to create a virtual storm of movement. Each time he re-emerges, that storm has greater intensity, greater self-assurance, until the end where he is joined by his brothers and the transition is made from the anguish of the *soleá* to the jubilant celebration of the *bulerias,* the celebratory flamenco dance for *fiesta* which ends the piece.

To summarise then, the invocation of García Lorca's *duende* in flamenco dance can be read as taking place in liminal space as defined here, in seclusion from everyday life. This is a liminal space which is informed by the subjunctive mode and characterised by metacommunication, the definition of which I have paraphrased here in terms of the non-verbal language of dance as involving embodied reflection. Flamenco dance, as performance and as ritual, thematically speaking involves then an endeavour to confront and navigate thresholds, whereupon the embodied knowledge of such transformative encounters is reiterated as habitus — a habitus that is articulated, reinforced and further developed through the compás and the dance itself, in a reciprocal act that is both formed and formative, by and for the dancer, through and within the creation of liminality as an embodied and shared spatiality.

Is flamenco a manner of being in the world or solely an art form? Interpreted here by dancer Patricia Ibañez from Jerez de la Frontera. Photographer: Pablo Leoni.

What's Wrong with this Picture?

There are, however, a number of problems that arise as a result of the above analysis. The first pertains to that of the particular narrative structure that is produced. The subjunctive mode defined as such and as employed in this model points forward, indicating a linear evolution; also, the aspect of transformation as described here by Turner implies an epic structure with a beginning, middle, and end, complete with conflict and epiphany followed by resolution in triumph. I would emphasise that this is just one layer of significance in the totality of the *soleá*, a layer that is informed by another, distinctive though related process.

This becomes clear when we understand that the narrative structure of the *soleá* is not a 'story', but rather a series of isolated reflections. Flamenco scholar José Maria Castaño specifies in *De Jerez y Sus Cantes* "one of the most precise definitions of the *cante* (song) for *soleá* could be to 'philosophise out loud', make public using the voice all of these internal thoughts that mark our existence" (Castaño 2007, 96, my translation). And further, Alfredo Grimaldos in *Historia Social del Flamenco* explains "The *cante* [singing] seldom relates complete stories, from beginning to end, like a song. Each verse usually constitutes an isolated reflection or memory" (Grimaldos 2010, 19, my translation). This is indeed the case for the *cante* of the performance addressed here: the narrative structure resembles more a series of isolated poems than a story, and the dancer's interpretation of the *cante* adheres to this structure. Each of the verses of the piece has a different theme, about estrangement, about loss, and about unrequited love, respectively. This lack of thematic unity in the classic sense has implications for the temporal space produced by both the music and the dance and for the structure of the *soleá* in and of itself. I will return to this below.

The second problem pertains to the aspect of ritual and transformation in the analysis, and the extent to which it can be (mis)understood as being descriptive of a type of mythology regarding flamenco and its origins: the idea that the *soleá* presented here is a stage version of a (originally) folkloric practice, in which roughly the same choreography was/is created in a familiar or community scene, taking place in some mythical "as" undefined moment and space, where people gathered and an individual dancer would work through their personal trauma, navigating thresholds in the context of public or community ritual. Nothing could be further from the truth, at least for the *soleá*. The *soleá* as a dance form came into being in the context of the *ensayos publicos* (public rehearsals) and the *cafes cantantes* — entertainment venues in which flamenco was performed – which arose first in Seville in the middle of the 19th century (Navarro and Pablo 2005, 45), and flourished throughout Andalucía in the period referred to here by way of introduction as flamenco's golden age. As such, the influence in the *soleá* of such moments of ritual and family celebration is far from straightforward. Evolving out of the *jaleo*, which for its own part, was characterised in terms of the dance by improvisation and spontaneity (Alvarez Caballero 1998, 23-24; Cabral Dominquez 2008, 85n), the *soleá* as a dance was produced specifically for a performance context, as a dance for the stage, with the date of its conception being situated by scholars as roughly 1850 (Navarro 2002, 271; Navarro and Pablo 2005, 46; Cabral Dominquez 2008, 85).[7]

What one is dealing with then is the distinction between resolution of personal trauma/crisis through ritual, versus the staging/performance of the resolution of personal trauma/crisis through art as performed ritual. As Turner would put it: "The reenactment is framed as a performance, but it is a metaperformance, a performance about a performance" (Turner 1988, 107). One must also keep in mind here the oral and hybrid nature of the evolution of flamenco as an art form. An important aspect of this evolution was a process of mutual influence between folkloric practices and dance forms produced for the stage. This was the case first for Andalucian dance, in "the establishment of a fertile dialogue between the dances of the countryside and the first dance professionals" (Navarro and Pablo 2005, 10), and later in the context of the public rehearsals and subsequently the cafés cantantes:

> ...in these academies, the seed of the future cafés cantantes, the first transcendental fusion in the history of flamenco dance was forged: that of the Andalucian bolero dances and the dances of the gitanos. (Navarro and Pablo 2005, 36-37, my translation)

Navarro and Pablo then quote from *De Telethusa a la Macarrona* that "they performed side by side, sharing the billing, the most accredited bolero dancers of the time and the gitanas of Triana who were also professionals in their art. There they learned from one another and influenced one another" (ibid., 37).

And herein lies the dig: how to account for the nature of the influence of folkloric practices in flamenco for the stage if it was not a matter of simply directly transferring a particular dance to another arena, polishing and adapting it, and then letting it loose on an audience? When it is rather a situation in which there has been an abundance of songs and dances, some traditionally Andalucian, others gitano, and mixtures of both, which were practiced in familiar/community scenes which both reflected upon and absorbed experiences from stage performances, and in their own right served to provide material for the same?[8] Not least because of this, the statement that 'flamenco is a way of being in the world' is the source of no small amount of controversy within flamenco studies. Dancer and choreographer Javier Latorre wrote in a commentary in connection with the Jerez Festival de Flamenco in 2011 "A way of life? I think that definition usually comes from those who aren't capable of rehearsing for two hours in a row ('because the nice thing about flamenco is the improvisation') and from those who scorn or simply ignore other forms of expression, or from those who, straight out, don't have a life outside of flamenco" (Latorre 2009/2011).

Latorre's comments here — however much they may appear to dismantle my analysis — serve to illustrate concisely the controversy I refer to above. However, I see no fundamental contradiction here, or where the contradiction lies is in a blurring of the difference between flamenco as performance art versus a folk tradition — a distinction that is often overlooked or, when recognised, tends to lead to disparagement or defense of the one to the benefit or disadvantage of the other. Latorre does not say here that no flamenco culture exists which defines itself as such. My understanding is that what he is reacting to is the definition and *privileging* of flamenco as exclusively about and defined through such a culture.

I would also hasten to add at this point that when I speak of habitus or the concept of flamenco as a manner of being in the world, I am not referring to a type of essence; neither am I maintaining that it is only the gitano or Andalucian practitioners who are capable of producing and/or embodying this particular qual-ity. My claim pertains more to the sources, tradition, and evolution of flamenco and *the living of these as cultural constructs used in processes of identity making*. This is significant in terms of exploring the issues of censorship and otherness which flamenco for me involves, particularly with respect to its embodiment of cultural hybridity.

Writing Hybridity

This of necessity involves addressing an intricate web of cultural assumptions within which flamenco as habitus, or a cultural construct for identity making continues to live, breathe and inspire. Just in the course of the past year I have come across a number of stories about flamenco's evolution which illustrate the apparent difficulties in finding a narrative voice for its hybridity, as well as a tendency to 'solve' these difficulties through the creation of a universal flamenco subject. A full presentation of this debate is far beyond the scope of this article, so I will limit myself here to a few, hopefully telling, examples.

The website Flamencoworld.com in its presentation of the history of flamenco makes the following observation which can serve to summarise a current and prevailing tendency in the ongoing debate: "There is an idea that although generally accepted is nevertheless subject to some questioning and states that the gypsies' contribution to flamenco relies more on the face of mimesis and interpretation and less on that of the actual creation itself" (Caldo 2011). The author does not actually take a stand here; he neither champions nor disputes this view. He merely presents a perspective, which I appreciate because my own experience in the community confirms the existence of such a view, and it corresponds with what I am trying to highlight here. What this view holds is that the gitanos did not actually produce anything — they copied the work of others and through interpretation somehow expropriated it, claiming it for themselves. The same claim is made by flamenco scholar Alvarez Caballero in *El Baile Flamenco*: "Although some are confused about this, these dances are not gitano, rather the gitanos give them a certain art in dancing them which in Andalucía is called *duende*" (Caballero 1998, 32, my translation). Here again the emphasis is on the gitanos not as founders or creators, but merely as talented interpreters, who add to flamenco a certain artistry.

These examples are representative of what I read as a tendency to edit and clean up the messy, unwieldiness of the flamenco story. Flamenco scholar and critic José Mariá Castaño resists this tendency in his meticulously detailed documentary work *De Jerez y sus cantes*, and the value of this particular piece of scholarship lies in among other things in the manner in which he presents the evolution of the *cante*, which to a very large extent begins to approach the type of narrative that a hybrid and oral flamenco evolution requires. He offers perspectives, presenting various voices, and schools within flamenco scholarship, and although obviously his selection is implicitly pedagogical in its own right, he for the most part exercises restraint in his presentation. He navigates the minefield of information with abundant care, and in so doing creates a text that gives voice for a diversity of perspectives within flamenco research. In the following example he enters the above debate from another vantage point:

> Here there is much talk by historians of the Moors, of the Sephardim, the black slaves, of the coming and going to and from the Americas, the gypsies, the influences of Castile, the Salon dances, the troubadours and so on. But, where have we left the common Andalucian man and woman? The failure to include them is one of the greatest injustices committed with respect to Andalucian music, the very seed of flamenco of today. (Castaño 2007, 45, my translation)

And on this point I agree with him, in particular to the extent that he is describing the consequences of the same old Orientalist story. Essentially he is reacting to the fact that flamenco scholars often seem to be looking for zebras when the horse is right in front of them. In this case, the difficulties in writing the flamenco story err on the side of exoticism. Somehow the 'common Andalucian folk' are not exotic enough, not 'other' enough to merit inclusion in the story of flamenco and that is absolutely, as he states, not only doing a great injustice to that population – the rectification of which is his primary objective here — but also to the art of flamenco itself. Flamenco could not have arisen anywhere except in Andalucía, and one part of the reason for this is the abundance of folk dances and songs found in that very culture, the seeds of the flamenco of today. But having said as much, it is not necessary to eliminate or downplay the role of the gitano population in order to make this point. Neither is it necessary to reject the role of the folkloric evolution, the living of flamenco prior to, alongside of and subsequent to the cafés cantantes; the existence of the one does not disallow the other.

Before the time of the cafés cantantes what exists in the way of written source materials about flamenco is a multitude of fragments — playbills, advertisements, newspaper clippings, and literary references by authors both Spanish and foreign. Subsequent attempts to compile and piece together these fragments have sought as well to coax them into some type of coherent linear narrative, a realist story if you will, but this very structuring is at risk of doing the history itself a great injustice. Not least because flamenco has evolved to a very large extent through oral transmission, also during and after the *café cantante* period, these fragments require a type of narrative that takes into account the diversity and often haphazard nature of influences, the hybrid nature of the practice of flamenco itself.

To summarise then, there appears to be not so much an outright denial, but rather a resistance or difficulty in including both the *gitano/payo* as mutually active subjects, and the parallel evolution of folkloric traditions/flamenco for the stage, respectively, in the narrative that is produced about flamenco — and this despite the fact that there is nonetheless a general consensus across the board that flamenco is hybrid by definition. It would appear, in short, that flamenco's very hybridity continues to present a snag in efforts to compose its history — and it is precisely here that a liminal space opens up — as a metaphorical wound which the dominant discourse continually seeks to recuperate or 'heal', in a representational closure. It's as if the hybridity itself *resists being written*.

The Third Space

The habitus of flamenco has been forged over the course of generations, through both folkloric practices and dance for the stage as mutually influential strains, a habitus which imbibes its hybrid nature and I would hold here, by virtue of this hybridity, opens up and inhabits what literary and post-colonial scholar Homi K. Bhabha in *The Location of Culture* (1994) refers to as 'the third space'. Bhabha defines this as "the inbetween space — that carries the burden of the meaning of culture. It makes it possible to begin envisaging national, anti-nationalist histories of the 'people'. And by exploring this Third Space, we may elude the politics of polarity and emerge as the others of ourselves" (Bhabha 1994, 56). An inbetween space, I would interject, is the very definition of liminality, and Bhabha connects it here to hybridity. An exploration of this third space "... may open the way to conceptualizing an *inter*national culture, based not on the exoticism of multiculturalism or the diversity of cultures, but on the inscription and articulation of culture's hybridity" (ibid.).

The flamenco dancing body is marked as both the 'other' and the 'same', and I would propose that herein also lies its survival mechanism, in this duplicity, this masking and unmasking. I both am and am not *gitano/payo*, a folkloric practice/performance art. This body contains as well a plethora of other influences, as outlined above, all of which are part and parcel of the habitus that is the flamenco dancing body. As such, any attempt to account for that body must of necessity seek to bypass the 'politics of polarity', and allow this hybridity to find voice.

As noted by Michelle Heffner Hayes in her work *Flamenco: Conflicting histories of the dance*, "if one examines the scholarly accounts of flamenco history, the problems of representing the dancing body become immediately apparent. The dancing body in performance carries with it the weight of corporeality. Dance cannot be divorced from the bodies that perform it" (Hayes 2009, 31). It is indeed then the weight of corporeality that I am addressing through the habitus of flamenco, the hybrid bodies that perform it. In so doing, the concept of flamenco as a manner of being in the world becomes not an ethnic slur or Orientalist generalisation that suspends flamenco in mythical space of an eternal past. It becomes a perspective that seeks rather to address the flamenco dancing body as lived, in all of its manifestations.

In Conclusion

Let us return now, in closing, to relate this to the structure of the *soleá*, which as specified above, is informed by a linear dimension, but also something else, a contrasting internal structure that is spatial. There are different types of energies emerging here; one, as outlined above, is the linear development of transformation as crisis-confrontation-resolution. The other is more about a state of being in and expansion of the state of crisis in its own right – an embodied reflection of an existential state, of 'man in his wholeness wholly attending'.

A number of flamenco scholars have documented that the music of the *soleá* was upon its initial creation quicker, lighter, and more danceable, created in effect for dance performance on stage. However, one of the features of the *cante*'s evolution, and correspondingly that of the dance, has been that of a slowing down, with the augmentation of precisely the spatial quality (Castaño 2007, 95-96) which I have defined here as liminal. So, on the one hand, the soleá acquires a linear structure involving transformation — the triumphant and celebratory *bulerías* that is now frequently employed to end the *soleá* in the dance also came at a later stage in the *soleá's* evolution. Simultaneous to this, however, the slowing down of the *cante* and the dance over the years has had the effect of augmenting a suspension within that same linear structure, through a series of poetic reflections on different themes, which albeit, share a common focus in the *soleá* on anguish, bereavement, estrangement, etc. This particular quality in the *soleá* then has the impact of subverting and opening up an otherwise linear narrative. As the story of the *soleá* as crisis resolution unfolds, it is informed by a spatial dimension, which serves to highlight liminality.

The hopeful turn of the subjunctive mode then unfolds within liminality, which is in turn augmented by the spatial elements of the *soleá*. If we agree with Bhabha that it is in liminality that hybridity finds expression, the crisis being resolved involves on the one hand the difficulties of living and negotiating a particular form of embodied subjectivity that is hybrid — hybrid in the sense of an array of different cultural influences but also influences from flamenco's evolution as both a folk tradition and an art form for the stage, the expression of which I have suggested continues to challenge scholars to this day. The state of yearning embodied by the flamenco dancing subject in the production of this liminal space proves then to contain a dense complexity. The crisis negotiated in liminal space, or to return to my opening quote, the 'wound' of flamenco, is a rupture that we should, in addressing the dance, seek to explore and articulate as a defining feature of flamenco as an art form, as part and parcel of its habitus — rather than 'heal'.

For as much as the subjunctive mode is directed towards crisis resolution, it is the embodiment of that space of yearning particular to crisis that is flamenco's primary distinguishing feature — or to employ another term introduced here — the moment of its *duende*.

BIBLIOGRAPHY

Bhabha, Homi. K. 1994. *The Location of Culture*. New York: Routledge Classics.

Butler, Judith. 1997. *Excitable Speech. A Politics of the Performative*. New York: Routledge.

Caballero, Alvarez Ángel. 1998. *El baile flamenco*. Madrid: Alanza Editorial, SA.

Cabral Dominguez, Miguelina. 2008. *La Identidad de la Mujer en el Arte Flamenco*. Sevilla: Signatura ediciones de Andalucia, SL.

Caldo, Sylvio; http://www.flamenco-world.com/magazine/about/historia_del_flamenco/ paginas/9.htm, accessed November 2011.

Castaño, José Maria. 2007. *De Jerez y sus cantes*. Cordoba: Editorial Almuzara.

Elmojama4, 2010. *Farruquito-Soleá-1/2-San Fernando* and *2/2-San Fernando*. [video online]. Accessed October 2010. http://www.youtube.com/user/elmojama4.

García Lorca, Federico. 1993. "Theory and Play of the Duende". Translated by A.S. Kline. Accessed October, 2004. http://www.poetryintranslation.com/PITBR/Spanish/LorcaDuende.htm

Grimaldos, Alfredo. 2010. *Historia Social Del Flamenco.*Barcelona: Ediciones Península.

Hayes, Michelle Heffner. 2009. *Flamenco: Conflicting Histories of the Dance*. Jefferson, NC, and London: McFarland & Company.

Latorre, Javier. 2011. Free Platform. Flamenco According to…Javier Latorre for Flamenco-world.com December 16th, 2009. Accessed March 2011. http://www.flamenco-world.com/magazine/about/tribuna_javier_latorre/ latorre16122009.htm

Leblon, Bernard. 2003. *Gypsies and Flamenco*. Hertfordshire: University of Hertfordshire Press.

Navarro, José Luis and Pablo, Eulalia. 2005. *El Baile Flamenco*. Cordoba: Almuzara.

Navarro, José Luis. 2002. *De Telethusa a la Macarrona. Bailes Andaluces y Flamencos*. Dos Hermanas (Sevilla): Portada Editorial.

Turner, Victor. 1988. *The Anthropology of Performance*. New York: PAJ Publications.

NOTES

1   The term hybridity as I employ it here refers to cultural hybridity and is indebted to Homi K. Bhabha's use of the term in *The Location of Culture* (1994). My argument pertains to what Bhabha's describes as "The social articulation of difference [...] [as a] complex, on-going negotiation that seeks to authorize cultural hybridities that emerge in moments of historical transformation" (1994, 3). It is my contention here that the liminal space produced by flamenco represents such a moment of historical transformation. I would also specify that the hybridity as will be shown here also pertains to the mixture of influences from flamenco as folkloric practice and flamenco as art for the stage.

2   I use the term *gitano* here to refer to the Romani population in Andalucía, or the Iberian Kale. In my experience the word *gitano* in Spanish does not carry the same derogatory associations as the word gypsy in English.

3   To say that there is no small amount of controversy regarding who in effect 'owns' Flamenco, would be an understatement and is an issue I will return to below. I begin based on the theory of flamenco scholar Bernard Leblon, who says in *Gypsies and Flamenco* that "The initial phase of flamenco's gestation and development was essentially Gypsy, whereas the second phase, which considerably expanded its repertoire and audience, was primarily *Payo* or Andalucian. The transmission within a number of gypsy families of certain songs, and above all of a particular interpretative style and a way of *living* the flamenco, is incontestable fact, but this must not blind us to the role played by *Payo* artists of genius..." (Leblon 2003, 73). Payo is the Andalucian Spanish word for non-*gitano*.

4   I employ here Bourdieu's concept of habitus, as this is discussed and applied by Butler in *Excitable Speech A Politics of the Performative* (1997). According to Butler "Bourdieu offers a theory of bodily knowingness in his notion of the *habitus*, but he does not relate this discussion of the body to the theory of the performative" (ibid., 152), something which Butler on the other hand does.

5   I would emphasise here that this is my perception and definition. Angel Alvarez Caballero in his work *El baile flamenco* makes the following observation which corresponds with the type of knowledge I am seeking to identify here, but he on the other hand calls this being *enterado*, or informed, "in the know", which consists in... "not solely understanding the rhythm one must follow in each dance, but as well to know at which precise moment to signal the guitarist, with a gesture or step, the changes one wants to make" (Caballero 1998, 33).

6   Cf. Judith Butler in *Excitable Speech*: "The body, however, is not simply the sedimentation of speech acts by which it has been constituted [...] something exceeds the interpellation, and this excess is lived as the outside of intelligibility" (1997, 155).

7   Dominquez does not narrow the date down any more precisely than to the 19th century, but there is general agreement among the authors quoted that the *soleá* evolved out of the *jaleo.*

8   Note here how this aspect of mutual influence between folkloric and stage practices corresponds with the definition of habitus presented earlier as reciprocal, both formed and formative.

INTERACTING SPACES IN ARGENTINEAN TANGO

Susanne Ravn

Abstract

Centred round the case of interaction in Argentinean tango the article is focused on exploring how theoretical descriptions of space and movement and the empirical realities of an actual movement practice might inform each other. Based on Doreen Massey's (2005; 2011) reconceptualisation, space is understood as a product of relation and, accordingly, unfolding in interaction. Philosopher Erin Manning's (2007a; 2007b; 2009) definition of how a relational interval can be expressed in the fluctuating duration in between actual movements is used constructively to relate Massey's theoretical propositions to micro-levels of creating space: two bodies interacting in tango. Exploring the empirical realities of tango reveals the potential of Massey's and Manning's conceptual frameworks, but also challenges their parameters. The article highlights how the conceptual frameworks unfold and open the descriptions and understandings of how space is created in movement. However, the discussion also exemplifies how it is a constant challenge not to take an *ideal of* tango dancing (as this ideal is known from being *in* practice) as a paradigm of how interaction is improvised and unfolded in tango. Following Massey's reconceptualisation, descriptions and analyses of tango dancing have to include both the *multiplicity* and *complexity* of the space(s) in creation.

Introduction

Prologue: Setting a Tango Scene

I began dancing Argentinian tango by accident. About five years ago I planned a three-week holiday to visit my sister, when she lived in Buenos Aires for a period. Somehow it seemed impossible to visit Buenos Aires as a dancer, and teacher and researcher in dance without having participated in a few milongas (places where tango is danced). So, despite the fact that I had never really been that interested in this kind of dancing, I tried to get just a bit familiar with the basic steps and the basic rules for improvisation in Argentinean tango some months ahead of my visit.

After a few workshops, which I had picked out rather randomly at a Danish Tango festival, I arranged for some private lessons with a local teacher. I learned to place my feet correctly in the basic cross step, to turn around the leader in the *giro*, and to recognise that the *boleo* was a bit tricky. According to my own judgment at that time I was doing okay in recognising the different movement signals for when certain steps were expected from me when dancing the follower-role. I felt a continuous progress during the private lessons. My posture as well as the way I shared the embrace with the leader became more relaxed. I became still better at taking the role of the follower without ending up trying to predict the steps to come and

Dancing couples from a tango festival in Malmö in Sweden, 2012. Photographer: Lars Kårholm.

I discovered that I actually enjoyed to be led in the dance. A bit untrained but not unfamiliar with the steps I arrived in Buenos Aires.

My sister introduced me to José, an experienced *milonguero*, who invited me to several different milongas during my stay. José and his friends thereby came to nurse my first meeting with the tango environment of Buenos Aires.

…So, there I was, a bit nervous, in a local milonga. I had survived some dances okay. I could follow the continuous sequence of steps that José and some of his good friends had offered me on the dance floor. I sensed that I could be still more relaxed in my body — however, the tension was not bad. It all seemed to work and I enjoyed the challenge and the intimacy of the improvised tango dancing.

Then this tall guy invited me 'through eye-contact' to dance. I took a deep breath, nodded a bit, smiled back to him and crossed the floor to meet him. (It was later that I learned that as a female follower in a milonga in Buenos Aires I am supposed to wait for him to come to me.) We established the embrace, and for some reasons I felt my body hesitating … and I began thinking. I felt as if I was nearly stumbling over my own feet and unable to follow the signals given through his movements. Nothing seemed to work … or rather: he walked and I tried to follow and recognise the steps, which I then did my best to follow. I felt the tension rise and my sense of centre lifting with this tension. Then he stopped. For a minute I feared he would leave me there on the dance floor without finishing the *tanda*,[1] and that I would have to find my chair alone — humiliated. I got totally confused when he began lifting me slowly and nearly off the ground. I just stood there on the absolute tip of my toe and he just waited … waited until I relaxed, stopped looking for signals and sequences of steps, and began to be there with his body in the movement… I gave up the idea of being in control of my body — I guess — accepted and went into the embrace and began dancing from the dynamic as created in the embrace. I don't remember that we did anything else but walk … that space opened and time left…

Space Unfolding as Interaction

The prologue is based on experiences from my first year of dancing tango. A period I, by now, about five years and many milongas later, remember as a confusing state of limbo despite all my prior dance experience. No doubt, I felt uneasy with being, on the one hand, an experienced dancer used to improvise and, on the other hand, realising that I was a beginner in Argentinean tango, struggling to find out what was requested and expected in this genre-specific kind of improvisation — dancing in a close embrace while wearing high heels.

As indicated in the prologue, the focus of this article will be the interactive movements when improvising in tango. More precisely, the aim of the discussions to be presented in the following pages is to explore how the actual practices of improvised interaction in tango can be tied to movement processes of creating space. I will specifically focus on discussing how conceptual frameworks of space and interaction might open a theoretical space for analysing empirical realities[2] of dance practices. The discussions will be tied to the two conceptual frameworks of human geographer Doreen Massey (2005; 2011) and philosopher Erin Manning (2007a; 2009), respectively. That is, after introducing Massey's propositions concerning space, I will explore interaction and space with reference to Manning's ideas. Accordingly, I will suggest how Massey's considerations can be used to look critically at which space(s) are opened and unfolded through Manning's conceptual articulations of interaction in tango. From the outset, the discussion focuses on theoretical approaches and related concept, but I intend to keep the practice present throughout. In other words, my own experiences with tango form a central track of my reflections on how the theoretical framework might shed light on what is going on in the practices of the dancing.

Massey's Concept of Space and Interaction

Massey's poststructuralist reconceptualisation of space provides the underlying basis for the exploration. In her writings, she confronts and rejects the idea of space as an abstract, but nevertheless relatively static dimension which we relate to in our mode of exteriority to our life-world (Massey 2005, 57). Rather according to Massey, space is to be understood as closely connected to the implicit structures, connections and tensions continuously created in interactions. Space is *in* movement — constituted and continuously created through different kinds of movement (Ravn 2009, 187ff). Based on, among others, the philosopher Henri Bergson's description of time as durational, Massey indicates that "the 'role of space' might be characterised as providing the condition for the existence of those relations which generate time" (Massey 2005, 56) — and "if time unfolds as change then space unfolds as interaction" (ibid., 61).

From a politically-oriented perspective, Massey throughout *For Space* (2005) exemplifies and emphasises how space can be understood as forms of processual existence in a multiplicity of ways. She sets out three propositions concerning space: space is to be recognised as the product of interrelations, to be understood as the sphere of the possibility of the existence of multiplicity/coexisting heterogeneity and to be recognised as always under construction (ibid., 9, 61). According to Massey (2005; 2011), space is the dimension of simultaneous existence of our stories so far and how they are weaved into each other. In this sense space "is the condition of the social in the widest sense and the delight and challenge of that" (Massey 2005, 105).[3]

In developing these propositions, Massey specifically points to the fact that the challenge of the latter two propositions in particular is to "argue not just for a notion of 'becoming', but for the *openness* of that process of becoming" (Massey 2005, 21, my emphasis). She emphasises her point by exemplifying and discussing how "power is embedded and embodied within relations that structure spatiality" (Massey 2011, 38). In several ways, Massey emphasises that she intends to challenge what she refers to as a modern view of social discourses. She insist that despite being embedded and embodied in power relations we should be constantly aware that space holds out the possibility of difference and surprise. She emphasises her reconceptualisation of space as being critically grounded in a poststructuralistic and postcolonial view of the world. In my view, Massey thereby also implicitly indicates that as practitioners struggling, experimenting and enjoying different practices of dancing, and/or as researchers juggling with theories, we should be aware that we might be partly blinded by the spaces we know through our own practices of dancing and/or through working with theories. Spaces might be more and sometimes different to the spaces we expect and know of in advance.

In line with Massey's work, the geographers Mike Crang and Nigel Thrift have pointed to the way different academic disciplines "do space differently" (Crang and Thrift 2000, 1). Space might be about the space of communication, the different social spaces within communities and the actual space of, for example, cities, architectures and physical activities. They further emphasise that no matter how academic disciplines 'do' space, space is also a representational strategy (ibid.). In the following exploration, the focus is directed towards the space created in the intimate connections of tango improvisation. Obviously, this means that the transnational context characterising tango today is not the primary focus of the discussions. However, in accordance with Crang and Thrift (2000), I still intend to include considerations of how the contextual space, the setting of the actual tango scene, somehow influences and is part of the interaction between the leader and follower dancing together. That is, I intend to recognise that the tango interaction of the couple is also taking form because of the coded and learned movement of tango and according to the implicit codes and rules of the tango setting, as these are influenced both by the transnational and local culture of the actual milonga.

Manning's Concept of Pre-accelerations and Intervals

Erin Manning is a philosopher and tango practitioner, who often describes dancing the leader role (2007a, 100; 2007b; 2009, 25). In her books *Politics of Touch* (2007a) and *Relationscapes* (2009) Manning focuses on foregrounding the body as a processual body and uses tango to prepare the way "for a thinking of the strange instability of bodies" (Manning 2007a, xvii). In her descriptions of our capacity to enter into relations, she emphasises how the bodies relating and interacting are to be thought of as extending bodies (ibid., 102). When a body in tango works as an extension of another body (and vice versa) this might concretely relate to when leaders, for example, refer to sensing their movements through and in the body of the follower. The conceptual framework of interactions, which Manning presents, specifies embodied levels involved in social relations. It is therefore relevant to suggest that Manning's framework might constructively contribute to exploring what can be considered as the micro-levels of Massey's propositions of space. In other words, I suggest that Manning's conceptual framework presents a constructive way of taking Massey's politically-oriented discussions into the micro-levels of socialising processes of two bodies acting and interacting together.

In her book *Relationscapes* (2009), Manning elaborates on the incipiency of movement by foregrounding sensations of the not-yet of movement as this is felt as part of and in the actual movement. She emphasises, in several ways, that her work is neither to be misunderstood as a description of pre-articulations nor as an elaboration on some kind of non-verbal authenticity of movement forerunning reflections (Manning 2009, 5-6, 18-19). Rather, her focus is on how movement can be felt in a *moment of not-yet* before it actualises, like *pre-accelerations* forerunning potential movement. Pre-accelerations are, according to Manning's descriptions given life and can be felt through relational *intervals of movement*, which is expressed in the fluctuating duration in between actual movements. The continuous changes in interactions and interrelations are central to how pre-accelerations come to life. To find movement is thereby about working pre-accelerations (ibid., 21) and to move relationally is, according to Manning's descriptions to create and move an interval together (ibid., 30). The interactive complexity of intervals and pre-accelerations are to be understood as central to processes of creating space in movement. In Manning's words: "I move not you but the interval out of which our movement emerges" (ibid., 17). It is the interval created in interaction which opens space(s) for movement.

To bring her philosophical writings and concepts closer to actual movements and interactions, Manning exemplifies how pre-accelerations and intervals might work when improvising in tango. She describes how dancing the leading role is not about deciding, but about initiating an opening, "I am not moving her, nor is she simply responding to me: we are beginning to move relationally, creating an interval that we move together" (ibid., 30). Manning also suggests that the dancers can work the interval *more or less* successfully by emphasising that "*When the relational movement flows*, it is because we surrender to the interval: the interval in-forms our movement. We re-form: we create a collective body" (ibid., 27, my emphasis).

The Promise of Manning's Concepts

In her descriptions of pre-accelerations, intervals (2009) and touching (2007), Manning from the outset foregrounds the body as processual. As she emphasises herself, through the prism of tango, she is not asking what a sensing body is but what a sensing body *can do* (Manning 2007a, xv). Manning's tango specific contextualisation of how bodies might compose and recompose through their "coupling or conjoining" (Blackman 2009, 137) with others exemplifies what this might mean in practice. In her descriptions of tango dancing, space becomes activated and created — in a continuous process of shaping both bodies and sensations. Philosophically and by presenting examples of practices, Manning confronts the idea that bodies, from the outset, can be understood as singular individualities and argues that individual bodies are rather to be understood as an outcome of individuation processes (Manning 2007a, xv, xvii, xx). Consequently, she indicates how descriptions of the movement created by the leader and follower in tango dancing cannot be reduced to a *system* of actions and reactions between individual bodies. In this sense, Manning's concepts of pre-accelerations and intervals are to be understood as focusing on the *process* of interaction as the first thing — and as forming the basis for generating the dance practitioners' sense of their individual body as well as their sense of space.

As emphasised in the introduction, it is the intention to keep empirical realities present throughout while exploring the potential of Massey's and Manning's theoretical insights. Before continuing the conceptually-oriented discussion, I will thus briefly relate to what Manning's conceptual framework might mean in relation to the analysis of actual tango practices. By drawing on Brandon Oszlewski's (2008) work I will exemplify how implicit theoretical presuppositions concerning the concepts of space and body direct the analytical outcome of empirical reality

— specifically, how space conceived as a passive background seems to forefront bodies as individual entities throughout the analysis.

Oszlewski (2008) has performed partly autobiographical and partly ethnographic fieldwork at milongas on the American West coast. Based on self-observations and informal interviews, he suggests that the intimate kinetic connection is central to the transcultural popularity of tango. In his comparison to other ballroom dances, which are also improvised, he characterises tango as "particularly spontaneous" (ibid., 65) and further characterises the tango improvisation by referring to the facets of interaction as "complementary movements" and "kinetic synchronicity" (ibid., 68). When describing the intimate kinetic connection, Oszlewski refers to the "physical fit" (ibid., 70) of bodies and points to how "everyone has a different body, and each couple somatically connects differently" (ibid., 69). Nevertheless, in reading Oszlewski's descriptions and analysis we do not really come to know what it means 'to connect' nor do we know how 'a good match of somatic bodies' might be further characterised and understood. In the analysis, space implicitly becomes reduced to being a passive background for the "personal transformations" (ibid., 78) of individual bodies. If we are to further understand how practitioners might end up matching or not matching and how personal transformations might be an outcome of the interaction in tango, we need a conceptual framework to be able to focus on the process of interaction. We need space to be conceived as something else than just a passive background. Manning's framework offers suggestions as to how the *process* of interaction might be approached and thought about as a central approach for analysis. This includes that space is created in and as part of the relational connection.

Activating the Multiplicity of Space(s)

As indicated in relation to Oszlewski's (2008) work in the previous section, Manning's conceptual framework of processual bodies, pre-accelerations and intervals might work constructively to generate new insights in relation to empirical realities. However, at the same time I am a bit puzzled about how Manning forefronts a smooth sensitivity in the touching and how she relates to flow in the practitioners interactive sensitivity. By emphasising tango as a desire for communication she comes to focus her descriptions on tango as being "the inner exchange between two silent partners moving quietly, eyes half closed, towards dawn" (Manning 2007, 2). From the presentation of tango dancing in the prologue, I want to remind the readers that as a beginner I primarily 'responded to movement signals'. It was only later, meeting this insistent leader in Buenos Aires, that I experienced that I was 'dancing from the embrace' and found myself in a situation where I was not sure of where my body ended and my leader's body began. Following Manning's elaborations on tango dancing, the latter description illustrates how movements flow when the dancers surrender to the interval, while the first description of handling the improvisation appears to be related to the unsuccessful struggle of beginners not being capable of surrendering to any interval. In contrast to Manning's descriptions, I do not find that we should only think of, for example, beginners in relation to an ideal of how the relative interval of movements (should) flow. Rather, in accordance with Massey's emphasis on the space as the sphere of multiplicity and always under construction, I find it important to be aware of the heterogeneity of expectations and motivations, which both characterise and shape the actual practice taking place in tango communities. Parallel to Heike Wieschiolek's (2003) descriptions of the differences within the shared discursive practice of salsa dancing in Hamburg, tango practitioners might on the one hand agree on striving for 'the good dance' and on the other hand relate to very different experiences of what is conveyed and how this is communicated during the dancing. Drawing on my own experiences, I find it relevant to add that depending on, for example, the leader's skills and personal style, I still find myself today, many milongas later, shifting between different ways of being in the improvised dynamics shaping the tango dancing. The improvised interactions I share with different dance partners during a milonga differ according to, for example, how he works the embrace in the leading, how I feel the strength of his upper torso in the leading, how he interacts with the music, the way he listens (or does not listen) to my responses, and how he dances in relation to the other couples on the floor. With some partners, the interactive improvisation feels like a sharing process of dancing the melody we listen to together, while others invite for playing around with turns, *boleos* and ornamentations while using the rhythm of the music as a baseline. Sometimes it changes — and the same partner leads differently. I might have certain expectations but I never really know how the improvised interaction will take shape. The differences and variations of the improvised interaction present themselves in expected as well as in unexpected ways. With reference to Massey's descriptions, the differences and variations of improvisation manifest an *openness* of the process of becoming.

Manning's descriptions of tango dancing (2007a; 2007b; 2009) appear to twist in and out of her development of the concept of pre-accelerations. In these descriptions, the *ideal* of how improvisation in tango dancing should be handled appears as an implicit paradigm of what tango dancing is. Her elaborations thereby

A couple dancing Tango in Malmø in Sweden, 2012. Photo by Lars Kårholm.

come to imply that dancing tango can be described according to whether the pre-acceleration and interval of movement and the continuous process of recon-nections are being worked on *more* or *less* successfully. It is this implicit absence of differences and varieties in how the process of pre-accelerations and intervals might take form that puzzles me. If Manning's elaboration on how space is created is to make sense in relation to Massey's conceptual propositions concerning space, then the possible ways of shaping and handling pre-accelerations and intervals are to be 'opened' so they can take form in a multiplicity of ways. Concretely, this means that, for example, the two different ways of handling the follower role in tango, as presented in the prologue, are to be understood as *two different ways* of working pre-accelerations and intervals. Some of these tango interactions might successfully adhere to Manning's descriptions of surrendering to the interval and others might not, but the dancing couple and their dancing is still part of characterising the practice of interaction in tango. I suggest that somehow they create another kind of interval, which stands out as very different to Manning's descriptions of an ideal tango interval.

Based on Marta Saviglioni's (1995a) historically-oriented descriptions and analysis of tango as a battlefield of colonisation and de-colonisation, Manning herself refers to the idea that tango "lives through flexibility, mutation, evocation, pluralization, and transculturation" (Manning 2007a, 4). However, when Manning turns to describing and analysing the tango dancing, I miss the diversity emphasised in her introduction. I miss the tensions and contradictions presented within the web of tango practices as described by Savigliano. In other words, Manning in many ways states that "tango is an improvised movement" (Manning 2007a, 28) and combines the concept of improvisation with focusing on an inner exchange between two partners (see for example Manning 2007a, 2, 27, 29, 38, 100-101). However, at the same time other and 'different ways' of approaching the improvisation process are only present in her descriptions when Manning characterises what tango dancing is *not*. For example, the way the improvised interaction is approached by beginners and by couples being more focused on handling an exchange of sequences of steps together (see for example Manning 2007a, 38).

If we take a closer look at the different kinds of tango Savigliano (1995a; 1995b; 2010) presents in her work, it is noteworthy that she does not identify one specific approach to improvisation as essential, but rather refers to different kinds of improvisations and how these run as important and different threads in the web of tango. Tango has not been and is not always improvised the way Manning suggests at the beginning of her description. Tango has been a battlefield of class-tensions, colonisation and decolonisation, and this means that improvisation has been downplayed or foregrounded in different contexts (see for example Savigliano 1995a, 149, 153-155). In accordance with Massey's politically-oriented discussions, Savigliano argues that tango as popular culture is to be viewed as a battlefield of powers at play. Tango is "the battlefield/dance-floor and weapon/dance-step in and by which Argentinean identity is continuously redefined" (Savigliano 1995a, 5). It is worth noting that in some versions of Savigliano's tango descriptions the tight connection between the leader's step and the music seems to be primarily what the improvisation is about, while the interaction with the follower appears secondary to the improvisation process (ibid., 40-41). Improvisation, what it means and how it is to be performed, is itself part of the tensions within the practices of tango dancing.

In the descriptions Manning (2007a; 2007b; 2009) uses for her analysis and discussions, she seems to end up working through a prism, which idealises the improvisation of tango. If tango dancing comes to be defined by an ideal, as in Manning's writings, this ideal also comes to predefine the structure of how pre-accelerations and intervals are given shape. The smoothness and flow of intervals in tango as described by Manning implicitly establishes a particular horizon of experiences for how tango can be danced. In that sense, the openness in relation to how spaces can be created becomes restricted. Following Massey's (2005, 21) discussion, Manning, in her descriptions of how space is created, thereby comes to argue for a notion of becoming. However, she does not take up the burden to also argue for the openness of this becoming. It is of course important to note that Manning is not exploring tango per se. However, her use of tango as a prism and her way of exemplifying her philosophical descriptions still reflect back, inscribing other and new meanings on the practices of tango dancing. In this sense, her ideal comes to work as an implicit paradigm of tango dancing.

I do not disagree that Manning's ideal of tango dancing can be experienced in practice. On the contrary, being a tango dancer myself, I think it can. Nor do I reject the importance of having an ideal *in* the practice of tango dancing. I simply want to stress that when, for example, a couple dancing focus on an exchange of steps, this is part of the heterogeneity of tango dancing. The couple dancing might not work their bodies in the same way as Manning chooses to focus on, but they still, somehow, interact according to a sense of the other's movement. Their dancing might be different to an ideal of tango improvisation, but still be part of the practices within the tango communities and thereby present a *difference of differences* of how we might create an interval together.

Manning's descriptions of ideal tango dancing works as a highlighter of how pre-accelerations and intervals work interactively. However, if her concepts are to work according to Massey's propositions concerning space and interaction, a non-ideal way of dancing tango may just as well be characterised by pre-accelerations and intervals. Again, drawing on the descriptions in the prologue, when dancing the follower role in tango, so that I focus on recognising steps and responding to signals, pre-accelerations are worked on differently compared to when my dance partner invites me to focus on interacting from a shared dynamic as created and felt from the embrace. Different kinds of intervals are to be understood as inviting different kinds of actual movements. In that sense, it is not only about how 'the flow' might feel different, but also about how the difference of different kinds of flow might unfold in interaction. Following Massey's (2005) propositions we are to be aware not only of the simultaneity, but also the multiplicity of how pre-accelerations and intervals come to life. From a researcher position, we have to take on the burden of being aware of the openness in the process of becoming. This includes, being aware of the multiplicities of possible spaces of interaction which might be created.

It Takes Three to Tango

As mentioned in the beginning of this article, the contextualised setting of the Milonga also influences how the improvised interaction takes shape for the couple dancing together. The way I touch my partner and the way pre-accelerations take form is also influenced by the way we are watched and the way we participate in the practices of tango dancing. The interactions at play include more than the two dancers in the couple. When Manning (2007a, 12) focuses on and emphasises how the physical touching produces an event, she also reminds us that the given setting which makes the touching possible also produces and influences the touching. Clearly, Manning also makes us aware of the contextual requests of the milongas, just as well as she emphasises the necessity of knowing how to "operate according to the codes of tango" (Manning 2007a, 100). One thing is to learn and know the language of tango but the "being-in-language" of tango is more than can be described by the language itself (ibid., 5). Manning stresses that the touch, touching and being touched at the same time is an engagement with the contextualised setting. Participating in tango, like participating in, for example, contemporary dance (Potter, 2008) or a boxing (Wacquant, 2005), involves figuring out what it takes to participate. Participation is not only about knowing the skills of the activity, may it be contemporary dance, tango or boxing, but also about how and when these skills are expected to be performed, how different meanings are communicated and how these are then talked about among participants (Goffman, 1990/1959).

Savigliano (1995a; 1995b; 2007; 2010) highlights the continuous political interest and tension at play when defining and developing the tango. As she exemplifies in several ways, the battlefield of tango became established through the gaze of Others (Savigliano, 1995a). The colonisers' gaze on the natives forms/informs and (re-)shapes the natives' look on themselves and what and how their culture presents authentic values of exotic interest for the coloniser. Concretely, Savigliano points to the facts that in the historical web of tango men also competed with other men over dancing skills (Savigliano 1995a, 63) and that the practice was a showcase of complex social tensions (ibid., 110). It took three to tango: a male master, a female to seduce and a gaze to watch (ibid., 74). As I will touch upon in the following, it still takes three to tango.

The tango being danced today generally takes place as a recreational activity of trying out the Argentinean tango culture "without the need to be or become native" (Savigliano 2010, 135). Rather, the practitioners of the transnational tango scene act like cultural consumers and "global customers" (ibid., 135). Their interest in tango tends to be dance-oriented and, in that sense, more or less formal (ibid., 140). So, it might be a little exaggerated to describe today's tango scene as if participants will experience tango dancing as a battlefield of tensions between race, gender, class, colonisation and decolonisation. However, the participation in the milongas and the challenge of finding a way of being part of the local and transnational tango scene somehow include that participants also find their way of dealing with the rules of the game — as these might be played out in Buenos Aires, Tokyo, Malmø and Odense.

Following the track of my own experiences with tango dancing, any tango event first of all begins by figuring out how to get the dance opportunities at the milonga. In a Danish context this might include a combination of both being invited or receiving positive responses, if I take on the initiative to ask. Sitting and waiting is never just waiting. Waiting includes watching the people dancing and being aware of how the different leaders lead. For example, if he takes care of his follower or continuously seems to let her bump into other couples on the dance floor. If he has got some experience or still struggles to get hold of steps. If he invites his follower to create a shared improvisation according to the pauses and hesitations of the melody, or if he dances on the rhythm and prefers to play around leading combinations of steps. Vice versa, I know that when I dance, I am watched by the other potential leaders at the milonga. I am aware of the gaze of the other dancers watching in the improvised interaction with the partner with whom I am dancing. The gaze of other dancers thereby adds to the complexity of interaction. It still takes three to tango, even when the tango is danced by cultural consumers and global customers.

Conclusions

As revealed in the prologue, my interest in tango begins in practice. Accordingly, I have presented a genre-specific case of how empirical realities of actual dance practices might inform theoretical discussions. Conceptual frameworks help unfold descriptions and understandings of what is going on in the practices of dancing, but the actual dance practices might also add to develop the conceptual framework. It has been central to the discussions to exemplify that, when drawing on experiences of a given practice in theoretical discussions we have to remember to be aware of the multiplicity as well as the diversity of the practice. In other words, we have to be aware that in practice certainly, ideals count and as practitioners we have opinions on what we intend to do, achieve or be part of when dancing. However, when looking into theories of how space is created through interaction and interrelations in (tango)dancing, we need to ensure that we do not end up taking ideals as implicit paradigms of the dances. We need to ensure not to end up neglecting the diversity within the practice because of theoretical preconceptions.

Throughout the article I have argued that Massey's (2005; 2011) and Manning's (2007a; 2009) conceptual frameworks concerning space and interaction are of constructive value when analysing embodied improvisation in tango. I have suggested and exemplified how Manning's concepts of pre-accelerations and intervals might work constructively in relation to Massey's reconceptualisation of space. In the discussion, I have also pointed to some of the challenges to be aware of when turning to Manning's concepts of pre-accelerations and intervals, specifically how we are to be aware of both the *multiplicity* and *complexity* of spaces created. As Massey has indicated in her work, there is a multiplicity of approaches and experiences to be included when describing the possible processes of interaction between bodies. Therefore, we have to keep an openness in our descriptions of the possible space(s) being created in the actual contextual setting of the milonga. In other words, we have to be critically aware and not blinded by our own ideals of the practices in the use of theoretical concepts.

Furthermore there is a complexity of simultaneity of the spaces created to be remembered when describing how space is created in movement. Different kinds of interactions affect how the actual space for movement between two bodies is created. So when dancing tango, not only my dance partner, but also the gaze of the other practitioners dancing tango influence and form part of how the interaction is shaped and how we create dance space together. In that sense, it still takes three to tango.

REFERENCES

Bergson, Henry. 1911. *Matter and Memory*. London: George Allen and Unwin. http://spartan.ac.brocku.ca.

Blackman, Lisa. 2009. "'Starting over': Politics, Hope, Movement." *Theory, Culture & Society* 26(1): 134-143.

Crang, Mike and Thrift, Nigel. 2000. "Introduction." In *Thinking Space*, edited by Mike Crang and Nigel Thrift. 1-30. New York: Routledge.

Goffman, Erving. 1990/1959. *The Presentation of Self in Everyday life.* London: Penguin Books.

Manning, Erin. 2007a. *The Politics of Touch: sense, movement, sovereignty.* Minneapolis: The University of Minnesota Press.

Manning, Erin. 2007b. "Incipient Action: the dance of the Not-Yet." Unpublished conference paper given at *TransLatinDance:Translocal dance culture tango* conference, University of Hamburg, Germany, date (e.g. November 21-24).

Manning, Erin. 2009. *Relationscapes: movement, art, philosophy.* Cambridge, Massachusetts: The MIT Press.

Massey, Doreen. 2005. *For Space.* London: Sage.

Massey, Doreen. 2011. For Space: Reflections on an Engagement with Dance. In *Proceedings from the 10th International NOFOD Conference, Spacing Dance(s) — Dancing Space(s)*, 35-44. Odense 2011, University of Southern Denmark, January 27-30.

Olszewski, Brandon. 2008. "El Cuerpo del Baile: The Kinetic and Social Fundaments of Tango." *Body & Society* 14(2): 63-81.

Potter, Caroline. 2008. "Sense of motion, senses of self: Becoming a dancer." *Ethnos* 73(4): 444-465.

Ravn, Susanne. 2009. *Sensing Movement, Living Spaces — An investigation of movement based on the lived experience of 13 professional dancers.* Saarbrücken: VDM Verlag Dr. Müller.

Savigliano, Marta E. 1995a. *Tango and the Political Economy of Passion.* Boulder and Oxford: Westview Press.

Savigliano, Marta E. 1995b. "Whiny Ruffians and Rebellious Broads: Tango as a Spectacle of Eroticized Social Tension." *Theatre Journal* 47 (1): 83-104.

Savigliano, Marta E. 2007. "Wallflowers and Femme Fatales: Dancing Gender & Politics at the Milongas." Paper presented at Agassiz Theater, Harvard University, Radcliffe Institute of Advanced Study, October 27 (the Case of Angora Matta p. 1-49).

Savigliano, Marta E. 2010. "Notes on Tango (as) Queer (Commodity)." *Anthropological Notebooks* 16(3): 135-143.

Wacquant, Loïc. 2004. *Body and Soul — notebook of an apprentice boxer.* New York: Oxford University Press.

Wieschiolek, Heike. 2003. ""Ladies, Just Follow His Lead!" *Salsa*, Gender and Identity." In *Sport, Dance and Embodied Identities*, edited by Noel Dyck and Eduardo P. Archetti, 115-138. Oxford and New York: Berg.

NOTES

1   A series of three, four or five dance melodies, similar in style. The *tandas* are sepa-
    rated by *cortinas*, which is a short musical interlude that breaks the flow of dance
    melodies. The *cortina* provides time for dancers to change partners.

2   'Empirical realities' here refers to how concrete practices unfold. However, it is not
    the intention to indicate that there is *'a'* concrete physical reality out there, which we
    (researchers) might uncover. Rather, the concept 'empirical realities' has been chosen
    to emphasise both the 'existence of entities, things and identities' (Massey 2011, 43)
    and that the experience of these existing things might take shape in different ways
    for the subjects involved. In other words, the plural is used to remind us how any
    experience of 'a reality' might take shape in very different ways depending on, for
    example, the subject's actual intentions, incorporated skills and habits as well as the
    prior experiences connected to a given situation.

3   Massey emphasises that the concept of 'social' is not to be misunderstood as if in-
    tending "to invoke the human (as social) as opposed to the non-human" (Massey
    2011, 36). Rather, social is meant as the multiple rather than the singular — and in-
    tended to include the non-human as well as the human as active and dynamic in the
    creation of the multiplicities of interactions (ibid.).

SPACE AND ARTISTIC PRACTICE

ON THE ROPRESENTATION OF SPACE

Camilla Damkjaer

Abstract

"On the Ropresentation of Space" is an examination of the specific spatial characteristics of the circus discipline vertical rope. Starting from the assumption that we
cannot compare the spatial characteristics of aerial disciplines to dance until we
have understood the disciplines' internal spatial articulation, this presentation leaves
the floor in order to go into that space, above, often vaguely understood as "in the
air". The presentation describes the space that the vertical rope articulates as a set
of interweaving aesthetic tensions, activated and intensified by the movement of
the human body in the rope.

At the same time, the text is a reflection on the different time-spaces that occur
in the event of a lecture-performance or a text, and the way these time-spaces condense or expand the information given. Through re-visiting the lecture-presentation
in vertical rope "On the Ropresentation of Space" and a shorted "Ropetition" of this
presentation, this text unfolds some of the information that was either condensed
or materialised in the physicality of the presentations, thus filling out some of the
blank spaces and creating new ones.

Introduction

Representation of Tension 0: Circus — Dance

> (…) This is where I was thinking to start: where the aerial disciplines of circus break
> with the horizontal space of dance. But in fact, we may have to break with the naïve
> assumption that the interest of aerial disciplines lies simply in the contrast they
> provide to moving on the ground.

The comparison of dance and circus would have built only on a distinction of genres: who says that dance has to be on the ground? Instead, I will have to start by analysing the rope in itself. I have to make a sketch of the space of the rope, a sketch of the "ropresentation" of space. Before anything else that is perhaps what the rope does to space: it renders vertical space visible. (…)

My sketch will be simple, but sometimes the simplest things are the most complex. For instance, a vertical rope has a very simple spatial design. But to understand the space of the rope, we have to see it not as a static set of dimensions, but as a set of aesthetic tensions.

So perhaps I should start by saying what I mean by aesthetic tension. I here mean a constellation where two or several aspects or qualities stand in a relation of difference that cannot be resolved. They are neither united, nor in opposition, but in a constant relation of paradoxical difference.

For instance there is such a tension between theory and practice in this presentation. It may seem that I rely only on practice in my analysis, but it is paradoxically influenced by theory. The two reinforce each other without ever merging totally. The more practical it seems, the more it is informed by theory. The more theoretical it seems, the more it is based on practice. (…)

Ropetition in Writing: Back to 0

This was where I started; where I stood underneath the rope, raised my hands to take a grip, slowly lifted my feet of the ground, inverted my body into a so-called "catchers" position, locked the rope around one thigh, and then started to read this "paper in the rope". And this is where I am planning to start now: where the physical presentation of the lecture-performance "On the Representation of Space" left a space to be filled out. "On the Ropresentation of Space" is a reflection on the space of movement in vertical rope, but it also became a reflection on the relation between movement and text, and the spatiality and temporality of written and spoken words.

When writing for a lecture-performance in rope, or as I call it: "ropeflections" or "ropresentations", I tend to try to condense the text, simply in order to be able to read it out loud even if the effort of being in the rope makes me lose my breath. But in between those condensed sentences a lot more material becomes folded away, folded into the movement: hidden, condensed or omitted, but still there. For instance two aspects were thus folded away in "On the Ropresentation of Space": the specific motivation of doing the presentation and exploring the space of the rope, and the specific physical objective of the presentation itself.

The academic alibi of this "ropresentation" was an exploration of the space of one specific vertical circus discipline in relation to or separate from dance. This seems particularly necessary to me at a time when contemporary circus is becoming more and more integrated with the other performing arts. However, out of necessity and lack of literature, much of the research on circus focuses on the history and characteristics of contemporary circus (Eigtved 2001; Guy 2001; Jacob 2002; Wallon 2002; Purovaara et al. 2012) and a more detailed scholarly exploration of the individual circus disciplines and their aesthetic potential still needs to be conducted.

In this kind of exploration the work done within dance studies might provide tools and directions, given that the specificity of the circus discipline is taken into account. Among other things the tools of spatial analysis developed and continued from Rudolf Laban, explained as choreology by for instance Preston-Dunlop and Sanchez-Colberg (Preston-Dunlop and Sanchez-Colberg 2010, 83-92) might be useful tools to analyse the trajectories of movement in space. However, what I was searching for here was not a description of the spatial trajectories of the art-ist's movement in vertical rope even though this approach could be very fruitful as well, but an understanding of the particular spatial conditions for movement in the rope. Before we can begin to study what happens to the kinesphere of the body in the rope, we need to get at least a preliminary understanding of the kinesphere of the rope, the way the rope structures space, or what I here called "the ropresentation of space". This obviously also includes the human body, as the rope becomes an apparatus when the body enters into it, but it starts from an understanding of the body of the rope and how it affects the spatial conditions of movement.

This search was linked to another motivation; the one I had as a practitioner. Part of the reason why it was urgent to do this presentation and explore the space of the rope, was a need to try to understand and rediscover the complexity of the rope at a moment when my interest in this discipline was suffering from doubt. To be honest the doubt actually came from a fascination with another circus discipline, which seemingly has little to do with rope, that spoke to my theoretical preferences: handstand, which speaks to that figure that lies close to my theoretical heart: the combination of movement and stasis, movement on the spot, the specific intensity that lies in this spatially condensed figure.

In the middle of a handstand, I one day realised that this practice was a varia-tion on this very same figure that I had spent more than four years of my life researching, especially the way it is choreographed in the philosophical work of

Gilles Deleuze (Damkjaer 2005/2010). As I have tried to show in my work (Damkjaer 2005/2010), Deleuze often uses figures of writing that combine movement and immobility; a figure that is linked to his understanding of intensity. Movement and immobility is a qualitative contradiction; however, to Deleuze this qualitative contradiction is only the external expression of intensity: "qualitative contrariety is only the reflection of the intense, a reflection which betrays it by explicating it in extensity. It is intensity or difference in intensity which constitutes the peculiar limit of sensibility." Deleuze (2004, 296) defines this intensity, that reveals itself externally as contraction, as an "intensive quantity":

> Intensity has three characteristics. According to the first, intensive quantity includes the unequal in itself. It represents difference in quantity, that which cannot be cancelled in quantity or that which is unequalisable in quantity itself; it is therefore the quality which belongs to quantity. (Deleuze 2004, 291)

Rather than assuming quality and quantity to be two separate entities in a way that leads us to assume that the spatial quantity is always the same, whereas the quality is what differs, Deleuze places difference within quantity itself. This becomes obvious in the exercise of handstand, where any change in the material and spatial outline of the handstand immediately changes the quality of the position and the movement; in this sense handstand is an intensive exercise, and this intensity shows in the way the artist is in constant movement, even though standing on the same spot. It is a "an intensive quantity" which "may be divided, but not without changing its nature" (Deleuze 2004, 297).

This particular characteristic also, I believe, aligns handstand with a tendency within contemporary dance, a tendency especially brought to the fore by André Lepecki in *Exhausting Dance — Performance and the Politics of Movement* (2006). In this book he examines the way in which some contemporary choreographers have tried to break with the ontology of dance in modernity and the imperative to move through the use of stillness and what he calls (after Nadia Seremetakis) "the still-act" (Lepecki 2006, 57). However, I would claim that handstand arrives at this stillness in a way that does not eliminate the movement, but makes it intensive.

If handstand spoke to me because of this characteristic (and the sheer impossibility of ever mastering this exercise completely, because of its physical complexity) — what was then so fascinating about the rope? Apparently the rope is more extended, more deluded in space, so what kind of intensity could the rope hold? The answer to this became an attempt to describe the different spatial tensions that the discipline of vertical rope holds and how the movement in the rope in different ways activates, creates and comments on these tensions.

Another aspect that was also condensed in the "ropresentation", and that may not even have appeared to others, was the very physical objective that I set out with. The lecture-performance was not intended to be a choreographic reflection on the different tensions that I was trying to explain and demonstrate. The movement in the rope was indeed very demonstrative and in that sense simple; the movement supported the text and in different ways visualised the tensions I am talking about, but it did not really undertake a choreographic exploration of it. Instead the objective of the presentation lay closer to performance art and its way of underlining one physical trait, preferably taking it to its extreme. The idea I set out with was quite simply to make a lecture-performance that underlined my final conclusion and the relation between space and time in the rope, through one simple strategy: staying as long as possible in the rope.

Normally, when working with vertical rope, the movement sequences are between 5-8 minutes long — not only because of the traditional format of the circus act, but also because the specific physical conditions in the rope make it hard to work longer than this. In this "ropresentation" I managed to stay in the rope approximately 20 minutes. Though it may have seemed fairly effortless — I had to construct the movement very simply, in order to be able to stay in the rope and sustain my energy — staying so long in the rope actually meant that I could not do handstand for several days afterwards; the muscles of my arms were so sore that I could not execute the fine-tuned nuances of balancing.

When I had the chance to perform "On the Representation of Space" a second time — "A Ropetition of the Representation of Space" — it became even more evident, how the physical presentation condenses the material. In this second presentation I only had maximum 7 minutes at my disposal, which meant that I had to cut the text to less than a third. My theoretical side is quite verbose and loves to unfold everything in text, but when working with physicality, I have been forced to dare to condense, to reduce and rely on the fact that the shortness of the text gives space and time for physicality and reflection. This is what remained in the condensed version of the text, but now you know some of the parts that were left out:

Ropetition 0:

(...) Before anything else that is perhaps what the rope does to space: it renders vertical space visible. My sketch may be simple, but sometimes the simplest things are the most complex. (…) For instance, a vertical rope has a very simple spatial design. But to understand the space of the rope, we have to see it not as a static set of dimensions, but as a set of aesthetic tensions. (…)

Representation of Tension 1: up — down

(…) The first tension in the rope is simply the one between the two directions of the rope: up and down. But is it really that simple?

As an object the rope has two ends, but when rigged they are held out in a tension created by the distance between those two ends. And when a body enters into the rope as it hangs from the ceiling this is intensified by gravity. The body is held in a tension between the muscular effort of holding on to the rope and the force of gravity drawing the body towards the ground, affecting all movement in the space of the rope. (…)

This distance and tension is also visualised in the difference between the body hanging close to the ground, and the body hanging at the top of the rope. However, this phenomenon is made even more paradoxical by the presence of the floor and the ceiling that the rope bind together. At the top of the rope a tension is created through the distance from the floor, but also the closeness to the ceiling. And at the bottom of the rope there is a tension between the body and the ground: so close and still not touching, a tension that adds itself to the distance between up and down, and is reinforced by the presence of gravity.

In other words, the tension between up and down is not only a tension between two ends kept apart by a distance and the surfaces of the floor and the ceiling that they bind together, it is also a tension between an effort of the body and a force of nature. (…)

Unfolding the Condensation: Staying up there

Is it really that simple? Given that my objective was to stay as long as possible (at least as long as a standard paper presentation) in the rope, my focus during the presentation — and in the preparation of it — was obviously how to make it possible to stay up there. The directions "up and down" were thus coloured by this objective. Though I started at the lower end of the rope, close to the floor with the tension of being suspended just above the floor and with the maximum distance to the ceiling, the direction "up" was given focus — and the direction "down", represented by the floor, was suspended from this beginning and until the end of the presentation, approximately 20 minutes later, when I finally let go of the rope.

This tension was also influenced by another aspect of what it means to do rope. The difficulty of staying in the rope for 20 minutes not only has to do with the physical force it requires, but is intensely related to the question of *how* to stay in the rope — a question that was complicated by the fact that this was a paper presentation. In vertical rope both hands and feet are needed for climbing and transitions, and it is only when the body is locked into the rope through different knots around the legs or the hips that it is possible to liberate the hands. As "On the Ropresentation of Space" literally is a paper presentation I was carrying the manuscript with me in the rope, thus further complicating the issue of how to stay in the rope. Thus it was only when positioned in different locks that it was possible to actually hold the manuscript with my hands and read the text, and the rest of the time I had to hide the manuscript under my clothes — or let the sheets of paper fall to the floor one by one once I had read the page, thus also pointing to the floor and foreseeing even the moment when I would finally go down.

However, even if this sounds like a solution it did not solve all problems; because of the time-scale of the lecture even staying in the knots, where I can apparently rest my arms, becomes a small challenge of endurance: the longer I have to stay in the knot, the more it hurts — in rope there is a visceral relation between not only space and time, but even pain and time. The longer I stay in the knot, the more the internal space of the knot is reduced, the more it hurts, the more I have to focus on speaking the text and not the lack of comfort of the position. Others may not notice this — unless my facial expression betrays it, as it probably did when one of the sheets of paper got stuck towards the end of the presentation. Hanging only a couple of meters above the floor, I had to search intensively to find the missing paper, then change the position as the pain got too bothersome, in order to finally find the sheet and read the second condensed version of the text:

Ropetition: up — down

(...) One tension in the rope is simply the one between the two directions of the rope: up and down. This distance and tension is also visualised in the difference between the body hanging close to the ground, and the body hanging at the top of the rope. (...) However, this phenomenon is made even more paradoxical by the presence of the floor and the ceiling. The tension can express itself in two paradoxical ways: so far from the floor! Or: so close to the floor and still not touching! (…)

What is condensed in this focus on the tensions imbedded in the directions of up and down is also a critique of the classical way of seeing height in circus, namely

Training the Ropresentation of Space. Photographer: Stacey Sacks.

as a way to increase the risk. Circus and circus techniques involve risk to the point that risk is sometimes seen as the center of the art form (Goudard 2002; Björfors 2011), But though it is important to recognise and understand this element of risk, it is just as crucial to remember that it can be used in multiple ways even within a particular discipline. Björfors names seven dimensions or ways of dealing with risk that she believes are inherent in all circus disciplines to different extents: "balance", "everything is possible", "collaboration", "failure", "presence", "confidence", "desire" (Björfors, 2011). Here, however, I wanted to approach risk through the spatial and durational possibilities of the vertical rope. Through focusing on the tensions in the spatial dimensions of the rope, and through focusing on the feat of staying in the rope rather than working at a height, I wished to see and use risk in rope in another perspective: not as a question of height, but one of duration.

Circus deals with risk not only because it can be dangerous, but even more fundamentally because it, just as performance art, "implicates the real through the presence of living bodies" (Phelan 1993, 148). According to Peggy Phelan certain forms of physical performance "attempt to invoke a distinction between presence and representation by using the singular body as a metonymy for the apparent nonreciprocal experience of pain" (Phelan 1993, 152). In this particular presentation I wanted to underline the physicality and risk of circus not as the performance of technically advanced tricks, but as an act of endurance: the endurance need to be suspended in between up and down, between muscular effort and gravity over a long time.

Ropresentation of Tension 2: Vertical — Horizontal

(…) Another tension that is just as obvious is the tension between vertical and horizontal. So obvious: the verticality of the rope, in contrast to the horizontality of the floor. But let us not be mistaken: the horizontality does not only exist in contrast to the floor, it is a tension that is at stake at any level of the rope. There is a horizontal angle on the rope at any height and it is constantly activated through the movement of the body, stretching out in space.

Though the tension horizontal/vertical may seem similar to the difference between up and down, they are different tensions. Whereas up and down is a tension between two directions on a vertical line, the tension between vertical and horizontal is the tension with the perpendicular cut that can be traced at any moment of this vertical line. (…)

So when sketching the space of the rope, it seems as if the different spatial dimensions of the rope overlap and tend to activate each other. And also: they may be there, drawn through the rope's visualisation of space, but they are further activated and brought into play, perhaps even constructed, by the moving body.

In fact, to really understand the space of the rope, we have to understand it in relation to the spatial dimensions of the moving body. However, through the interaction with an object, the spatial complexity of the human body is also multiplied. (...)

Re-membering Friction

In this part of the "paper in rope" there is a moment where I visualise the tension between the horizontal and vertical planes in the rope. From the position in the rope called "the scissors" or "hip-lock" I twist my body into a horizontal position, mirroring the horizontality of the floor that I am looking at beneath me in such a way that my body becomes a horizontal cut across the rope. As I twist, the rope pushes against some indefinite organ in my body, and produces a squeaking sound. It is with this kind of concreteness one is confronted when addressing questions of theoretical and philosophical interest through a discipline such as vertical rope. The tension between horizontal and vertical in this particular figure is so dense, and my body in the rope is caught in it, literally squeezed by it — and the seriousness of the matter is brought back to its concrete matter-of-fact consequences in the rope.

The vertical and horizontal planes have strong historical and philosophical connotations. Verticality is often linked to representation, hierarchy, phallic structures or even religion. Horizontality is often linked to flat hierarchies and community, and perhaps even a critique of representation. These dimensions and what they stand for also seem to be a part of the discussions of post-modern and contemporary dance, although sometimes in a paradoxical way. For instance, it is remarkable that whereas much of post-modern discourse in the arts and philosophy in the 1960s and 1970s focused on horizontality (we can just think of Deleuze and Guattari's concept of the rhizome as a root-structure spreading in all directions (Deleuze and Guattari 2003, 3-25)), post-modern dance also went into vertical space (Bernasconi and Smith 2008). As modern dance had been conducted mostly on the horizontal ground, one way of over-throwing the tradition was to start bringing it into the vertical, most symptomatically perhaps with Trisha Browns *Man Walking Down the Side of a Building* (1970) (Brown DVD 2004). Nevertheless, verticality is still associated with representation, and in an interpretation of a more recent work of Trisha Brown (*It's a Draw/Live Feed*, 2003), in which she dances and draws on a horizontal plane, André Lepecki interprets the final gesture when the paper is lifted into verticality, as re-entry into representation: "it is in the final rising of the sheet of paper (...) from the horizontal into the vertical plane of representation and contemplation, that we may find the limits of Brown's radical deterritorialization" (Lepecki 2006, 75).

Though vertical rope has not been included in this kind of discussion of horizontality and verticality, for the reason that circus only recently has begun to be considered an art form, these cultural associations are also present in this discipline. On a critical note, one could of course say that it is the very verticality of the rope that makes the articulation of the movement possible, and that brings it into the realm of representation. At the same time this very articulation is only made possible through the horizontal dimension, allowing for the use of the whole kinesphere of the body, and the entire range of tensions in the rope. The rope may be vertical, and as such very hierarchical, structured, or to use Deleuze and Guattari's distinction between smooth and striated space (Deleuze and Gattari 2003, 474-500): it seems "striated" as it "relates to a more distant vision, a more optical space" (Deleuze and Gattari 2003, 493). But the movement that the body produces in the rope also reorganises the human perception of space — one of the first things to learn in the rope is to be able to distinguish directions such as right and left when hanging upside down. Moving in a vertical rope even makes space more tactile or haptic, as Deleuze and Guattari would say of smooth space (Deleuze and Guattari 2003, 494) — while climbing in the rope, the rope does not seem vertical in the same way that it does at a distance, instead my focus is on the vital aspect of holding onto the rope, the texture of the rope and the friction it creates in my grip.

Though the use of the vertical dimension to produce clear lines of articulated movement may be a classical form of (circus) representation of movement, the physical difficulty of producing such movement in the element of the rope thus nevertheless attracts my interest. The physical experience brings me back into the concrete materiality of the rope and the simple effort of creating enough tension in the space, enough friction between my body and the rope in order to be able to hold a horizontal position. When I execute this horizontal figure on the left side of my body, I manage to push enough with my hip to create this tension, and I am used to the pain on this side. If, however, I try to execute it on the other side, I immediately start to slide and get blue marks from the rope — and the aesthetic satisfaction from the tension disappears, as my body is less horizontal against the rope. Understanding the spatial tensions in the rope also means trying to understand the kind of aesthetic pleasure produced in and by the rope, within its specific vertical and horizontal conditions.

My theoretical persona tells me that this is obviously not the only possible way of understanding the spatiality of rope, and my practioner's persona tells me that other aspects of the rope may produce similar satisfaction as well. Nevertheless, as it is physically difficult to obtain clarity in the rope due to the multiple factors of gravity, friction, effort, time and space and the way they influence the possibility of movement, it seems necessary to try to obtain a basic understanding of the spatial tensions created when moving in a rope. Thinking in terms of tensions practically helps me produce more clarity and a spatially wider range of movement in the rope, thus using the tactile friction of the grip even more, and theoretically underlines the aesthetic complexity in the rope in a way that goes beyond the awe that we often connect with circus. It is a seemingly simple theoretical grip, but it activates a set of historical, philosophical and aesthetic assumptions that help us unfold the pleasure held within this simple plaited object when a human body moves in it:

Ropetition: Vertical — Horizontal

(...) A tension that is obvious is the tension between vertical and horizontal. But let us not be mistaken: the horizontality does not only exist in contrast to the floor, it is a tension that is at stake at any level of the rope. (...) It is the horizontal angle or the perpendicular cut on the vertical line of rope at any height. This tension is constantly activated through the movement of the body, stretching out in space. (...)

Ropresentation of Tension 3: Two-Dimensional — Three-Dimensional

(...) One part of the spatial dimensions of the rope that becomes more visible through the action of the human body is the space around the rope. When we look at the rope on its own from the distance of the spectator, the rope seems almost flat, as if it would create an almost two-dimensional picture. But when the human body enters into it, it becomes obvious that it is not two-dimensional, but three-dimensional.

However, there is a tension between the two- and the three-dimensional space of the rope. When performing in a frontal space, the moving body is struggling to emphasise the two-dimensional picture of certain figures and avoid unintentional turning. But when performing in a circular space, the performer must struggle to satisfy the frontal perspective of each spectator. (...)

The tensions created in the space around the rope, also have to do with the effect that the body's weight has on the rope, making the upper part of it tight and the lower part of it loose. When trying to reach around the rope, at the same time as the weight of the body tightens it, it creates distorted tensions in the relation between the body and the rope. (…)

The Three-Dimensional, Reaching Out of the Fourth Wall

Already when using the horizontal and vertical dimensions of the rope to create movement, the three-dimensionality of the rope inevitably becomes involved. The kinesphere of the body and the kinesphere of the rope interact in complex ways that create angles in between the body and the rope, and the rope twists the kinesphere of the body into other directions compared to on the ground. But the three-dimensionality of the rope does not only include the figures created in the rope, but also the space beyond the one the performer can physically reach.

When presenting "On the Ropresentation of Space", I had decided to have the listeners seated around the rope — especially in view of the section on the two- and the three-dimensional sides of the rope. Often rope is performed in a frontal theatre setting, leading to some difficulties of controlling the image transmitted to the audience, as the rope may turn in ways that are hard to predict and often depend on the way the rope is rigged. However, having people seated around the rope does not take this tension away — it just makes another aspect of it visible. If an audience is seated around the rope, they help underline the three-dimensional aspect of the rope, but the images the audience sees also vary more.

Presenting this "ropresentation" made this even more evident, as it was simultaneously a paper presentation and I was addressing the audience verbally. As performer/speaker I had to take special care to try to talk in different directions and address all sides of the audience (just as circus performers in a big top also do). I had to work with the three-dimensional space of the rope, even deliberately making it turn.

The necessity of including the three-dimensionality of the rope also forced me to attempt to open up another dimension: the one of interaction during the presentation. This became even more obvious in the shortened repetition of the presentation. For the sake of change, and as a reaction to comments, I decided to make the relation between the text and the movement more arbitrary — thus underlining that all tensions are at stake in all movement in rope, in different degrees and in different ways. I therefore asked the audience to place the sheets of paper with the manuscript in my clothes, thus connecting more concretely to the audience before starting the presentation. Without an explicit element of humor, this was a reference to the technique of clowning; as Lecoq wrote in his characterisation of this technique: "As the clown comes on stage, he establishes contact with all the people making up his audience and their reactions influence his playing" (Lecoq 2002, 157). Obviously, some of the sheets of paper were particularly difficult to find — leading to more interaction with the audience, as they tried to help me find it. This also underlined the performative objective of the presentation: the decision to stay in the rope throughout the whole presentation. As I could not find one of the papers I kept searching, insisting on the necessity of finding it ("I mean, this is a paper presentation") but also refusing to go down until I had found it. Eventually, I did find it and I could hold onto the rope, simply hanging, until I could no longer hold on, my hands slid off the rope and I eventually landed on the ground.

Opening up and extending the three-dimensionality of the rope thus even contains the possibility of including not only the space around the rope, but also those who may be present in that space. Through using the three-dimensionality it may be possible to break through the fourth wall, taking inspiration for instance from the technique of the clown and the clown's interaction with the audience (Lecoq 2002; Wright 2006; Peacock 2009), or even the circular performance space. Performing in a circle is associated with traditional circus, but the circular space has also been reinvested by many contemporary circus companies (Goudard 2001), even if performing in frontal (theatre) spaces has become the most common. In the choice of the circle, this space is sometimes associated with a less divided meeting with an audience, or as Goudard writes: "Spontaneously, we group ourselves in circles, everyone in this disposition having an equal and reciprocal view of the spectators in front and the space thus limited: the circle" (Goudard 2001, p. 161, my translation). Even something as seemingly non-theatrical and yet extremely staged as a paper presentation can be performed with or without a fourth wall, and this choice urges us to think of it not only as a paper presentation but as a specific performative event in a specific space with those that inhabit it. Though we can never be sure that the communication succeeds, we can try to make an effort of making it possible, of reaching those that we wish to communicate with:

Ropetition: Two-Dimensional — Three-Dimensional

(…) In the rope there is a tension between the two-dimensional and the three-dimensional space of the rope. This becomes apparent when the body tries to reach around the rope, though the weight tightens the upper part of the rope. (…) But it also appears when trying to emphasise the two-dimensional picture of certain figures and avoid unintentional turning, or when struggling to satisfy the frontal perspective of each spectator. (…)

Representation of Consequential Tensions: Time and Space

(…) The sketch I have made only draws the most simple spatial dimensions of the rope. But out of this simplicity we begin to see a picture of the "ropresentation" of space, the space that the vertical rope makes visible and articulated, a space that we often just conceive of vaguely as "in the air".

And through these simple dimensions, a set of complex tensions begin to emerge and multiply. Each of them are in themselves complex. Each of them interacts with the other tensions. And all of them interact with and complicate the spatial dimensions of the human body. That is the paradox of the simplicity of the rope. (…)

Furthermore, the spatial tensions of the rope even interact with other factors. For instance effort and also time. In fact, the spatial dimensions of the rope are influenced by the time that is stretched out between the moment you leave the floor and the moment you come back to it. The longer the body is up in the rope, the more evident it becomes that is suspended. And the more it is suspended, the longer the time span seems.

Perhaps that is the ultimate consequence of the spatial tensions in the rope. Through the tension between up and down, between horizontal and vertical, between two- and three-dimensional, another tension is reinforced: the one between gravity and effort. And this in its turn reveals a tension between the spatial conditions of the rope and the time it is possible to stay there. Or in other words: through the effort of moving in the space of the rope, time becomes visible. (…)

Re-Thinking some Time after

Through writing the text for the presentation and rehearsing it in the rope, I began to aesthetically appreciate the rope in a slightly different way, understanding some of its possibilities differently, underlining other aspects of the movement in the rope. I still have moments of doubt, when the difficulty of this particular practice overwhelms me, or when the aesthetic pleasure of practicing or watching it simply does not appear. But in my mind there is a still picture, a drawing of the tensional lines in the rope and the possibilities of exploration that they open, that I can return to in order to remind myself of the complexity of the simple apparatus of the rope. It may not be as condensed as the intensive movement on the spot of handstand, but its extendedness holds similar intensities that can be manipulated through the use of the different spatial tensions.

One way of understanding the difference between the intensity of handstand and the intensity of rope would perhaps be to see them through the relations between movement and time that Deleuze describes in cinema as "the time image" and "the movement image" (Deleuze 2005a, Deleuze 2005b). Perhaps one could compare handstand to the crystals of time that Deleuze conceptualises in *Cinema 2 — The Time Image* (2005b). In handstand we see time that changes and splits into past and future with every little variation of tension in the body, as the muscles try to adapt to the inverted position in space, "Time consists of this split, and it is this, it is time, that we see in the crystal" (Deleuze 2005b, 79). Handstand could be seen as "the smallest internal circuit" (Deleuze 2005b, 68) in which the relation between spatial position and gravity, between time and space becomes visible. Whereas the discipline of the rope is more extended, comparable to the movement-image and its "mobile section of duration" (Deleuze 2005a, 12). The relation between movement, space and time is also intrinsic, but across another duration — and in the rope I would add extension. Through this work I think I got a better glimpse of the rope-sequence as a "mobile section of duration" and how it is linked to a mobile vertical section of space; the rope sequence as "a block of space-time" (Deleuze 2005a, 61).

As I worked on "On the Representation of Space", my understanding of time and space in the rope clarified, nuanced, became concrete, and literally stretched. Physically my understanding of the space-time of the rope also changed. When starting to rehearse the presentation I could hardly manage the needed 20 minutes, but as I rehearsed that limit stretched, and I could stay in the rope with more and more ease as I found ways of sustaining the energy and accepting the pain in the rope. In the end, the very "feat" of staying for 20 minutes was thus less of a feat, and perhaps no one other than myself noticed this particular aspect of the presentation. This way of stretching the time possible in the rope had already become naturalised. Curiously, this stretching was partly made possible because of the text — as the necessity of staying in the rope was caused by the text, and as reading the text helped me focus on something else than the fatigue and the pain.

But also in other ways the space-time of the text, the presentation and this text have intertwined, and this has stretched the time frame of the "ropresentation", through the way the rope sequence contains the time of its preparation as well as it reaches forwards towards this text. And within this extended time frame the "ropresentation" and this text have folded, highlighted and hidden different aspects of the ropresentation of space. When preparing the presentation the relation between the spatial and temporal aspects of the text were highlighted — first through the necessity of keeping the text at a length possible to say (and read on one single page at a time), then condensing it even further in the shortened version. The text was plaited into the physicality and the rope and the movement spoke between the lines, filling out the space that the text left unsaid. But when writing this text the relation was inversed: it was no longer the physicality that folded away the possible meanders of the text, but the physicality was now rendered invisible in the text, only indirectly visible through its absence. Only through some examples and some strategic placing of markers of its absence (…) this text still contains some reminiscences of it. However, the text also re-expands other aspects, filling out some of the blank spaces that the physicality filled in the original version, unfolding some other details. Each of these versions: the "ropresentation", its "ropetition", and this rewriting of the "ropresentation" highlights different aspects of the spatial dimensions of the rope. Each event condenses and expands different elements, in different materials, in the particular space-time of their experience. As these forms and experiences multiply and overlap, the time embedded in their production also materialises and continues to grow in the gaps of space-time that physicality and reflection are left to fill out:

> (…) Out of the apparent simplicity of the rope, we begin to see a picture of the space that the vertical rope makes visible and articulated. Through these simple dimensions, a set of complex spatial tensions begin to emerge and multiply. (…) Furthermore, the spatial tensions of the rope even interact with other factors. For instance effort and also time. Perhaps that is the ultimate consequence of the spatial tensions in the rope: that even time becomes visible. (…)

BIBLIOGRAPHY

Bernasconi, Jayne C. and Smith, Nancy E. 2008. *Aerial Dance*. Leeds: Human Kinetics Europe Ltd.

Björfors, Tilde. 2011. "Ur kaos födas allt — om risker, möjligheter och nycirkus som gränsöverskridare." In *Form och färdrikning — strategiska frågor för den konst-*

närliga forskningen, edited by Helena Bornholm, 108-131. Stockholm: Årsbok KFoU— Vetenskapsrådet.

Brown, Trisha. DVD, 2004. *Trisha Brown — Early Works 1966-1970*, San Francisco: Artpix.

Damkjaer, Camilla. 2005. *The Aesthetics of Movement — Variations on Gilles Deleuze and Merce Cunningham*. Stockholm: STUTS. Also published as:

Damkjaer, Camilla. 2010. *The Aesthetics of Movement — Variations on Gilles Deleuze and Merce Cunningham*. Saarbrücken: Lambert Academic Publishing.

Deleuze, Gilles. 2004. *Difference and Repetition*. London: Continuum.

Deleuze, Gilles. 2005a. *Cinema 1 — The Movement-Image*. London: Continuum.

Deleuze, Gilles. 2005b. *Cinema 2 — The Time-Image*. London: Continuum.

Deleuze, Gilles and Guattari, Felix. 2003. *A Thousand Plateaus — Capitalism & Schizophrenia*. London: Continuum.

Eigtved, Michael, ed. 2001. *Det teatrale cirkus — Essays om cirkus, artister, kunst och kultur*. Copenhagen: Multivers.

Goudard, Philipe. 2001. "Le Cercle Recyclé." In *Avant-Garde, Cirque! Les arts de la piste en revolution*, edited by Jean-Michel Guy, 157-173. Paris: Les Éditions Autrement.

Goudard, Philipe. 2002. "Esthétique du risqué: du corps sacrifié au corps abandonné." In *Le cirque au risque de l'art*, edited by E. Wallon, 23-41. Arles: Actes Sud.

Guy, Jean-Michel, ed. 2001. *Avant-Garde, Cirque! Les arts de la piste en revolution*. Paris: Les Éditions Autrement.

Jacob, Pascal. 2002. *Le cirque — du théâtre équestre aux arts de la piste*. Paris: Larousse.

Lecoq, Jacques. 2002. *The Moving Body — Teaching Creative Theatre*. Great Britain: Methuen Drama.

Lepecki, André. 2006. *Exhausting Dance — Performance and the Politics of Movement*. New York: Routledge.

Peacock, Louise. 2009. *Serious Play — Modern Clown Performance*. Bristol: Intellect.

Phelan, Peggy. 1993. *Unmarked — The Politics of Performance*. London: Routledge.

Preston-Dunlop, Valerie and Sanchez-Colberg, Ana. 2010. *Dance and the Performative — A Choreological Perspective, Laban and Beyond*. Hampshire: Dance Books.

Purovaara, Tomi; Damkjaer, Camilla; Degerbøl, Stine; Muukkonen, Kiki; Verwilt, Katrien and Verwilt Katrien. 2012. *An Introduction to Contemporary Circus*. Stockholm: STUTS.

Wallon, Emmanuel, ed. 2002. *Le cirque au risque de l'art*. Arles: Actes Sud.

Wright, John. 2006. *Why is That so Funny?* Great Britain: Nick Hern Books Limited.

FROM BODY PSYCHOTHERAPY TO A PERFORMATIVE INSTALLATION ENVIRONMENT: A COLLABORATING PERFORMER'S POINT OF VIEW

Leena Rouhiainen

Abstract

As an ethnographic narrative about artistic research, this article discusses the dramaturgy of the performer and the creation of a performative installation environment from the perspective of the dance member of the collaborating group of artists. The article describes an open artistic process that utilised the collaborating actor's and dancer's embodied experiences in constructing the installation environment. More specifically, it introduces how the construction of this environment drew on insights from body psychotherapy and displays how they informed the development of the spatial dramaturgy of the performance. By describing some of the premises, the process and the end result of the artistic project, the article discusses how the embodied practice of the performers pervaded the staging and influenced the manner in which visitors were invited to participate in the installation as a form of shared emplacement. In so doing, it addresses some aspects of dance dramaturgy and new choreographic forms.

Introduction

In this article I address an artistic research project the overall aim of which is to apply insights and practices from a form of body psychotherapy to the artistic undertakings of the contemporary dancer engaged in recent forms of European concert dance. This is done in order to further understand and facilitate the work of dancers, who are involved in collaborative and improvisatory forms of dance-making that, among other things, rely on their immediate reactions as well as use of voice and speech in performances (cf. Rouhiainen 2012). The more specific focus is on the first artistic phase of the research, in which I, as a contemporary dancer, collaborated with a group of artists in the performing arts and created what we originally termed a 'participatory performance'. Taking my cue from dance artist and scholar Sarah Rubidge (2009), I have here chosen to call it a 'performative installation environment'. An emerging understanding of a spatial dramaturgy informed by features of the body psychotherapeutic encounter guided the construction of the performance, in which the audience-visitors were invited to take part in diverse perceptive and physical tasks. In discussing how themes that arose in collaboration with the artists and from body psychotherapy influenced the spatial structure of the performance, this article outlines some of the complex implications this setup had for the performers and participants. In doing so, it contributes to the topical discussion on dance dramaturgy and new modes of choreographic activity from a dance-maker's and performer's point of view (deLahunta 1999; Rubidge 2009; Wildschut 2009).

An Ethnographic Take on Artistic Research: On Producing this Text

As artistic research, by definition, is research through art practice, in the performing arts some of its persuasive quality lies in the embodied process of actual performance (Borgdorff 2011; Arlander 2012). In this article, I can only allude to the quality of the concrete artistic process and performance through verbal description and analysis as well as some photos of the performance process that are included in the article below. What I attempt to address in more detail, are features of the emerging process: some decisions we made as a group and their impact on our more overt and tacit efforts from my point of view. Co-relatively, artistic research is often also considered to be a process in which artists unravel the tacit knowledge that is involved in their explicit artistic undertakings. Yet, doing so is challenging: the unconscious features as well as habitual skills and assumptions involved in art-making are often difficult to grasp and to articulate in writing (Borgdorff 2006; 2011; Rouhiainen 2008; Arlander 2012).

In taking on this challenge, I accept that I can only manage a partial solution. By assuming an ethnographic stance, I connect recollections of my personal experiences of being emplaced in the midst of the artistic process with other empirical data retrieved from it and link them with theoretical considerations related to dance studies, body psychotherapy and the performing arts more generally. In the ensuing multiple narrative event I therefore address the assumptions and practices of my own professional field by focusing on my engagement in an artistic collaboration that was, to a degree, influenced by body psychotherapy (cf. Tedlock 2000). Even if the artists I worked with were important negotiating partners who shared an investigative orientation to artistic processes, in this article I deal more with how and what I learned through my embodied and emplaced experiences about our undertaking.[1] Here, I consider writing as a process of learning. In venturing into what at least partially was not-yet-known and unthought-of when initially writing this article, I repeat with a difference that which has already passed and that which has been engraved in me. Divergence seeps into the narrative through the form it takes and through the interlinks the article makes with other ideas and texts (Richardson 2000; Tedlock 2000; Pink 2009; Borgdorff 2011; Johnson 2011).

Ethnographer Sarah Pink (2009) opines that, as evocative narratives of embodiment, ethnographic places are something ethnographers make while communicating about their research to others. She suggests that ethnographic reports should be understood as emplaced events — permanent texts whose meaning is reinvented and reconfigured according to what is going on around them (Pink 2009, 41-42). A similar notion is increasingly discussed in the realm of artistic research. It is considered to be performative in the sense that it has consequences and produces things in the world. Artistic research explores material, affective and discursive effects which performance acts have on the world (Haseman 2006; Bolt 2008; Rouhiainen 2010; Borgdorff 2011; Arlander 2012). While attempting to evoke insights for its reader, this article interweaves theory, experience, reflection, memory, imagination and discourses as well as explores some of the effects opened by the performance I engaged in.

Some Insights on Space

Before venturing into describing and analysing the process of constructing the installation environment, I will offer a few words on how space can be understood to be an active process of construction involving the body, others and the environment. This I believe will help to understand the spatial motives of our artistic work and to interlink this article with the main theme of this anthology.

Finnish phenomenologist Jaana Parviainen (2006) argues that the lived body is a place that transcends the body's material basis and that we inhabit. According to her, it is a topographical terrain in which different kinds of sensations spring forth and which is moulded by habits, learned skills and techniques as well as moral codes. It contains different points, paths and routes the transitions of which we can recognise and follow. Parviainen calls the sensuous experiences the body renders through its actions in a first-person modality *kinesthetic knowledge*. She underlines the fact that this kind of knowledge concerns not only one's own bodily experiences, but allows for the epistemic access that individuals have to the world more generally. Bodily knowledge requires functional interaction with the world (Parviainen 2006, 74, 76). In this sense exploring embodied experiences is at least tacitly about figuring out how one is related to one's situation. This is not an unfamiliar view to body psychotherapists. They likewise rely on the understanding that subjective experiences extend over the body, space and world of a person. As a consequence, instead of simply working on the inner state of patients, body-oriented psychotherapists also focus on their lived spaces; their embodied and implicit way of relating to others and their environment (Fuchs 2007; Totton 2008).

Another phenomenological thinker, Edward Casey (1998), underlines that place is an event — a process in constant change in which the lived body and its environment are interdependent. This view comes close to cultural geographer Doreen Massey's understanding of place as contingent and active. Massey (2005; 2008) argues that space is the simultaneous existence of more-than-one and is produced through social practices and interactions. She considers space as the simultaneity of stories-so-far and places to be collections of these stories — articulations of the wider power geometries of space. In this sense, place is an encounter, a moment in networks of social relations, understandings and experiences. It is the coming together of the previously unrelated, a constellation of processes rather than a thing. For her, there is a thrown-togetherness of place. Massey argues that space involves a contingency that can never be completely eliminated; it is the continuous happening of place that we need to bear responsibility for and understand (Massey 2005, 130, 139, 153; 2008; 29, 184, 199).

While relating to the notions of Casey and Massey, Pink turns to use the term emplacement. According to her, emplacement relates to the body-mind-environment intertwinement and accounts for the relationships between bodies, minds and the materiality and sensoriality of the environment (Pink 2009, 25). Following her suggestion, I link the kinesthetic knowledge rendered by the lived body with place as an encounter between the subject, others and the environment, and refer to them together as emplacement.

While addressing emplacement, I take heed of Massey's suggestion that as the dimension of the multiple, of coexisting difference, space brings forth the question of how we are going to live together. This I do, as I believe that the questions of who I am, who you are and how we relate to each other are basic questions attended to in both psychotherapy and the performing arts.[2] Working with both of them and offering possibilities for emplaced encounters in performative installation environments with different visitors is one way of setting up an opening in which it is possible to address these questions. The following paragraphs describe and discuss an artistic process that relates to these themes by especially focusing on how the performers' bodily explorations instigated a physical environment in which audience-participants could share into this exploration through their own activities. The mentioned questions informed the dramaturgical set up of the installation.

Avenues into the Artistic Process

The group of collaborating artists with whom I worked included especially the actor-researcher Helka-Maria Kinnunen, the lighting designer and researcher Tomi Humalisto, the dancer and videographer Riikka Theresa Innanen as well as the sound designer and researcher Antti Nykyri. I invited these artists, whom I all knew from before, to participate in exploring how they, with their skill sets and interests, could relate to and expand the thematic that was of relevance to me. They all were established professionals in their field and were occupied with artistic research by having been involved in similar projects before or working with their respective doctoral and postdoctoral research. I wished to explore how body psychotherapy could inform the construction of a performance. The collaboration mainly took place in the fall of 2011 and culminated in four performances titled *Who Are You — Breath, Steps, Words and Other Things* at the Theatre Academy Helsinki in December 2011.[3]

Some Notes on Character Analytic Body Psychotherapy

My interest in body psychotherapy emerged from personal observations. I was familiar with some of the work done in this form of psychotherapy through my practice of somatically-oriented dance.[4] As well as supporting increased bodily awareness and self-understanding, I felt it especially boosted my ability to utilise my immediate reactions as a base for artistic actions in performance, helping me become more engaged with the dance tasks I worked with while dancing. This I learnt in the years 2006-2009 when I explored my bodily experiences in a post-Reichian body psychotherapy training programme that was run by the Finnish Institute for Character Analytic Vegetotherapy (www.luonne.fi). Following Wilhelm Reich's early formulations, vegetotherapy here means therapy of the vegetative nervous system that is nowadays called the autonomous nervous system and mediates the involuntary aspects of our embodiment. Character, in turn, refers to habitual mental and physical patterns with which persons defend themselves from perceived internal and external threat (Totton 2008, 90).

The various post-Reichian forms of body psychotherapy[5] usually consider awareness of and surrendering to bodily sensations and emotions important.[6] The practice that I was involved in included breathing and physical exercises both to balance bodily tension and to increase awareness of bodily sensations as well as verbal articulation of one's experiences and dialogue with an intuitively, emphatically and occasionally confrontationally functioning psychotherapist (Reich 1990/1949; Välimäki & Saksa 2006; Totton 2008). These were the basic means used to support the client's development of a more flexible or creative identity.

Like in many instances in current dance performance, the focal concern in body psychotherapy was the actuality of the situation and allowing what is emergent in it to take form. What was paramount was perceiving what happens now together with one person or several persons and making decisions on the basis of what one sees, hears and feels (Reich 1990/1949; Mannila 2009). Psychotherapist and theorist Nick Totton (2008) describes body psychotherapy as essentially embodied relating, a process of illuminating and affecting the client's style of relating to the self, the other and the environment in the present moment. Instead of simply attempting to adjust or realign the body energetically and physically through corrective exercise and treatment, the post-Reichian form of therapy in which I was involved allows the client's body-mind to guide the therapeutic journey, to act rather than be acted on, and to generate images and motifs freely and playfully (Totton 2008, 20, 53, 58). In my experience, this process-oriented approach worked with supporting awareness, tolerance and regulation of one's experiences and actions for the sustainment of a satisfactory life.

On the Dramaturgy of the Performer

I perceived a link between body psychotherapeutic practice and the way in which dancers' self-awareness and interactional skills are utilised in dance-making and performance. The shift in the past decade in the role and agency of performers within contemporary dance that challenges the traditional competencies and tasks of the dancer has been addressed increasingly. The task of the dancer has moved from being a skilled interpreter of a choreographer's intentions by dancing to working more collaboratively in planning, making, practicing and performing the creative undertaking (Preston-Dunlop and Sanchez-Colberg 2002; Arlander 2011; Foster 2011; Roche 2011; Rouhiainen 2012). The dancer is positioned as a self-reflective and creative entity in the process of co-constructing and performing dance together with others (Roche 2011, 106). Likewise, she is often well-rehearsed in utilising her kinaesthetic experiences to guide her movement and interaction with others and the environment.

The actor Helka-Maria Kinnunen and I shared an interest in this framework. Of the group members she was the one I worked most intensely with in planning and rehearsing for the performance. Our roles as performers and makers of the performance as well as our professional expertise in dance and theatre interweaved in the process. We both introduced ideas and exercises to explore with each other, discussed our experiences, gave each other feedback and negotiated how the emergent materials we were working with could produce a performed score. The following quotation that we presented in a seminar during our collaboration summarises the shared premise we considered ourselves to be exploring:

> Both dancers and actors work in increasingly egalitarian and collaborative ways as well as rely on immediate forms of interaction with their co-performers, audiences and environments. They explore embodiment, perception and sensation as forms of or basis for "thoughtful action". (Kinnunen and Rouhiainen 2011)

In the past few decades, contemporary theatre, dance and performance art have been in the process of pervading each other (Lepecki 2010; Numminen 2010). Dance, for example, often utilises text, speech and voice in performance; and has adopted as one of its sub-disciplines that of the dance dramaturge. Theatre, by contrast, has turned to other dramaturgical means than text that often underline embodiment in different ways (Lehmann 2009; Wildschut 2009; Helavuori 2011). The ensuing cross-disciplinary and new modes of performance in the dance and theatre arts often draw upon a rather general definition of dramaturgy.[7] Dramaturgical practices are concerned with how to deal with the performance material — visual, musical, textual, filmic, philosophical, etc. (Van Kerkhoven according to Theodores 1999). The dramaturgical process involves observing, doing, reflecting and conversing to organise, order and structure almost any material to weave them into a performance (Theodores 1999; Hotinen 2008). When dramaturgy is thus associated with the composition of a work, it is concerned with the functional logics of the levels, materials and agents of a performance (Turner and Behrndt 2008; Behrndt 2010; Hulkko 2011). According to performance theorist André Lepecki, new performance dramaturgy implies the reconfiguration of one's whole anatomy, not just the eyes, as it explores possible sensorial manifestos (Lepecki according to deLahunta 1999).

With the rise of post-dramatic forms of theatre, director Katarina Numminen (2011) even claims that in contemporary performance everyone is a dramaturge. She suggests that the responsibility for the dramaturgical logics of the performance lies on all members of the collaborating artistic group (Numminen 2011, 35). In line with this approach, director-researcher Pauliina Hulkko (2011) argues that there is a new self-regulatory requirement for performers in the kind of contemporary dance and theatre that utilises multiple and cross-disciplinary approaches in constructing performances. Instead of following conventional rules, the performer needs to assume what Hulkko terms 'the gesture of self-regulation' in each production. The performer needs to establish relationships between the performance materials and reveal how she regulates them to produce holistically embodied and sensuously evocative performing. Expanding on theatre director and pedagogue Eugenio Barba's conceptualisation, Hulkko calls this approach to acting and performing the actor's or performer's dramaturgy (Barba 2010, 23; Hulkko 2011, 17, 24).[8]

I consider the practice of body psychotherapy a tool that can support the self-regulatory gesture of the performer. Relying on an empathic attitude,[9] together with Helka-Maria, we considered this gesture by investigating breath work and physical awareness exploration as well as written, drawn and spoken articulation of our experiences with each other. We likewise discussed the varying roles of, for example, the researcher, producer, facilitator, practitioner, performer, observer, listener and commentator that we felt we occupied at different points in the process. We also kept negotiating and re-formulating the tasks, the setting and the parameters of our collaboration as it proceeded and brought in new experiences, questions and elements. Usually we began each rehearsal by discussing where we were at and what we would like to work on that day. We used our drawings, personal notes and occasional interviews[10] we conducted with each other as forms of post-rehearsal reflection.

However, we did not delve deeply into observing and interpreting issues of transference that belong to character analytic body psychotherapy, which has strong roots in psychoanalysis. Transferences colour any dialogical process, in the sense of scripts of internalised relationships that are projected into and replicated in new relationships (Ormont 1984; Soth 2005). I believed tackling them belonged to a truer therapeutic process in which the roles between therapist and patient are clear and ample time is given to working through transference issues. Our open creative collaboration had a production schedule and strove for an artistic end product and therefore did not entail a setting stable, containing and sustainable enough for such work. Instead, we utilised our experience and understanding of the way we related to each other firstly to understand what kinds of materials we wanted to be working with, how we could do so and to support each other in addressing them, and secondly to determine the tasks each one of us worked with in the process.

A Spatial Dramaturgy

From the beginning it was clear to us that we were interested in our embodied experiences and how they could inform the construction of the performance. In exploring breathing and diverse physical routines drawn from body psycho-therapy together with Helka-Maria, we paid attention to our observational and emotional attitudes and how they affected our postures, movement, and use of voice. We used these insights to recite texts we wrote and edited about the history of our bodies. We created short scenes of exaggerated or reversed physical characters that exemplified typical attitudes we found that we often embody in our everyday lives. Through this kind of pre-performance exploration we were creating the groundwork of our performer's dramaturgy that became translated into a dramaturgy of the whole performance.

Besides creating the above described partially improvisatory materials for us to perform, it became increasingly important for us to engage the audience or visitors in physical self-exploration themselves. We wanted to offer them means to tune into their own embodied experience and awareness of how they related to the performance on both a more experiential and reflective level. We anticipated that by becoming sensitive to their bodily experiences, the way they perceived or witnessed the environment and contents of the performance would somehow be affected. Our anticipation resonates with postmodern choreographer Simone Forti's words:

An awareness of yourself comes from a certain amount of activity and you can't get it from just thinking about yourself. You do exercises, you have certain kinds of awareness that you don't have if you read a book. (Forti according to Rosenthal 2010, 13)

Instead of imposing predetermined forms of performed embodiment and a chronologically evolving dramaturgy, we wanted to offer the visitors an arena for finding their own way around. We aimed at creating a sufficiently comfortable and safe environment in which they could choose the degree of participation they found enticing and suitable for themselves and in this sense explore their view and knowledge of themselves within the emplacement the performance evoked. We thus had an agenda of offering the visitors a chance to explore how they were emplaced and inhabit the performance through paying attention to their embodied reactions and actions — as potential ways of living and relating to others, the environment and potentially the world (Bourriaud 2002). Here we attempted to follow the ideology of what contemporary performance is said to do: it presents and engenders alternative modes of living and unconventional patterns of action (Helavuori 2011).

We began thinking about the performance both in terms of exploratory tasks offered to the visitors as well as our own improvisatory performance scores. One impetus for this was that in the psychotherapeutic process, it is not the therapist but the client who produces the material analysed and interpreted, and in that way guides the process. The therapist is there to follow and support the client's process — to work out what is trying to happen and let it happen (Totton 2008). Consequently, we felt that the members of the audience should be given, at least to some extent, the chance to manage and influence the performance as well as generate performed material. In order to achieve this, we drew imaginatively on principles involved in the body psychotherapeutic encounter to construct the soundscape, lighting design, video-projections, staging and task instructions for the audience. These principles related to themes of empathic encountering, containing interaction, contact, the use of breath and voice as well as body awareness work. They intuitively informed our construction of the performance environment in which the visitors could explore how they are emplaced, who they are and how they ask the question of who they are (Kinnunen and Rouhiainen 2011).

In one of our conversations, sound designer Antti Nykyri began thinking of the performance in terms of a spatial dramaturgy. After all, we were constructing a performance environment with a rather high level of interactivity, where the visitor was expected to construct at least a fragmentary narrative, make choices, adopt a position, and engage directly in action (cf. Turner and Behrndt 2008). From that point onwards we thought about our performance in terms of a spatial composition, an architectural structure to be journeyed through and to provoke a shared event. The rhythm of sound, degrees and direction of light, movement, architectural structure and the audience's bodily journey acted as dramaturgical material (cf. Turner and Behrndt 2008).

The tasks were located and defined by constructed spatial areas within the black box theatre where the performance was staged. The audience actually became immersed in the performance space by sitting, standing, moving from one location to another and by actively engaging in diverse exercises. The space of the performance and observation overlapped. The tasks we offered to the visitors included simple physical actions such as slow walking and deep breathing. The first is considered a grounding exercise by some body psychotherapists. It refers to engendering a relaxed and active connection between the weight of the body and the ground that supports it that also fosters postural aliveness and a sense of where one stands as a person (Conger 1993; Totton 2008). Paying attention to breathing was understood as helping to anchor the visitors' awareness in the present moment and their bodies. In body psychotherapy, this is considered a pathway for better connection with or awareness of bodily sensations and emotions. (e.g. Totton and Edmonson 2009; Martin et al. 2010). Slow walking and breathing exercises were something we ourselves repeated at the beginning of each of our rehearsals. The tasks offered to the visitors also included an adaptation of Twister, a physical skill game played on a mat designed for it (cf. http://en.wikipedia.org/wiki/Twister_(game)). The visitors could randomly pick from a box of instruction notes requesting them to do specific physical acts in a specific location. We likewise built a circle of chairs in which visitors were asked to face each other in pairs and answer the question: "Who are you?" with one word ten times in a row. The space also included a large video screen with video material on feet probing the sand and water on a beach shoreline, a small video projection of the legs of people walking up and down a staircase as well as chalk with which to draw on the floor and walls. The soundscape was constructed of sampled sounds of breathing, voices talking, and bells. The lighting design highlighted activity areas and changed slightly according to the way the visitors and performers positioned themselves in the space.

An Outline of the Performance

We invited the people to attend the performance with the following description in the leaflet on ongoing performances at the Theatre Academy Helsinki:

> **Who are you — breath, steps, words and other things?** The participatory performance invites you into actions that identify bodily experiences. What kind of breathing feels most familiar to you today? Can you walk slower? What do you hear right now? (Who speaks?) Whom do you watch and what do you see?

Each performance lasted for two hours. The audience-visitors were invited to stay as long as they wished after entering. A group of them was allowed to enter every fifteen minutes in pairs of two. Helka-Maria and I welcomed the visitors at the entrance to the space. We gave them a small booklet we called the performance passport that contained material from the body stories that we had written and which we used for dialogue intermittently in the performance as well as space in which to draw and write with the attached pencil. We stroked the visitors' backs from head to heels and drew their footprints on the floor before sending them into the space, where they could roam as well as observe and do things at their own pace. The spatial set-up involved the following nine scenes that were introduced in the handout by the italicised text and by an accompanying map that was drawn by Helka-Maria:

1. *A video asks questions.* As an introduction to the performance, we placed a video in the entrance hall waiting area that showed the front landscape view of a walking person seen from knee level with the edited text: Who is walking? Where? Why?
2. *Gravel path: slow down.* A six-meter long gravel path for slow walking.
3. *Sounding boxes: touch and try out.* The "Sonic Sandboxes" are the creation of Antti Nykyri.[11] Two large boxes covered with small stones and underlying contact microphones to be played by touching or placing weight on them.
4. *Chair circle task.* Visitors were asked to sit opposite each other in pairs and to ask "Who are you?" The pair was asked to answer with one word. This task was repeated ten times.
5. *Position game area*: An application of Twister that asked people to take diverse positions or do simple movements and pay attention to their sensations and perception.
6. *Drawing wall:* A wall on which visitors were invited to write and draw their observations and thoughts.

Gravel path in Who Are You — performance, 2011. Photographer: Hannele Kurkela.

Score wall in Who Are You — performance, 2011. Photographer: Hannele Kurkela.

Chair circle in Who Are You —
performance, 2011. Photographer:
Hannele Kurkela.

Breathing corner in Who Are You
— performance, 2011. Photographer: Hannele Kurkela.

7. *Breathing corner:* An area with two screens featuring video material of body parts moving to the rhythm of breathing and a rug and pillows to recline on. The area also had six iPods for the visitors to use. They contained taped instructions to listen to the breathing on the tape and to slow down one's own breathing.

8. *The path of light and darkness: listen and roam*: An in part brightly and in part dimly lit hall contained a soundscape with a mixture of bells and humming sounds sung by Helka-Maria and I as well as the video projection of a staircase.

9. *Turning point*: At the end of the hallway there was a full-body mirror and a large bowl of chocolates. The chocolates had notes attached stating that: "You are a riddle", "You are soft breath", "You are a visionary", "You are soft breath" etc.

10. *Return to the hall:* Here the performance ended.

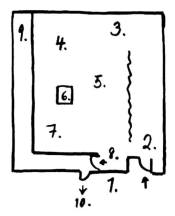

The space had posters taped to the floor or the walls that gave detailed instructions on what the audience was asked to do in the different areas. In the midst of greeting the visitors and sometimes guiding or participating in their explorations in the space, Helka-Maria and I improvised with the short scenes we had been working on. We gave non-sensical names to our materials and wrote them on one of the walls. We silently agreed on moments when to turn to performing them, and as we had done so, we crossed over the related chalk writing on the wall.

Here are a few excerpts from the written feedback we received from the audience.[12]

※ This kind of participation in which one can reflect and experience things without a compulsory plot or sitting in an auditorium is wonderful. There were only a few other people present, which made the space more intimate and gave permission to explore, lay around and linger — if there had been a lot of other participants, I would not have dared.

※ I was quite tired and chilly when I entered the space. The space received me with its peace, warmth and freedom. I felt that I was not obliged to do anything, so I first went on the rug to rest. I remember thinking that "this is exactly what I need" and "if one could always take a rest position in performances".

※ Sensing is so recuperative, it was fun that there were different kinds of stimuli, sounds, feelings…

※ I felt as if I was at the core of some kind of humanity or life: words were not important…There was nothing to understand, I only needed to feel and experience what happens in the space, in me and the others.

※ A situation with a near stranger without words in the midst of a childish act made me feel like a child, who doesn't have to rationalise the importance of the situation. This was important for me for totally irrational reasons. I have never been in such a situation and with exactly this person. I immediately liked this person and only because I experienced that he/she "understood" how wonderful and unique the situation was.

※ The greatest joy was to do the "who are you" game with a total stranger, how much happened, how I played a dramaturge became more intense through the repetition, meanings were created from delicate nuances. It was pure joy and I thank you for the chance to encounter another person!

※ The breathing corner had a special impact on me: Here we breathe together and everything is all right. Almost a very early, perhaps prenatal experience.

From Spatial Dramaturgy to a Performative Installation Environment

What was our performance structure finally like? Most theatre and dance performance is centered around the exchange and community that is built between the audience and performers in live events. In this sense they always rely upon participation by performers and members of the audience alike. Performance, dance and theatre art therefore involve different forms of relational encounters

(Bourriaud 2002; Fischer-Lichte 2008 38, 40). We used the term 'participatory' to indicate that the performance we constructed involved the members of the audience in physical action, verbal interchange and contact with each other or the performers outside a proscenium stage setting. However, on post-performance reflection, the term participatory did not quite seem adequate in describing our project and I searched for a new concept to describe it. In our conversations with the artictic group owing to the cross-artistic and spatial set-up, the term installation was mentioned. Generally, in the realm of visual art, installation art relates to an artistic genre of three-dimensional works that are set in an interior space and designed to change the perception of that space. This resonated with our work and as I familiarised myself further with the topic, it became very evident that since the late 1950s, aside from dance, the term choreography has been applicable to painting, sculpture and installation art. In these instances, works of art have invited visitors to an exhibition to perform certain movements, effectively creating choreographic performances in them (Rosenthal 2010).

In her article on choreography and installations Sarah Rubidge makes a distinction between performance installations and performative installations. The latter she qualifies with a strong sense of performativity and describes them as events "not concerned with representing the known, but rather with bringing new state of affairs into being" (Rubidge 2009, 364-365). With repetition of predetermined performance, performance installations establish new identities or eventualities only provisionally. In performative installations performers and members of the audience actively intervene in the development of the performance event as it unfolds and influence or even change the performance environment. In Rubidge's view, performative installations are about spatio-temporal events in either constructed or site-specific non-conventional theatre spaces and in which viewer's stage their actions actively, flexibly and reflectively. As they give rise to new circumstances, they are likewise improvisatory in one sense or another (Rubidge 2009, 365, 369). She writes:

> ...the installations guide the visitors' behaviour as they negotiate the installation environment and bring a variety of unique virtual 'worlds' (or new states of affairs) to presence. (Rubidge 2009, 374)

Considering our *Who are you — breath, steps, words and more?* as a performative installation environment, underscores its immersive spatial design and audience-activating tasks both of which were meant to allow the visitors to make new observations about themselves — their embodied way of relating to themselves, the other visitors and the performance materials. It likewise offers the possibility of understanding the visitors as performers. Their actions and the way they invited each other as well as Helka-Maria and me to participate in the tasks they explored produced something that could be described as sensorial, concentrated and lingering embodied interactivity and co-emplacement.

Further Post-Reflection

The spatial set-up of audience-activating areas that set them on an embodied journey became the logic of our performance. Our performer's dramaturgy extended from the personal bodywork exploration and feedback between Helka-Maria and me to us sharing experiences and goals together with the collaborating group and thus moving to work with a spatial dramaturgy. The latter design extended our embodied practice into an environment in which the visitors could similarly explore their embodiment and emplacement. This was the manner in which we developed our staging strategies to explore "the function, condition and course of the encounter and interaction between performers and members of the audience" as an experiment on how to work with themes drawn from body psychotherapy (Fischer-Lichte 2008, 40). This established a performance in which role reversals between performers and visitors, the modes of contact between them as well as the issue of concerning the individual and the communal or the private and the public were addressed. The previous feedback material alludes to both personal and shared experiences between the members of the audience. The recording of the audience discussion after the second performance contains comments on how the members of the audience felt they themselves became performers in the installation, especially when exploring the position game area.

Dance scholar Susan Foster (2010, 32) and art curator Stephanie Rosenthal (2010, 4) point out that in contemporary dance, choreography is increasingly understood as a somewhat open frame or set of principles that structure movement — suggestions for possible courses of action to be taken by performers and the members of the audience or both of them together. These frames provoke the exposure of both personal and social kinaesthetic values and practices to their participants. Ever more often constructed performative installations are a case in point. However, there is still lack of discussion on how they come into being and what concrete implications they have on the performing artists and audience participants. I have tried to answer to this gap, with describing how personal and shared bodily exploration can foster a shared space, a place of encounters.

ACKNOWLEDGMENTS

This article was written with the support of the Academy of Finland that funded my Academy Research Fellow position.

REFERENCES

Arlander, Annette. 2012. "Santa Marian suola-altaat — epäpaikoista ja performatiivisen tutkimuksen haasteista (The Salt Pools of Santa Maria — On Non-Places and Challenges of Performative Research)." In *Näyttämöltä tutkimukseksi: esittävien taiteiden haasteet metodologiset haasteet* (From State to Research: The Methodological Challenges of the Performing Arts), edited by Liisa Ikonen, Hanna Järvinen and Maiju Loukola, 9-25. Helsinki: Teatterintutkimuksen seura.

Arlander, Annette. 2011. "Tekijä esiintyjänä — esiintyjä tekijänä (The Author as Performer — the Performer as Author)." In *Nykyteatterikirja: 2000-luvun alun uusi skene* (The Contemporary Theatre Book — The New Scene of the 21st Century), edited by Annukka Ruuskanen, 86-100. Helsinki: Theatre Academy Helsinki and Like Kustannus oy.

Barba, Eugenio. 2010. On Directing and Dramaturgy. Translated by Judy Barba. London and New York: Taylor & Francis Group.

Batson, Glenna. 2009. "Somatic Studies and Dance." Accessed August 15, 2011. http://www.iadms.org/associations/2991/files/info/somatic_studies.pdf.

Behrndt, Synne K. 2010. "Drama, Dramaturgy and Dramaturgical Thinking." *Contemporary Theatre Review* 20 (2): 185-196.

Bolt, Barbara. 2008. "A Performative Paradigm for the Creative Arts?" *Working Papers in Art and Design 5.* Accessed October 20, 2009. http://sitem.herts.ac.uk/artdes_research/wpades/vol6/bbfull.html.

Borgdorff, Henk. 2011. "The Production of Knowledge in Artistic Research." In *The Routledge Companion to Research in the Arts*, edited by Michael Biggs and Henrik Karlsson, 44-64. Abingdon, Oxon: Routledge.

Borgdorff, Henk. 2006. "The Debate on Research in the Arts." *Sensuous Knowledge: Focus on Artistic Research and Development 2:* 7-28. Norway: Bergen National Academy of the Arts.

Bourriaud, Nicolas. 2002. *Relational Aesthetics.* Translated by Simon Pleasance and Fronza Woords with participation of Mathiue Copeland. Dijon-Quetigny, France: les presses du reel.

Casey, Edward. 1998. *The Fate of Place: A Philosophical History.* London: The University of California Press.

Conger, John P. 1993. *The Body in Recovery: Somatic Psychotherapy and the Self.* Berkeley, California: Frog Books.

deLahunta, Scott. 2000. "Dance Dramaturgy: Speculations and Reflections." *Dance Theatre Journal* 16 (1): 20-26.

Fischer-Lichte, Erika. 2008. *The Transformative Power of Performance: A New Aesthetics.* Translated by Saskya Iris Jain. London and New York: Routledge.

Fortin, Simone. 2009. "Presentation of Somatic Research." In *Somatic Approaches to Movement: Interview with Founders, Teachers and Choreographers* [DVD], directed by Lila Greene and film by Gabriele Sparwasser. Pantin, France: Recherche en Mouvement.

Foster, Susan L. 2011. *Choreographing Empathy: Kinesthesia in Performance.* Abingdon, Oxon: Routledge.

Foster, Susan. 2010. "Choreographing Your Move." In *Move Choreographing You: Art and Dance Since the 1960s,* edited by Stephanie Rosenthal, 30-39. Southbank Centre London: Hayward Publishing.

Fuchs, Thomas. 2007. "Psychotherapy of the Lived Space: A Phenomenological and Ecological Concept." *American Journal of Psychotherapy* 61 (4): 423-439.

Haseman, Brad. 2006. "A Manifesto for Performative Research." *Media International Australia Incorporating Culture and Policy* (theme issue "Practice-led Research") 118: 98-106.

Helavuori, Hanna. 2011. "Mitä esiintyjä tekee nykyteatterissa (What Does the Performer Do in Contemporary Theatre)?" In *Nykyteatterikirja — 2000-luvun alun uusi skene* (The Contemporary Theatre Book — The New Scene of the Early 21st Century), edited by Annukka Ruuskanen, 101-116. Helsinki: Like.

Hotinen, Juha-Pekka. 2008. "Dramaturgia (Dramaturgy)." Teatterikorkea 1/08. Accessed February 15, 2012. http://www2.teak.fi/teak/Teak108/default.htm.

Hulkko, Pauliina. 2011. "Ruumiinsyntaksista näyttelijän dramaturgiaan (From Body Syntax to Actor's Dramaturgy)." In *Nykynäyttelijän taide:horjutuksia ja siirtymiä* (The Art of the Contemporary Actor: Shifts and Staggerings), edited by Marja Silde, 15-50. Helsinki: Teatterikorkeakoulu.

Johnson, Mark. 2011. "Embodied Knowing Through the Art." In *The Routledge Companion to Research in the Arts,* edited by Michael Biggs and Henrik Karlsson, 141-151. Abingdon, Oxon: Routledge.

Kinnunen, Helka-Maria and Rouhiainen, Leena 2011. "Approaching Embodied Respons(e)ability: Explorations in Mindful Interaction." Lecture-demonstration at The Politics of the Psychophysical Symposium, Theatre Academy Helsinki, Helsinki, November 16-17.

Lehmann, Hans-Thies. 2009. *Draaman jälkeinen teatteri* (Postdramatic Theatre). Translated by Riitta Virkkunen. Helsinki: Theatre Academy and Like.

Lepecki, André. 2010. "Zones of Resonance: Mutual Formations in Dance and the Visual Arts Since the 1960s." In *Move Choreographing You: Art and Dance since the 1960s*, edited by Stephanie Rosenthal, 152-163. Southbank Centre, London: Hayward Publishing.

Lepecki, André and Banes, Sally. 2007. "Introduction: The Performance of the Senses." In *The Senses in Performance,* edited by Sally Banes and André Lepecki, 1-8. New York and London: Routledge, Taylor & Francis Group.

Mannila, Laura. 2009. "Esiintyjä, ohjaaja, esitys kehopsykoterapian valossa (The Performer, Director and Performance in Light of Body Psychotherapy)." In *Kehospykoterapian ja esittävän taiteen risteyksessä: Luonne 2* (At the Crossroads of the Performing Arts and Body Psychotherapy, Character 2), edited by Laura Mannila and Janne Maarala, 8-87. Helsinki: Multiprint.

Martin, Minna; Seppä, Maila; Lehtinen, Päivi; Törö, Tiina and Lillrank, Benita. 2010. *Hengitys itsesäätelyn ja vuorovaikutuksen tukena* (Breathing as A Support for Self-Regulation and Interaction). Helsinki: Mediapinta.

Massey, Doreen. 2008. *Samanaikainen tila* (The Space of the Simultaneous). Translated by Janne Rovio. Tampere: Vastapaino.

Massey, Doreen. 2005. *For Space.* London: Sage Publications.

Numminen, Katariina. 2010. "Tekstin ja esityksen suhde nykyteatterissa (The Relationship Between Text and Performance in Contemporary Theatre)." In *Nykyteatterikirja — 2000-luvun alun uusi skene* (The Contemporary Theatre Book — The New Scene of the Early 21st Century), edited by Annukka Ruuskanen, 22-39. Helsinki: Like.

Ormont, Louis R. 1984. "The Leader's Role in Dealing with Aggression in Groups." *International Journal of Group Psychotherapy* 34 (4): 553-572.

Parviainen, Jaana. 2006. *Meduusan liike: Mobiiliajan tiedonmuodostuksen filosofiaa* (The Move of the Meduse: The Philosophy of Knowledge Construction in A Mobile Era). Helsinki: Gaudeamus.

Pink, Sarah. 2009. *Doing Sensory Ethnography.* London: Sage.

Preston-Dunlop, Valerie and Sanchez-Colberg, Ana, 2002. *Dance and the Performative. Laban and Beyond.* London: Verve Publishers.

Reich, Wilhelm. 1990/1949. *Character Analysis.* Translated by Vincent R. Carfagno. Third, Enlarged Edition. New York: Farrar, Straus and Giroux.

Richardson, Laurel. 2000. "Writing: A Method of Inquiry." In *Handbook of Qualitative Research* 2nd ed., edited by Norman K. Denzin and Yvonna S. Lincoln, 923-948. Thousand Oaks, CA: Sage.

Roche, Jenny. 2011. "Embodying Multiplicity: The Independent Contemporary Dancer's Moving Identity." *Research in Dance Education* 12(2): 105-118.

Rosenthal, Stephanie. 2010. "Choreographing You: Choreographies in the Visual Arts." In *Move Choreographing You: Art and Dance Since the 1960s*, edited by Stephanie Rosenthal, 7-19. Southbank Centre London: Hayward Publishing.

Rouhiainen, Leena. 2012. "An investigation into facilitating the work of the independent contemporary dancer through somatic psychology." *Journal of Dance and Somatic Practices* 3 (1-2): 43-60.

Rouhiainen, Leena. 2008. "Artistic Research and Collaboration." *Nordic Theatre Studies* 20: 51-60.

Rouhiainen, Leena. 2010. "Dancing Emplacement in an Installation Entitled Passage." In *Norsk Dansforskning*. Edited by Sidsel Pape, 15-36. Trondheim: Tapir Akademisk Forlag.

Rubidge, Sarah. 2009. "Performing Installations: Towards an Understanding of Choreography and Performativity in Interactive Installations." In *Contemporary Choreography: A Critical Reader*, edited by Jo Butterworth and Liesbeth Wildschut, 282-378. London and New York: Routledge.

Soth, Michael. 2005. "Embodied Countertransference." In *New Dimensions in Body Psychotherapy*, edited by Nick Totton, 40-55. Maidenhead, England: Open University Press.

Theodores, Diana. 1999. "Choreographing the Question: A Dramaturg and Choreographer in Dialogue." In *Dance theatre: an Internatinoal investigation. Proceedings from the first MoMentUm conference*, 23-38.The Manchester Metropolitain University, September 9-12 1999. Accessed January 10, 2012. http://sarma.be/docs/719.

Tedlock, Barbara. 2000. "Ethnography and ethnographic representation." In *Handbook of Qualitative Research* 2nd ed., edited by Norman K. Denzin and Yvonna S. Lincoln, 455-483. Thousand Oaks, CA: Sage.

Totton, Nick and Edmonson, Em. 2009. *Reichian Growth Work: Melting the Blocks to Life and Love*. Ross-on-Wye, United Kingdom: PCCS Books.

Totton, Nick. 2008. *Body Psychotherapy: An Introduction*. Berkshire, England: Open University Press.

Turner, Cathy and Behrndt, Synne K. 2008. *Dramaturgy and Performance*. New York: Palgrave MacMillan.

Wildschut, Liesbeth. 2009. "Reinforcement for the Choreography: The Dance Dramaturge as Ally." In *Contemporary Choreography: A Critical Reader*, edited by Jo Butterworth and Liesbeth Wildschut, 383-398. London and New York: Routledge

Young, Courtenay. 2010. "The History and Development of Body-Psychotherapy: European Diversity." *Body, Movement and Dance in Psychotherapy*, 5 (1): 5-19.

Välimäki, Markku and Saksa, Sirkka. 2006. *Lyhyt katsaus kehopsykoterapian synty- ja kehitysvaiheisiin* (A Short Survey into the Birth and Development of Body Psychotherapy). Helsinki: Psykoterapiakeskus Gestalt Oy.

NOTES

1   The other members of the artistic group were asked to read and comment on the text.

2   Obviously, these questions are approached in different ways and degrees of explicitness as well as for different reasons in the two fields.

3   The production was supported by the Training Theatre and Performing Arts Research Centre of the Theatre Academy Helsinki as part of the artistic research project that I am conducting in the institution as an Academy Research Fellow. Here I cannot go into the details of the production support, but we had a small budget, technical help as well as the use of the props and wardrobe.

4   This is dance training, pedagogy and art that is related to what is variously termed *somatics*, *somatic studies*, or *somatic education* (Bateson 2009). The terms denote a field of study and movement practices, which combine different learning methods to foster awareness of the body within its environment. Some of the general goals of the related practices are to develop individuals' sensory and perceptual sensitivity as well as to increase flexibility in their movement skills for a variety of personal options to act in the world to emerge (Fortin 2009).

5   Many of the currently practiced and recently developed forms of body psychotherapy are in some manner or another indebted to Wilhelm Reich (1897-1957). He took Sigmund Freud's argument that our psychic life is rooted in our bodies seriously, developed a psychoanalytic method that observed the body's expression and finally endorsed bodywork as a therapeutic tool (Välimäki and Saksa 2006; Young 2010). Nowadays Reichian work includes many different approaches, as Reich himself worked in different ways during different phases of his career.

6   In addition, post-Reichian therapists have adopted some of his ideas while changing and developing others that are now considered dated. According to body psychotherapist and theorist Nick Totton (2008), what most agree upon is the importance of awareness of and surrender to bodily sensations and emotions, while downplaying Reich's emphasis on sexuality. Many also question Reich's alleged notion of unearthing the healthy genital character in the therapeutic process, even if he himself was of the opinion that each one of us is more or less neurotic and that the healthy character is an ideal.

7   Indeed, dramaturgy has evolved into an influential sub-discipline in dance and choreographers often rely on dance dramaturges in constructing performances. Liesbeth Wildshut (2009) explores the role of the dance dramaturge as an ally for the choreographer. She notes that the professionalisation of dance dramaturgy is gaining impetus with e.g. the Utrecht University now offering MA courses in dance dramaturgy (Wildschut 2009, 383).

8   Hulkko formulated these ideas in the final report of the research project entitled Actor's Art in Modern Times. The project explored Finnish pedagogy for actors at the Theatre Academy Helsinki between 2008-2011.

9   By empathic attitude I refer to both an altruistic and accepting attitude towards another person as well as a kinesthetic level of recognition of the behavior of this other (cf. Foster 2010, 10).

10   We asked each other among other things the following kinds of questions: "What was challenging today?", "What did you become aware of today?", "Where there moments when you surrendered to your body or you surroundings? Describe them." "Describe one perception you made of the environment, me or your own body." "What kind of time, space and rhythm did you experience during the rehearsals?" "What kind of roles did you assume in today's rehearsals" and "Who are you now?"

11   For further information on these instruments that have been set up in different locations see Antti Nykyri's website at http://www.anttinykyri.com/portfolio/prod_sound_sources.html.

12   We received written feedback from fourteen audience members via email. These excerpts are from this feedback and have been translated from Finnish into English by me. The overall project fostered feedback in other forms as well: There are the written and drawn comments on of the feedback wall of the installation. The audience discussion after the second performance was also recorded. Additionally, we discussed our experiences and showed video and photo material of the performance at a seminar at the Theatre Academy. The feedback we received there is also recorded. All this feedback material will be analysed and discussed in more detail in a later publication.

DANCING IN NATURE SPACE — ATTENDING TO MATERIALS

Paula Kramer

Abstract

The following text draws from practice-as-research engaged with outdoor dance. It firstly discusses the topos 'space' from the perspective of working in *nature space* and moving in the natural environment, principally arguing for an understanding of space as 'alive and happening'. Secondly, it addresses the position of the human dancer within this space, emphasising the potentials of a *decentralised* position of the human being. This has relevance beyond the realms of creative practice and performance, as it offers a changed perspective on how to live and act in this world shared by humans and non-humans alike. Thirdly, it explores a *research installation* as one possible dissemination mode for practice-as-research, which allows for the practical engagement of the research process to extend into its dissemination. Rather than reducing the three-dimensional, spatial and embodied practice of dance to a text on a page, an installation introduces possibilities of continued embodied engagement and participation in a research process.

Introduction

Nature Space

In my dancing and researching I work with the natural environment as a field in which body, imagination and 'worldly' (human and non-human) materialities meet through creative practice in ways both knowable and perceivable, yet also in ways partially exceeding my understanding. My way of working is strongly influenced by somatic and improvisational practices and rather than superimposing movement material on a location, both my teaching practice in workshops and my performance-making rely on repeatedly spending time onsite and developing movement and workshop material from there. The movement practice *Amerta*

Movement (or *Joged Amerta*) by Javanese movement artist Suprapto Suryodarmo is one of the strongest influences in my practice, mainly as developed by the dance and performance artists Bettina Mainz (GER), Helen Poynor and Sandra Reeve (both UK), all of whom have worked extensively with Suprapto in Java and Europe since the late 1980s and early 1990s. In its literal translation Joged Amerta means 'the moving-dancing nectar of life' (Reeve 2010, 189) and Reeve further defines it as "a somatic and performance practice", which "foregrounds the notion of 'non-self' ... as well as the notion of 'surrendering' the self" and "pays attention to environmental embodiment and attaches crucial importance to the mutual interdependence and co-creation of organism and environment" (Ibid., 189-190).[1]

It is no easy feat to speak and write about dance in the natural environment, as 'nature' is a strongly contested and humanly constructed entity, discussed throughout the history of philosophy. As philosopher Kate Soper (1995, 1) notes in *What is Nature?* it is a term "both very familiar and extremely elusive", and certainly not free from conflict, inscriptions and desires. As one possible descriptor of this contested field I have adopted the term *nature space* from Bettina Mainz. Working in Berlin and its surrounding areas she was the first movement teacher to take me outdoors to dance in the late 1990s and subsequently became a significant teacher throughout my twenties. Based on her studies at SNDO (School for New Dance Development, Amsterdam) and Amerta Movement, she developed her practice *Body of Becoming*, which she teaches both indoors and outdoors.[2] For her outdoor work in the natural environment she employs both the German term *Naturraum* and its poetic English translation *nature space*, a term not commonly used in English, yet fully comprehensible. *Natur* is German for *nature* and *Raum* means *space*. Other possible translations of *Raum* include *area* as well as, in a less geographical and more domestic sense, *room* or *chamber*. As a scientific term *Naturraum* describes a specific geographical or geological region.

In my work with and about outdoor dance practices in the natural environment, *nature space* has become one way of referring to nature as a 'space' for artistic engagement. The term, especially in its English 'not fully existent' translation, offers a poetic opening in the difficult dealings with nature, a way to speak about nature as a location of practice, rather than suffocating amongst the many contested constructions of nature. Yet even within *nature space* one is 'inside dispute'. Here I follow philosopher of science Bruno Latour's (2004) lecture remarks to steer clear of suggesting an unbroken or unilateral notion of nature: "[...] we are actually in the dispute about nature, constantly [...]. So to be close to nature is not to be close to outside, undisputable entities, but actually to be inside dispute".

Or, as he extensively argues in *We Have Never Been Modern*: "It is as impossible to universalize nature as it is to reduce it to the narrow framework of cultural relativism alone" (Latour 1993, 106).

When I asked Bettina Mainz for an explanation of her use and understanding of *nature space*, she wrote the following:

> I understand the word 'nature space' always in relationship to space being 'alive and happening', which is true for any kind of space.
>
> 'Nature space' is filled with simple and universal things, like the sound of the wind and the trees, the scent, quality and texture of the ground, the space in between and the distance to the blue and grey of the sky, to the tree tops, the play of light and so forth.
>
> All of this has a specific being, a momentary atmosphere, a density, pressure conditions, openings, movements, stillness, proportions and rhythms, in which I can move. (Mainz 2011, personal communication, my translation from German)

Mainz was initially introduced to the idea of space as 'alive and happening' in the context of studying with Adam Bradpiece between 1995 to 1998, one of the first Westerners to work with Suprapto in Java in the late 1980s. What is especially notable in her account of *nature space* is the close attention she pays to spatial relationships and to material, textural and sensual stimuli present in this realm, to which I will return later as relevant aspects for dancing in *nature space* as well as for working with *research installations.*

The understanding of space as 'alive' seems a shared concept among practitioners working in the lineage of Amerta Movement, as well as beyond. One of the most experienced in the UK, Sandra Reeve (2010, 200), for example, speaks of "our surroundings as a world-in-motion, as a becoming-world — not as a static environment" when describing her practice 'ecological movement'. Albeit from a different discipline, political geographer Doreen Massey (2011, 35) offers similar notions in her writing on space, with one of her key objectives being to "bring it alive", for which she strongly argues in her seminal book *For Space* (2005). Here she contests the "reduction [of space] to a dimension" (Massey 2005, 7) and supports the understanding of space as a "product of interrelations", as "never finished; never closed" (Ibid., 9). Dance researcher Susanne Ravn connects her thinking on space to Massey in similar ways as I am doing here. In her book *Sensing Movement, Living Spaces* she argues: "It is to move from the image of space as being a textuality to be looked at to the recognition of space as a continuous and multiple process of emergence in which one is placed" (Ravn 2009, 276).

Space as inert, empty or static is hard to conceptualise when spending time outdoors, in *nature space*. Exposed to the constant changes of weather, the sensual and spatial stimuli, as mentioned above by Mainz, the movements of other creatures as well as the multiplicity of materials present as respondents to and elicitors of movement, the notion of space as emergent, interrelational and alive is particularly apparent. Thus, this context might offer a specifically fertile ground to study the vitality of space, materials and the position of the human being within.

Decentralisation and Materiality

In the following section I argue for a *decentralised* position of the human (dancer) in *nature space*, not only for dancing but also for living and acting in the world at large. Whilst it can be cold, wet and tiring as much as warm and comforting, exposing the body to the liveliness of *nature space* positions the dancer as one creator of movement amongst many. In field notes during a workshop in which I was a participant I write, "life happens no matter what we do" (field notes Kramer 2011c, April 21). This sense of moving alongside a multitude of change and movements already happening has a crucial impact on creative practice — it can be experienced as inspiring and reassuring in the sense that life, movement and dance are plentiful and happening anyway, as well as limiting and frustrating, as the human artist is neither the sole 'creator' nor able to fully dictate what happens on a site, but is continuously asked to adapt. In an essay on working with dance pioneer Anna Halprin the movement artist Helen Poynor (2009, 127) explains this dynamic of changes onsite and the relinquishing of human control as follows: "For Halprin, the fact that nature is in a state of constant flux requires the performer to be able to respond instantaneously to changing conditions rather than attempting to control them". Apart from 'severe' weather conditions or the cold temperature of a river it can also be the size and magnitude of materialities in the natural world that highlight the decentralised position of the human (dancer). Working with Poynor, for example, it is at tidal sites, underneath cliffs or amongst big boulders that she brings conditions of potential danger to the attention of workshop participants and speaks of the environment as larger and more powerful than the mover (field notes Kramer 2011a, January 23). It is from dancing in *nature space* that I have learnt most clearly that I am present only as one materiality amongst many and am thus required to find form and possibilities between adaptation, intervention, co-existence, resistance and play rather than from trying to exercise control. Influenced and fed by such experiences I became interested in exploring the position of political theorist Jane Bennett (2010, 30), who proposes a "more radical displacement of the human subject than phenomenology has done". In *Vibrant Matter* Bennett (Ibid., 48) develops a "theory of materiality as *itself* an active, vibrant power", thus challenging the position of the human as an autonomous agent over inert matter and arguing for agency as always shared between humans and nonhumans, though not necessarily in equal parts.

Massey (2011, 36) very similarly states that "the material world itself *is* dynamic". In *For Space* she describes how she came to understand differently and anew the quality of change even in a material as steady as a mountain. Whilst always well aware of the historical movements of rock formations and indeed continents, it was on a specific occasion in the English Lake District, when she was staying near Mount Skiddaw and in her room at night "poring over local geology" (2005, 133), that Massey fully realised that even these rocks had been and were moving too:

> When the morning came I could not but look at Skiddaw in a different light. Its timeless shape is no such thing. Nor has it been 'here' for ever … the rocks of Skiddaw are immigrant rocks, just passing through here, like my sister and me only rather more slowly, and changing all the while. (Massey 2005, 135-137)

I would argue that experiences of "thing power" (Bennett 2010, 6) and the liveliness and mobility of materiality as heavy and seemingly inert as mountains, can support the appreciation of a post-humanist and decentralised position of a dancer. This argument is not meant to displace, annihilate or expel the human being, but instead offers a dynamic potential of simultaneously finding one's place and "becoming part of a larger whole" (Poynor 2009, 126). Massey (2011, 37) describes this as "one's appreciation of one's very place on the planet". To act and exist as a dancer as one part within *nature space* also offers the possibility of establishing a clarified (albeit temporary) sense of self and placement as part of the world. In my own practice I often experience this as a sense of ease in my body and mind and an appreciation of 'being here' (now, in this location, in this world). Yet my practice in *nature space* is not, and does not intend to be, an experience of unbroken harmony. It also includes feeling lost, dislodged and overcome by the puzzled insecurity of 'what the hell am I doing here?' It is thus in a continuous dynamic of losing and finding form, sense and meaning, that movement material as well as an appreciation of my own practice and being can emerge in relation to the specific conditions of a site.

In my experience it is particularly the attention to the materiality of the human

Workshop at Bordes d'Olp, Pallars Sobira (ES), 2009. Photographer: Vanesa Freixa.

body that can foster a sense of belonging in the midst of *nature space*. Supporting a clear sense of one's own body and its material, physical structure, nudges those perceptual capacities of the body into action that often fall by the wayside in the (western) world in which the mind and the visual sense are often prioritised. Dance anthropologist Andrée Grau (2011, 9) draws on Alan Dundes' (1972/1980) essay *Seeing is believing* when discussing this "prerogative of the visual" that comes to the fore for example when "'seeing' is equated to 'understanding'". In her 2011 brochure Helen Poynor writes: "Grounding ourselves through an embodied encounter with the land which refreshes both body and spirit we rediscover our 'place in the family of things'"[3]. In my experience of Poynor's work, the emphasis on the physicality of the body (as well as the land) is, for example, encouraged through practicing the clear placing of one's feet, supporting one's awareness of the body's skeleto-muscular structure and being reminded not to gaze out too soon, which holds the risk of losing all sense of one's own body. In an hour of practice by the sea during a weekend workshop, Poynor referred to this as "not getting seduced by the sirens of the sea" (field notes Kramer 2011b, April 3), i.e. to not look out to the far away horizon and the vastness of the sea too soon, but to keep one's visual attention in the first instance close to the body and the materialities nearby.

Writing about the experience of a workshop I taught in 2009, dance and movement therapist Teresa Bas noted the following in an email about her workshop experience:

> I felt a sense of heightened sensitivity in myself. It's strange because I could have lost myself in watching the landscape, but nothing like that happened. On the contrary, I felt my body was very present in this environment and my concrete physical as well as my intuitive feelings were heightened through the contact with the natural materials (through vision, smell, touch, etc.). This gave me a better focus to guide my movement from inside, however in relationship to the outside. It was really very surprising! I have never experienced this so clearly. (Teresa Bas 2009, personal communication, my translation from Spanish)

This workshop took place in an impressive mountain range of the Catalan Pyrenees, and I specifically used strategies to emphasise the materiality of the body before opening into the wider space in individual and group improvisations. One such strategy was based on an exercise I have learned from Bettina Mainz: a group structure that revolves around the placing and taking away of stones on each other's bodies whilst lying on the ground. Sensing one's body covered by stones offers a physically immersive experience of rocks as well as of oneself as a sensitive and vulnerable, yet also resilient and substantial human being, able to carry and appreciate weight.

The examples above speak about embodiment, materiality and physicality in the context of working in *nature space*. My argument is that it is decentralisation coupled with a clear sense of the human body and its materiality amongst other materials, which supports creative movement practice and renders moments of finding and sensing one's place in the world possible. Going further than dance, I propose that such a decentralised position of the human, this sense of not-being-fully-in-control whilst simultaneously belonging and being part of the environment, has relevance and potential beyond the realms of creative practice and performance. Experiencing the possibility of embodied co-habitation within *nature space*, rather than aiming to control it, offers a possible and necessary practice of repositioning human beings in the context of the current ecological crisis. Bennett argues that we need to devise new [...] regimes of perception that enable us to consult nonhumans more closely, or to listen and respond more carefully to their outbreaks, objections, testimonies, and propositions. For these offerings are profoundly important to the health of the political ecologies to which *we* belong. (Bennett 2010, 108)

It seems to me that outdoor dance practices can be considered one such 'regime of perception' that offers a direct relationship to and ways to experience and engage with the material presence and aliveness of *nature space*. Reeve makes a similar proposal drawing from her practice:

Ecological movement ostensibly has nothing to do with carbon emissions or global warming. But, in its emphasis on community and context, on being 'among' and being 'part of', on being constantly in flux in a world that envelops us (rather than being scenery or a backdrop), it encourages a sense of belonging rather than longing and a sense of the world as a shared habitat rather than owned territory. This sense of belonging and sharing is profoundly ecological. (Reeve 2010, 201)

It is thus my hope that movement practices which expose themselves to the continuous changes of the natural outdoors yet pay close attention to the human and non-human materialities at hand, constitute a potent tool that allows us to understand and practice our being in this world in a way that fosters what Bennett (2010) might call a "vibrant" co-existence.

Practice-as-Dissemination

I will now take the discussion around materialities further and into the realm of thinking about dissemination practices in the context of practice-as-research. How can experiences and insights gained through artistic and embodied research be extended into practice-as-dissemination? What might be adequate ways to document and communicate insights stemming from a reflective engagement with dance? From my perspective there is still a need to develop and discuss formats that hold and meet bodily experiences as well as their analyses and allow to diverge from repeating an event (like a performance) or writing a text 'about' it. The academic text still features as the most recognised communication tool, or, as performance studies scholar Lynette Hunter (2009, 232) notes "The academy values words above all else". Certainly since the ample investigative project PARIP (Practice as Research in Performance, Bristol University 2001-2005) there has been a great extension in thinking about and doing practice-as-research as well as about documentation and dissemination practices in the performing arts. However the bulk of the discussion related to dance seems to have revolved around how to fruitfully combine dancing and 'academic writing'. One such engagement with dancing and writing is the work of dance scholar Kim Vincs (2007), who helpfully argues for a radical democratisation between writing and dancing. She argues for not understanding one a priori to the other and instead moving beyond the hierarchical concept of "the dance produces; the writing articulates that production" (Vincs 2007, 106). Some modalities of disseminating practice-as-research that reach beyond the written word are available, including the DVD *The Suchness of Heni and Eddi* (2007), co-produced by choreographer Rosemary Lee and video artist and scholar Ludivine Allegue. This DVD includes excerpts of rehearsals, feedback to the dancers, materials that influenced the process of making, as well as a filmic documentation of the final performance. A shared intention is often to "continue rather than merely document" (Garrett Brown et al. 2011, 75) a process, as articulated in a collaborative photographic essay and interview on the movement and photography project 'Enter & Inhabit'.

Key to the discussion of practice-as-research in dance is the understanding of thought processes and physical action as intertwined, what dance scholars Fiona Bannon and Duncan Holt (2011, 216) refer to as "embodied encounters with thought, a place that affords a rich potential of thinking through the body". In the context of this writing I would thus like to propose that working with an installation to disseminate practice-as-research allows for a continuation of such 'embodied encounters with thought'.

I began to work with *research installations* for pragmatic reasons. I was looking for ways to communicate my research on dance in

Installation at Coventry University. Photographer: Paula Kramer.

Installation at the University of Southern Denmark, 2011. Photographer: Paula Kramer.

the natural environment, first to my academic supervisors and then to larger audiences, in a way that didn't reduce the research only to the spoken or written word, but allowed people to walk 'into' the research, without having to travel to a specific outdoor location. In order to take others into my research I thus began to place objects, writings, books, drawings, photographs etc. in indoor spaces, first spread out on a studio floor and later suspended three-dimensionally into the space. I have since developed the practice of working with installations as a dissemination tool integral to my research. An installation has material as well as metaphorical properties, it is some*thing* that is both static and there, yet it is also processual and changing, as I generally invite participants to intervene in the construction.

A specific installation with an intermediate overview of my research was presented twice at my home University (Coventry), and once at the Nordic Forum for Dance research in Odense (all in 2011). Poetry, photographs, interview excerpts, materials, quotes and drawings from movement practice were suspended in the space on thin white thread. A big ball of coarse string anchored in the middle of the room, with two ends floating upwards, interweaving with the thin thread. A sound score was audible, composed of a mix of field recordings from research sites and collaborative improvisations with musicians. The images and words in the installation stemmed from my entering the work-zone of other artists as well as from reflecting on my own outdoor movement, teaching and performance practice and the widespread reading and writing related to the topic of outdoor dance. Those present to engage with the research installation were invited to enter and move within the woven network of threads, materials, utterances and images. Provided with note cards, they were encouraged to comment on what they saw, did and experienced in the installation. In the end they were prompted to remove one item from the installation, which was later shared in a collective round of reflection.

Follow your curiosities, dwell where you like.

You are invited to leave your reflections, drawings or comments hanging in the installation or anywhere else. You may also comment on comments. You don't have to be silent, but you can. Don't hesitate to touch what you would like to.

(Excerpt from the installation guide available for participants)

Comments by installation visitors, left on the threads (January 17th and 29th 2011), included:

"A feeling of bringing the outside in ... And the inside, into ourselves."
"Heavy, weighted, textures — I can smell the sea, I can feel that weight."
"Around through, ducking over under, ideas, experiences, emotions."
"It moves as I move and connects me somehow."
"We can become part of this environment. I am part of this now ... will I be when I have left?"

This installation offered the possibility to literally step into the research process and engage with its current form and state in a temporary stability. The comments quoted above highlight the potential for embodied experience, a sense of feeling aspects of the research within the installation — for example specific textures of outdoor locations. Its delicate and slightly 'messy' way of being hung, criss-crossing the space, made touching the thread unavoidable and demanded physical attention, but also allowed for feeling connected as expressed in "it moves as I move". In further developments of this initial installation I have used both digital (film) and analogous materials (paper, wood, plastic bags, fabric etc.), as well as clarified different ways of engagement. These include physically moving/ improvising/playing with the objects, immersing oneself in reading/looking at specific items or walking/brushing past many with meandering attention. Most people choose combinations of these possibilities, yet enter with a specific affinity — some react more strongly to the visual and text-based information in the first instance, others are drawn to engage with the material and textural invitations.

Due to its inherent spatiality, the requirement to keep the body in motion in order to engage with it and the presence of objects with inherent aesthetic, metaphorical and material properties, I have found installations a valuable tool for practice-as-dissemination in dance. It allows for a simultaneity of moving, thinking, seeing, reading and engaging that I have not found in my preceding attempts of combining 'dancing and writing', which easily resulted in the frustration of impossibility, especially when I took this idea all too literally.

Tying the Threads Together

As for an installation, I have threaded together lines of thought and possibility in this text — the argument that an understanding of space as 'alive and happening' is a shared concern across disciplines as diverse as dance, geography and political theory which might strengthen the case across these distances. Outdoor dance practice in *nature space*, I have argued further, offers a context in which this concept of space can be physically explored and appreciated. I have introduced the decentralisation of the human as one specific aspect of outdoor dancing, which holds possibilities beyond dance and reaches into political ecology. When coupled with a clear sense of one's own materiality and the materialities sharing a site, such a decentralisation of oneself can offer profound experiences of belonging. Finally I have proposed working with a research installation as a useful dissemination mode for practice-as-research in dance. Whilst each thread deserves further twists, turns and knots, I hope these initial arguments elicit further spinning and weaving, and foster interdisciplinary collaborations between dancers and other creative practitioners and researchers exploring (for example) the topoi of movement, materiality, embodiment and space.

BIBLIOGRAPHY

Bannon, Fiona and Holt, Duncan. 2011. "Touch: Experience and knowledge." *Journal of Dance & Somatic Practices* 3 (1+2): 215-227.

Bas, Teresa. 2009. *My Memories* [email] to Paula Kramer. 24 August 2009.

Bennett, Jane. 2010. *Vibrant Matter: A Political Ecology of Things.* Durham: Duke University Press.

Dundes, Alan. 1972/1980. "Seeing is believing." In *Interpreting Folklore*, edited by Alan Dundes, 86-92. Bloomington, IN: Indiana University Press.

Garrett Brown, Natalie; Kipp, Christian; Pollard, Niki and Voris, Amy. 2011. "Everything Is at Once: Reflections on Embodied Photography and Collaborative Process." *Journal of Dance & Somatic Practices* 3 (1+2): 75-84.

Grau, Andrée. 2011. "Dancing Bodies, Spaces/Places and the Senses: A Cross-Cultural Investigation." *Journal of Dance & Somatic Practices* 3 (1+2): 5-24.

Hunter, Lynette. 2009. "Theory/Practice as Research: Explorations, Questions and Suggestions." In *Mapping Landscapes for Performance as Research: Scholarly Acts and Creative Cartographies*, edited by Shannon Rose Riley and Lynette Hunter, 230-236. New York: Palgrave Macmillan.

Kramer, Paula. 2011a. *Field notes Walk of Life Foundation Training in Non-Stylised and Environmental Movement with Helen Poynor*, 21-25 January 2011.

Kramer, Paula. 2011b. *Field notes Spring Awakening Workshop with Helen Poynor*, 1-3 April 2011.

Kramer, Paula. 2011c. *Field notes Workshop 4x4 Dance, Body & the Environment*, 19-26 April 2011.

Latour, Bruno. 2004. "Air Conditioning." Lecture Series Nature Space Society at Tate Modern London. Accessed February 10, 2011. http://channel.tate.org.uk/media/27686262001.

Latour, Bruno. 1993. *We Have Never Been Modern.* Cambridge, MA: Harvard University Press.

Lavelle, Lise. 2006. *Amerta Movement of Java 1986-1997: An Asian Movement Improvisation.* Lund: Centre for Languages and Literature.

Lee, Rosemary and Allegue, Ludivine. 2007. *The Suchness of Heni and Eddie*: *An interactive document and investigative research resource.* [DVD] London: ResCen Publications/ Bristol: PARIP.

Mainz, Bettina. 2011. *Nature Space* [email] to Paula Kramer. 7 January 2011.

Mainz, Bettina and Kramer, Paula. 2011. "Body of Becoming and Progressing into No-Progress", Part 1 (Mainz) and Part 2 ([1]), *Journal of Dance & Somatic Practices* 3 (1+2): 145-150.

Massey, Doreen. 2011. "For Space: Reflection on an Engagement with Dance". In *Spacing Dance(s)-Dancing Space(s) Proceedings*, 10th International NOFOD Conference, January 27-30, Odense 2011, edited by Susanne Ravn, 35-44. Odense: NOFOD and The University of Southern Denmark.

Massey, Doreen. 2005. *For Space.* London: Sage Publications.

Oliver, Mary. 1992. *New and Selected Poems.* Boston: Beacon Press.

Poynor, Helen. 2011. *Walk of Life Workshops and Training Brochure 2011.*

Poynor, Helen. 2009. "Anna Halprin and the Sea Ranch Collective, An Embodied Engagement with Place." *Journal of Dance and Somatic Practices* 1(1): 121-132.

Poynor, Helen. 1986. "The Walk of Life." *Human Potential Resources* Autumn: 3-5.

Ravn, Susanne. 2009. *Sensing Movement, Living Spaces: An Investigation of movement based on the lived experience of 13 professional dancers.* Saarbrücken: VDM.

Reeve, Sandra. 2010. "Reading, Gardening and 'Non-Self': *Joged Amerta* and Its Emerging Influence on Ecological Somatic Practice." *Journal of Dance & Somatic Practices* 2 (2): 189-203.

Reeve, Sandra. 2008. "The Ecological Body." PhD diss., University of Exeter.

Soper, Kate. 1995. *What is Nature? Culture, Politics and the Non-human.* Oxford: Blackwell Publishers Ltd.

Vincs, Kim. 2007. "Rhizome/MyZone: A Case Study in Studio-Based Dance Research." In *Practice as Research Approaches to Creative Arts Enquiry*, edited by Estelle Barrett and Barbara Bolt, 99-112. London: I.B. Tauris.

NOTES

1   Further useful resources on Amerta include Lavelle 2006, Poynor 1986 and Reeve 2008.

2   For a first short publication on *Body of Becoming* see Mainz and Kramer 2011.

3   With 'place in the family of things' Poynor quotes Mary Oliver's poem Wild Geese (Oliver 1992: 110).

SPACE AND EMBODIED COMPETENCE

THE LIVED SPACE OF ARTISTIC PRIMARY SCHOOL EDUCATION: THE SIGNIFICANCE OF EMBODIMENT AND VULNERABILITY

Charlotte Svendler Nielsen

Abstract

This article takes its point of departure in two stories produced from an interview with the Danish and music teacher of a second grade class involved in a six month project with a dance educator. Through a hermeneutic phenomenological approach (van Manen 1990) the article seeks to illuminate what the characteristics of artistic-educational spaces of primary school teaching and learning can be. The article also seeks to cast light on embodiment and vulnerability as significant phenomena in artistic-educational teaching and learning spaces. Embodied processes of teaching are explored, and it is discussed how skills and tools that foster embodied awareness and confidence to teach dance as an artistic subject area can be developed. Finally, the article reflects on how tools from dance can broaden understandings and practices of teaching in the artistic areas in general with an embodied perspective.

Introduction

Every teacher expresses a certain "tone of teaching" (van Manen 2002) in different situations. This tone comes forth in the pedagogical actions of every moment and is coloured by different bodily tools (use of space, use of gesture, etc.). The aim of this article is to explore embodied processes of teaching in artistic-educational spaces at primary school level. The artistic-educational space is looked upon as a lived and contextual space that gives certain possibilities for relating, communicating and thus also learning.[1] Through hermeneutic phenomenological analyses (van Manen 1990, 92-95) themes that turn out to be central in the processes between the participants in this space are illuminated. Max van Manen's (1990; 2002) thoughts are especially useful for the grounding of this research, as he is one of few pedagogues writing within a phenomenological tradition, thus emphasising on the lived and embodied dimensions of both spaces and experiences. Moreover, he is writing about some of the same themes I have found to be significant in my observations and analyses and can thus also be used in the interpretations and discussions of those.

In his book *Researching lived experience* from 1990, van Manen writes that phenomenological research always begins "in the lifeworld" (van Manen 1990, 7), and has as its aim to create deeper understandings of what meaning people make of experienced phenomena. He also mentions that descriptions of "significant moments" are central when we want to understand human experience and lived meanings (ibid., 163). Those moments can come forth in "concrete stories that present moments of teaching" and "may provide opportunities for reflecting pedagogically on actions, situations, and relations of teaching" (van Manen 2002, 54).

Both van Manen and psychologist Les Todres (2007) whom I will turn to later in the article are inspired by the existential branch of phenomenology rooted in the writings of Maurice Merleau-Ponty (e.g. 1962; 1968). They use phenomenology as both a philosophy of the body as lived and a method that highlights the experiential dimension of human actions. Van Manen applies a hermeneutic (interpretive) perspective to his way of working with phenomenology. This I find significant as my research is also pedagogic and as van Manen (2002, 29) states: "pedagogy requires a phenomenological sensitivity to lived experience" and "a hermeneutic ability to make interpretive sense of the phenomena of the lifeworld in order to see the pedagogic significance of situations and relations of living with children."

Doing Embodied Research — With Inspirations from Phenomenology and Ethnography

In the research process I collect data through "videographic participation" (Svendler Nielsen 2012) and interviewing in the pedagogic practice I am studying. The research methods come from the field of ethnography. As a researcher of a certain practice one will unavoidably be present as an experiencing subject. With the aim of exploring and understanding the embodied processes of the practice I am studying, I choose to also highlight and give room for my own embodied involvement in the research process. In phenomenologically-based research the embodied experiences of the researcher are of great importance to the knowledge that can be created (Snowber 2002; Depraz et al. 2003). This belief, hence, makes the grounding of how phenomenology is inspiring my ethnographic data collection. The phenomenological approach is at the forefront when I communicate people's experiences as they are described with their own words. But my own experiences also guide my analyses and interpretations. This sense- and meaning-making of my experiences happens already while I am engaged in collecting data, but when withdrawing from the field I start a deeper analytic work.

A hermeneutic phenomenological approach highlights that interpreting a social situation is to treat the situation as a "text" and look for meanings and metaphors that appear in the text. In the analysis I therefore "feel into" which words, associations and metaphors come forth about the role of the body in the artistic-educational spaces I study. As a researcher in the process of hermeneutic phenomenological analysis I hence move between moments of closeness and moments of distance (Todres 2007, 58) in relation to the phenomena and the people whose experiences and practises I am exploring. The moments of closeness happen when I am involved in collecting and communicating the participants' and my own experiences in narrative form. The moments of distance happen when I intend to pull meanings forward from the texts through hermeneutic interpretations. In the interpretations I constantly move between single sentences and the whole story in order to get to a deeper understanding of the themes that are communicated about the phenomena in focus. The analysis is done in a three-step process: first I read the text as a whole and feel into what word or concept might describe the overall theme which is communicated (van Manen (1990, 93) calls this "the wholistic[2] reading approach"). The next steps are the selective and detailed reading approaches (ibid.) in which I mark certain phrases that tell me something about the overall theme and then go into exploring what the selected sentences reveal about the theme.

Concrete Stories of Teaching that Gives Space for Artistic-Educational Processes

In the following I will present a "concrete story" which illustrates a significant moment in a teaching process. During an interview with the Danish and music teacher of the second grade class, we discuss what it takes to teach in the artistic-educational space in primary school classes. The example is not from dance, but it serves to illuminate and later on discuss how tools from dance could broaden understandings and practices of teaching in the artistic areas in general with an embodied perspective and why this could be important:

"It was just as if you were naked!" — a significant moment in teaching of music

If you don't dare yourself you cannot make the children do it. It is the same in drama and music. I remember an experience I had in a music lesson once. I sang a song to the children. I sang without playing the piano or anything. When I finished there was complete silence in the room for some seconds, but then the children suddenly started to laugh and laugh and laugh. I asked: "But, what are you laughing at?" and they continued to laugh and laugh and laugh, but finally a boy raised his hand and said: "It is not because it sounds awful, it actually sounds very, very good, but it was just as if you were naked!" The teacher continues: "I think it was such a fine way of expressing their experience. They thought I had exposed myself so much by standing there singing to them without anything to hide behind. They were touched, but their reaction was — we need to laugh, we need to do something and spontaneously they just started to laugh, because they were touched and didn't know what to do. The teacher says that she also thinks that this is central in dance teaching: "As the teacher and the adult you need to dare being a step ahead of them all the time. You need to dare being on the floor and act 'strangely'. If not you will not be able to teach in that subject. Of course you can teach a subject without being an expert, you don't need to be an author to teach Danish, but in the artistic subjects you need to dare.

To Dare — a Theme Coming Forth in Relation to Creating an Artistic-Educational Space

To dare is the theme I find to be central through a "wholistic reading" (van Manen 1990, 93) of the part of the interview when we talk about what it takes to teach in the artistic-educational space. Through a "selective reading" (ibid., 93) I see some sub-themes in relation to this theme as it is unfolded in the pedagogical context of an artistic-educational space. These sub-themes will be explored below. As the teacher takes this example forth in our talk about what it takes to teach in the artistic-educational area it must be an experience that has had a certain significance to her. She seems touched by the very reflected way of expressing what the children feel that the boy proposes through his use of the image: "It was just as if you were naked!"

If we wish to understand what is happening in the situation described above, we can start by exploring what the teacher *does* in the situation: the teacher's reaction when the children start laughing is one of wonder, but she also shows an open curiosity to what the children have experienced. She accepts their reaction and shows respect for them in her way of dealing with what to her probably is a very vulnerable situation. Indirectly she shows that she accepts to be in a vulnerable position and through this an atmosphere is created which holds that it is okay to be honest about what one is thinking and feeling. But let us get a little closer to what the teacher is *doing* through interpretations and discussions of the sub-themes which to me seem central in order to understand what is characteristic in this lived and contextual space of teaching in the artistic-educational area.

The Teacher's Attentiveness and Showing of Wonder

The teacher wonders. She does not understand why the children are laughing and chooses to show curiosity about the children's experience. When the teacher shares her wondering with the children, it shows her ability to be attentive in her professional practice. Through what she is doing the children see what she values and perhaps this will make them dare to share their wondering in the future. Van Manen (2002, 19) asks: "Can wonder be taught?" "Can we bring children to wonder?" He reflects upon the concept of wonder and says that "perhaps wonder is a state of attentiveness" (ibid., 21). In this moment one could say that the teacher through embodied communication helps the children learn to wonder by *showing* the way.

The Teacher's Attention to the Unique

In this situation the teacher pauses for a moment and wonders about the children's reaction. With van Manen (2002, 31) this could also be interpreted as if she *'sees'* the children and is attentive to the unique quality of the situation. According to van Manen (ibid., 23) *what* and *how* we see depend on who and how we are in the world, what our prior experiences are and how they guide us. This is perhaps also important in relation to what we *do* with it? The teacher pauses and makes room for the children and therefore has to listen to them as someone who might have a different viewpoint from her own. When one experiences being seen, one is "confirmed as existing, as being a unique person" (ibid., 31). The boy who finally says something may experience being seen by the teacher as she acknowledges his participation in the situation.

The Teacher's Creation of an Open Atmosphere

Van Manen (2002, 54) states that "spaces also have their atmospheric, sensual, and felt aspects" and that

> many teachers intuitively understand that the daily activities of teaching and learning are conditioned by such ineffable factors as the atmosphere of the school and classroom, the relational qualities that pertain amongst students and teachers, and the complex and subtle dimensions of temporality and lived space of the school. It is sensed or felt, rather than thought or reasoned. (van Manen 2002, 53)

The atmosphere is created by the people who inhabit the space, what they say and what they do. The teacher participates in this situation as herself, as a human being. With her lived experiences and preferences coming forth, she creates an open atmosphere. The words that the teacher says are important, but the way in which she says them and the pauses she makes, which make room for the children's initiative, are even more important. If one as a teacher shares some of one's experiences, worries and mistakes, one enables the creation of a space in which is okay to experiment and to make mistakes. But it is also important to pause and listen and wait for initiatives and responses. The open atmosphere is perhaps also what encourages the boy to finally share his thoughts about the reason for the children's reaction. Van Manen (2002, 71) emphasises that: "A teacher has to learn to become sensitive to the ways children experience the complexity of elements that contribute to the atmosphere of the school and classroom". This might be especially important in artistic-educational spaces as both the teacher and the children become vulnerable when they engage in expressive activities. If we want to work with creative processes it is necessary to pay attention to the atmosphere we create both by what we say and what we do.

The Teacher's Openness and Acceptance of Being in a Vulnerable Position

When pausing and being open to the children's response, the teacher "stands open and trusting to what may come" (Todres 2007, 155). With regard to openness van Manen (2002, 85) writes that "we truly open ourselves to a Childs's way of being when we are able to experience openness ourselves." So the teacher might be able to be open to the children's viewpoints because she herself is open to the fact that different people might have different viewpoints and ways of understanding situations. In the interview the teacher expresses her vulnerability standing in front of the children singing. In the openness she gives something of herself as a person and does not know how the children will receive it. But she explains that she is conscious about the fact that she needs to be one step ahead of the children in the sense that she needs to give something of herself and to show the way. It is her experience that showing the way inspires the children to take the challenge of expressing themselves musically. And this is something she thinks teachers need to *dare.*

Later during the same interview we talk about what is significant about the educational space in the dance lessons that her class has with a dance educator who comes into the school as part of a community-based project organised by a local dance theatre:

Using the body brings the feelings forth — significant moments in dance

When they run around like airplanes, I see that they use the space in a different way. I see how wonderful they feel using the space, how great it is to throw one's body around — look at this one! We cannot help being happy. Nobody looks angry when they move around like airplanes. That is simply not possible. So this happiness — you feel that they are having a great time, right? However, in the beginning it was difficult. There was resistance. But now they enter the space with 'the palms up' — if I can express it with a metaphor — there is opened up now. And that is why they are also vulnerable. Like Bea who was crying this morning. Perhaps she had had a hard morning and then when they enter this space something happens, they use their bodies and that brings the feelings forth. You can also see how the boys sit and cuddle, how they just need to touch and lean on one another.

A Different Space — a Theme Coming Forth in Relation to Creating an Artistic-Educational Space in Dance

The teacher chooses these examples to illustrate what she thinks is significant in the dance lessons that her class has with a dance educator who comes to the school once a week. The teacher participates in the classes in the periphery assisting the dance educator when necessary and I am there as a researcher 'taking notes' with a video camera (see Svendler Nielsen, 2012 for further elaborations on the videographic method used to capture lived experiences of children and teachers). The first thing the teacher emphasises is that she sees the children *use the space in a different way*. This to me is the overall theme in a "wholistic reading" (van Manen 1990, 93) of this story. She does not describe what the dance educator is doing, but even so from what the teacher expresses in the interview we can look at what seems to be significant for the pedagogical space that she creates. And in order to understand and be able to describe the situations that she mentions I also look at video recordings from the lessons with the following question in mind: what is it that makes the dance lessons 'different' from other ways of being in an educational space?

Creating Space for Feelings

In this story it appears that characteristics of an artistic-educational space in dance can be that it is a space which is used in a way that influences the atmosphere and the mood of the children. It is a space that makes room for a broad variety of feelings. The children are usually happy, but it also happens that someone is crying because of personal issues that may come forth when they move around. When moving around in the physical space many processes are going on at the same time, both with regard to the social and the personal sensing of one's own body. Moving creates a different way of being present than sitting in the classroom writing. This presence is the same phenomenon that appeared to be central in the analysis of the story where the teacher told about her experience of singing solo to the children. When the body is used in creative processes there will be a certain openness that not only makes the teacher vulnerable, but also the children.

The balance between education/learning and therapy/development can sometimes be fine-drawn. The dance project takes place in an educational context and the purpose is therefore not therapeutic, but this does not mean that there should not be room for different kinds of feelings if they appear. This can happen in all educational areas and is part of being human, but when there is 'opened up' for sensing oneself like in dance it is more likely to happen than in e.g. a maths class.

As a teacher one needs to consider what to handle in the situation and what to consult parents or other professionals about.

Making Space for Relations

The artistic-educational space of dance is a space with a very caring physical contact and it is a space that nurtures new relationships (this aspect is explored further in Svendler Nielsen 2009b). The teacher mentions the boys cuddling each other. When observing the class in dance I saw this caring physical contact between them a number of times. In other contexts I saw them being physical in more playful fighting ways. That the way of being together physically is so different is perhaps due to the fact that the creative processes creates room for an involvement through which the children's ways of being present is opened and widened. When they are in a state of openness they practice their sensitive involvement and widen their consciousness about and abilities to understand other ways of being and expressing. This is probably one reason why many children when I talk to them about what they think is significant to dance mention that they have "got new friends" or have become "better friends" with some. They do not mention that when I talk to them about other subject areas.

Opening Up a Space of Resistance

The teacher mentions that in the beginning of the dance project there was resistance. This resistance was expressed by both boys and girls. Many boys felt that "dance was for girls" and many girls felt that the dance they met in the project was not the dance that they knew (hip hop, disco and other dance styles). In the project they were presented with creative dance and tools for developing their own choreographic work which they had to perform at a professional theatre. The resistance, hence, was due to different expectations. After a while the boys forgot that dance was "for girls", because they became very involved in creating their own movements and the girls found ways to include their "own" dance movements in the choreographic work. This seemed to happen because the dance educator was open and accepted to be in a vulnerable position bearing the resistance of the children on her shoulders while showing the children a way to go. As such she was "one step ahead of the children" just like the class teacher in the story where she tells about singing solo to the children. Through her openness and acceptance of the children's viewpoints the dance educator managed to create a space where the children after a while came "with the palms up" as expressed by the teacher, in the sense that the children became more open to this way of working with dance.

Characteristics of an Artistic-Educational Space

In the analysis of both stories created from extracts from the interview with the teacher some common themes have come forth in relation to the characteristics of an artistic-educational space. Teaching as a concept and field of practice is closely linked to learning. When learning happens in areas of movement it is because an expansion of consciousness in-and-about movement is going on. It is an expansion of ability, knowledge, understanding or change of ways of experiencing or expressing oneself, in relation to others or a subject area (Svendler Nielsen 2009a, 243). The ability to sense differences in dynamic qualities of movements is rooted in this consciousness in-and-about movement which the children develop through *different* movement experiences and ways of engaging in movement. Both teaching and learning can be linked to embodiment and vulnerability as overall themes that permeate what goes on when we are with other people in a teaching space where the objective is to make room for creative and artistic learning processes.

Vulnerability in Creative Processes of Teaching and Learning
Vulnerability has been a theme appearing in the analysis of both stories presented in this paper. How can vulnerability be understood? And how is it possible to work with it in an artistic-educational setting? Todres (2007) explores the phenomenon of human vulnerability as an existential given. To be in a vulnerable position or situation metaphorically speaking makes a 'passage' (an openness) to other existential possibilities — possibilities of learning and development. This openness is what makes us vulnerable. We cannot control what will happen, are in a state of change and might be unsuccessfull, be laughed at, etc. It is about an ontological dimension (our being). Opening ourselves means 'disconnecting' from continuity, "a tear in the sense of simple going-on-being (...) a stretching towards what may come" (Todres 2007, 154). To dare being open and in a vulnerable position, one must have a firm assurance of oneself as someone who is able and capable in most situations. To some extent this can have to do with experiences of one's skills. If you know you can sing and it usually sounds good you will probably be more likely to try out singing in new ways or new places.

The same counts for teachers of dance when they act with their own lived bodies as 'instruments' in the space.

A Lived and 'Soulful' Space that Embraces Vulnerable Processes

When it works as truly open and fostering creative processes, the artistic-educational space can be a space of vulnerability, but also of deeply involved participation, learning and development in both professional and personal areas. A kind of human openness is needed to feel touched, an openness which Todres (2007) calls the 'soulful space'. 'Soulful' is used as an adjective meaning "'full of sentiment or emotion', 'evoking deep feeling', and 'not mechanical or heartless'" (Allen 1990 and Makins 1995 in Todres 2007, 152). 'Soulful space' refers to a "'spaciousness' that can tolerate or embody the vulnerability of 'soulfulness'" (Todres 2007, 152). It is a space where there is a possibility of being wounded psychologically, of feeling ashamed or weak. But with a skillful teacher, a 'soulful space' holds a spaciousness in which vulnerability is not avoided, but rather embraced (ibid., 162). The soulful space provides a foundation for empathic connection with others (ibid., 150).

The Role of the Lived Body and Kinaesthetic Empathy in Teaching Processes

Do all teachers see, feel and react to the subtle bodily signs expressing the feelings and experiences of the participants in the lived space of concrete moments? Most people react to expressions of feelings and bodily expressions in their everyday life and teachers react to their experiences with the participants in the class room. According to Finnish dance researcher Jaana Parviainen (2002), a dance teacher makes use of his or her own embodied experiences and kinaesthetic empathy to understand the participants' experiences, and to help learners in their learning process. Parviainen (ibid.) claims that especially dancers have a well-developed kinaesthetic empathy based on the ability to distinguish between different dynamic qualities in movements. A dance teacher hence has a special opportunity to make use of his or her embodied experiences in the endeavour to understand the participants' experiences from their viewpoint and be able to help them learn and develop.

The concept of empathy means the ability to put oneself in another person's place. Parviainen (2002) is inspired by the doctoral thesis of Edith Stein from

1917 titled *On the Problem of Empathy*, and describes kinaesthetic empathy as the appreciation that one can have of another person's kinaesthetic sensation. It is "a particular form of the act of knowing" (Parviainen 2002, 147), "an act of knowing within others" (ibid., 151). When we interpret what is going on amongst our students we make use of our own experiences. As van Manen (2002, 23) says: "we never see anything purely. How and what we *see* depends on who and how we are in the world." But when we 'feel' the kinaesthetic sensations of the other it does not mean that we either experience them ourselves, in the original, or know what the other person is feeling (Parviainen 2002, 147). We recognise the sensation, because it resonates with some of our lived experiences. Stein (in Moran 2003) calls the relationship between subjectivity and empathy a "co-experience," and emphasises that there is a connection between how you understand others and how you understand yourself: "you bring yourself along when you understand others" (quoted in lecture by Dermot Moran, 2003 (see details in the bibliography)).

Former dancer and now phenomenologist Maxine Sheets-Johnstone (1999, 57) highlights that "we can distinguish kinetic bodily feelings such as smoothness and clumsiness, swiftness and slowness [...] we make bodily-felt distinctions." To be able to conceptualise such nuances in movement requires sensitivity to differences in movement qualities. Moreover, in order to delve into and understand other people's movement experiences from their viewpoint we need embodied sensitivity (Parviainen 2002, 148), i.e. a well-developed kinaesthetic empathy. If and when we pay attention to subtle dynamic differences in peoples' movements it can be based on a certain training in being sensitive to differences in qualities of ways of moving. This sensitivity to the movement of others makes the base for kinaesthetic empathy and for what Sheets-Johnstone (1999, 229) calls "kinetic inter-attunement."

In this research it has shown to be significant to the artistic-educational space of dance that kinaesthetic empathic skills are developed through choreographic processes. Kinaesthetic and social empathy seem to be closely connected when the children in creative movement processes and body-awareness exercises open their attentiveness towards others. Parviainen (2002) and also Sheets-Johnstone (1999) can help get closer to what happens at the relational level in the educational space of dance as with the concepts of kinaesthetic empathy and kinetic inter-attunement it becomes evident that movement is foundational in our social relations and processes. Kinaesthetic empathy and kinetic inter-attunement can hence be the foundation for understanding social learning both as socially and learning about being social.

Significance of Enhanced Focus on Embodied Processes when Teaching

The elements that I have pointed out from the teacher's stories are all indicators of certain bodily based "tones of teaching" (van Manen 2002) and of teachers with a certain "pedagogical thoughtfulness" which is "sustained by a certain kind of seeing, of listening, of responding to a particular child or children" (ibid., 10). The stories that I have presented here show that the "tones" of both the practice of the teacher and the dance educator are based on a certain embodied awareness. The themes, that in dialogue with especially van Manen (2002) and Todres (2007), have become visible in their practice point in more general terms to a number of skills that could be relevant to focus on when highlighting embodied processes of teaching in the artistic-educational space. The following would be important:

※ To have a well-developed "kinaesthetic empathy" rooted in the ability to bodily distinguish different dynamic qualities.
※ To be aware, able to 'see' and sense what happens in the space, both in relation to the unique and common of individuals and the social processes.
※ To be able to (re)act on both verbal and non-verbal processes.
※ To be able to wonder, make room for feelings and to create an open atmosphere.
※ To be able to accept resistance and handle situations when oneself and the participants may experience being in a vulnerable position.

Development of Skills and Tools that Foster Embodied Awareness and Confidence to Teach Dance as an Artistic Subject Area

How can we become good at creating 'soulful' spaces that make room for artistic processes? And learn to dare teaching in areas where we may feel vulnerable? As underlined by van Manen (2002, 49):

> a living knowledge of teaching is not just head stuff requiring intellectual work. It requires authentic body-work. True pedagogy requires an attentive attunement of one's whole being to the Childs's experience of the world.

A body-anchored "tone of teaching" is not something which can be developed by reading books or following guidelines. It is "knowledge that issues from the head as well as from the heart" (van Manen 2002, 9). To develop this form of knowledge demands training of attentive awareness of one's whole being. One needs to learn to 'see' with the whole body. Many teachers are very good at this, but we can all become better. How do we learn to *see* the children in an open and curious way? For example by practicing to see differences instead of communalities? As teachers in the area of body, movement and dance, in order to 'understand' other people's movement experiences from their viewpoint we must also continuously practice our awareness and sensitivity to dynamic differences in movement qualities. Dance educators that I have interviewed suggest that this can be done through exercises that focus on paying attention and being bodily aware. They experience that working with body-mind techniques (such as yoga, Feldenkrais, butoh, etc.) and with the movement theory of Rudolph Laban (1963) in practice can help develop abilities to see and feel subtle differences in dynamic qualities.

Closing Remarks on the Development of an Embodied Pedagogy

As phenomenologically-based research, teaching based on phenomenological pedagogical theory seeks to create connections to the participants' experiences. Knowing that lived experiences and feelings are significant in order to understand, actively make use of and develop knowledge makes it important that teaching creates resonance in and among the participants by making what they are presented with meet their lived experiences and involving them emotionally.

An embodied and experience-based pedagogy takes as its point of departure the fact that knowledge about embodied processes is important in relation to the development of didactic approaches that emphasise how children and young people learn to develop strategies for living a good life, feel good and not forget to be engaged in movement in a world where body and movement plays a continuously less important role. The embodied dimension is present in much dance teaching and has been explored by some scholars in the area of artistic education (e.g. Anttila 2003; Bresler 2004; Green 2007; Powell, 2007). This is, however, a dimension which could be explored further and which could also inspire other areas of education in order to create more knowledge and experience about the connections of the body-mind in learning and development in general.

BIBLIOGRAPHY

Anttila, Eeva. 2003. *A Dream Journey to the Unknown: Searching for Dialogue in Dance Education.* Doctoral dissertation. Helsinki: Theatre Academy Finland: Acta Scenica 14.

Bresler, Liora (ed.). 2004. *Knowing Bodies, Moving Minds. Towards Embodied Teaching and Learning.* Dordrecht: Kluwer Academic Publishers.

Depraz, Nathalie; Varela, Francisco J. and Vermersch, Pierre (eds). 2003. *On Becoming Aware.* Amsterdam: John Benjamins Publishing Company.

Green, Jill. 2007. "Student Bodies: Dance Pedagogy and the Soma". In *International Handbook of Research in Arts Education*, edited by Liora Bresler, 1119-1132. Dordrecht: Springer.

Laban, Rudolph. 1963. *Modern Educational Dance.* London: MacDonald & Evans.

Merleau-Ponty, Maurice. 1962. *Phenomenology of Perception.* London: Routledge.

Merleau-Ponty, Maurice. 1968. *The Visible and the Invisible.* Evanston, Illinois: Northwestern University Press.

Moran, Dermot. 2003. "The Problem of Empathy: Husserl and Stein." Lecture 11 March 2003. Copenhagen: Center for Subjectivity Research, University of Copenhagen.

Parviainen, Jaana. 2002. "Kinaesthesia and Empathy as a Knowing Act." In *Dance knowledge — Dansekunnskap. International Conference on Cognitive Aspects of Dance*, edited by Anne Margrete Fiskvik and Egil Bakka, 241-247. Trondheim: Norges Teknisk-Naturvidenskabelige Universitet & Rådet for Folkemusikk og Folkedans.

Powell, Kimberley. 2007. "Moving from Still Life: Emerging Conceptions of the Body in Arts Education". In *International Handbook of Research in Arts Education*, edited by Liora Bresler, 1083-1086. Dordrecht: Springer.

Sheets-Johnstone, Maxine. 1999. *The Primacy of Movement.* Amsterdam: John Benjamins Publishing Company.

Snowber, Celeste. 2002. "Bodydance: Enfleshing Soulful Inquiry through Improvisation." In *Dancing the Data*, edited by Carl Bagley and Mary Beth Cancienne. 20-33. New York: Peter Lang Publishing.

Svendler Nielsen, Charlotte. 2009a. "*Ind i bevægelsen — et performativt fænomenologisk feltstudie om kropslighed, mening og kreativitet i børns læreprocesser i bevægelsesundervisning i skolen*". [Into the Movement: A Performative Phenomenological Field Study about Embodiment, Meaning and Creativity in Children's Learning Processes in Movement Education in School]. PhD.diss., Copenhagen: Department of Exercise and Sport Sciences, University of Copenhagen.

Svendler Nielsen, Charlotte. 2009b. "Children's Embodied Voices: Approaching Children's Experiences through Multi-modal Interviewing." *Phenomenology & Practice* 3(1): 90-93.

Svendler Nielsen, Charlotte. 2012. "Looking for Children's Experiences in Movement: the Role of the Body in Videographic Participation." *Forum Qualitative Social Research* Accessed December, 2012. http://nbn-resolving.de/urn:nbn:de:0114-fqs1203165.

Todres, Les. 2007. *Embodied Enquiry. Phenomenological Touchstones for Research, Psychotherapy and Spirituality*. New York: Palgrave Macmillan.

van Manen, Max. 1990. *Researching Lived Experience: Human Science for an Action Sensitive Pedagogy*. New York: State University of New York Press.

van Manen, Max. 2002. *The Tone of Teaching*. London, Ontario: The Althouse Press.

NOTES

1 The concept of learning that this research leans on is defined in more detail on page 180.

2 There are historical and contextual differences in the use of the words "holistic" and "wholistic" see e.g. http://www.merriam-webster.com/dictionary/wholistic

A CONTEMPORARY DANCER'S KINAESTHETIC EXPERIENCES WITH DANCING SELF-IMAGES

Shantel Ehrenberg

Abstract

In this article philosopher Maurice Merleau-Ponty's (1945, 1968) idea of reversibility is put in conversation with a professional contemporary dancer's descriptions about her dance experience in a particular context. More specifically, the concepts intertwining and chiasm are utilised to conceive of a spatial relation according to her descriptions of a co-construction of the look and feel of her dancing. This article supports the argument that the dancer, at times, embodies two (or more) perspectives at once and yet also, at other times, experiences gaps between what might otherwise be deemed 'internal', such as kinaesthetic experience, and 'external', such as video self-images. The work contributes to a growing area of dance scholarship giving voice to individual dancers' practice and expertise (Rouhiainen 2003; Potter 2008; Ravn 2009; Albright 2011).

Introduction

This article conceives of a professional contemporary dancer's described effort to co-construct the look and feel of her dancing as a spatial relation. The spatial relation discussed here resides with the dancer, who attempts to present movement to an audience (which can be conceived as 'external' to the dancer) *and* who is kinaesthetically sensing and feeling that same movement (which can be conceived as 'internal' and a privately felt experience for the dancer). I primarily utilise philosopher Maurice Merleau-Ponty's (1945; 1968) concept of reversibility to argue that, on the one hand, the dancer indicates a communion with the external performative space in her descriptions — she actively *intertwines* what she sees

Shantel Ehrenberg spinning. Photographer: Frank Peters.

and wants others to see with what she kinaesthetically feels and wants to feel in her dancing experience. On the other hand, the dancer indicates that her kinaesthetic and imaginative experiences, and what she imagines that others see, do not completely melt into each other; there are also times when the dancer confronts *chiasm* between how her movement feels and how her movement might appear from an external perspective. The focus is explicitly on the visual-kinaesthetic relationship in dancer experience.[1] The purpose is to challenge a spatial distinction between what is internal and external in a dancer's perception of her own movement in a specific context, and yet also acknowledge that a gap will always exist with video-based self-reflection because she can never see her own movement from a 'purely external' perspective.[2a]

Methodology

The main fieldwork for the study was a series of three qualitative interviews utilising a phenomenological and sociological approach and including video-based self-reflections. The material presented serves as part of my PhD research project (Ehrenberg 2012).

The methodological approach is phenomenological in that it is informed by Merleau-Ponty's (1945; 1968) phenomenology and designed to investigate a dancer's 'lived experience' (van Manen 1990; Creswell 2007; Ravn 2010). In other words, the interest is investigating how the dancer perceives and describes her dancing and how she makes meaning of her 'lived' dancing experience in terms of phenomenological concepts. As Albright (2011, 8) describes, "Generally speaking, phenomenology is the study of how the world is perceived [...] It is a way of describing the world as we live it — a philosophical approach that positions the body as a central aspect of the lived experience". And as Ravn (2010) clarifies, the aim is to give an *account* of subjective experience, rather than prove an already established hypothesis or theory or to simply give a *subjective account* of experience (Gallagher and Zahavi 2008, 19).

The methodological approach is sociological in that contemporary dance is viewed as a type of culture, and the dancer as a participant in that culture (Crossley 2001). Contemporary dance is conceived as culture in the way Chiseri-Strater and Sunstein (1997, 3) describe it: "An invisible web of behaviours, patterns, rules, and rituals of a group of people who have contact with one another and share common languages". Cynthia Novack (1990, 115) likewise argues that contact improvisation is a shared practice with "core movement values" which distinguish it and in turn impact on those who train, rehearse, teach, and perform in the style. More specifically, I focus on one kind of "somatic mode of attention" in the culture of contemporary dance (Csordas 1993, 135).

The research centres on descriptions of experience, primarily from semi-structured interviews, which is important to both phenomenological and sociological approaches (van Manen 1990; Kvale and Brinkmann 2009). However, the interviews included dancing and watching videos of the dancer's movement and thus also incorporated non-verbal aspects of dance practice. These non-verbal aspects at times inspired unexpected discussion, similar to other sociological research (Mason and Davies 2009). For instance, sometimes what was *not seen* on the video became a talking point for what the dancer kinaesthetically remembered feeling when she did the movement.

General information about the project was provided for the dancer, especially for informed consent purposes, and an interview guide was used, however care was taken to allow the dancer to frame her experience in her own ways as much as possible. By using an open-ended approach, "the participant has a chance to define what is meaningful or important about the dance experience, rather than simply responding to what the researcher feels is important" (Green and Stinson 1999, 102).

The Dancer

The featured dancer is an American national. She was in her mid 20's, had 5 years of professional international dance experience, and was working in a touring professional company in the United Kingdom at the time of interviews.

Interviews

Three interviews of about one hour each were conducted over a one-month period in London, UK. For the first interview the dancer and I met to discuss her particular training background and initial exploratory questions, such as "do you think you can imagine what you look like dancing?" For the second and third interviews, we met in a dance studio convenient for the dancer. The second interview consisted of the dancer doing a short movement phrase (~1 minute), from choreography she was currently rehearsing, then filming the movement, watching the filmed movement, and filming again. Discussion regarding her experience was strewn throughout. For the third interview, we met to discuss her experiences of the previous interviews, in rehearsal after the second interview, and reflections overall. The third interview was also a chance to address questions which emerged during transcription of the first and second interviews, i.e. to clarify meaning (Kvale and Brinkmann 2009).

Interview Analysis

The transcripts[2b] were primarily analysed utilising the approach suggested by Kvale and Brinkman (2009), which is:

> entering into a *dialogue* with the text, going into an imagined conversation with the 'author' about the meaning of the text. The reader here asks about the theme of the texts, goes into the text seeking to develop, clarify, and expand what is expressed in the text. (Kvale and Brinkman 2009, 192)

However, the dancer is not taken as sole 'author'; rather, the transcripts are conceived as intersubjective and fluid. As Kvale and Brinkman advise: "The analysis of the transcribed interviews is a continuation of the conversation that started in the interview situation, unfolding its horizon of possible meanings" (ibid., 193).[3]

The interviews were analysed and re-analysed into key themes, or 'codes', aiming to develop, clarify, and expand on what was discussed (Kvale and Brinkmann 2009). The theme of a visual-kinaesthetic spatial relation emerged after detailed line-by-line reading and several iterations of coding as part of the above analytical approach.

The research is interpretive and not meant to proclaim a universality or 'truth' about dancer experience, but to try to understand some of a dancer's reflective processes in a particular context.

> Interpretive research is most helpful in allowing us to understand how participants in dance are making sense of their experiences…The interpretation offered by the researcher can give readers an opportunity to reflect, to pay attention to what they might otherwise miss in their own [dance] settings. (Green and Stinson 1999, 104)

The research is designed to open out and question what a dancer's individual experiences are like and how she makes meaning and is situated in the dance world (Csordas 1993; Aalten 2004). The fieldwork is also interpreted by me as researcher. As Mason (2002, 52) articulates in her description of qualitative methodologies, "the researcher is seen as actively constructing knowledge about that world according to certain principles and using certain methods derived from, or which express their epistemological position". Indeed, my own experience as a trained contemporary dancer impacts on the research. That is, my previous and current experiences in dance inform the design, fieldwork, and analysis of the project, in keeping with the work of other dance scholars (Rouhiainen 2003; Potter 2008; Ravn 2009, 2010; Albright 2011). My experience gives me a certain kind of knowledge of the field and provides insight to aspects of the research which might go unnoticed if I did not have this particular access (Ravn 2010). For instance, my experience meant that the dancer and I share 'the language' of contemporary dance (Kvale and Brinkmann 2009). In addition, during fieldwork, I engaged experientially with the research problems, such as in my dance classes or in recording and watching my own video self-images. However, being a contemporary dancer also meant that it was important for me to create critical distance to the research and field at times. I continually tried to be aware of biases during design, fieldwork, and analysis (Green and Stinson 1999). I developed a critical stance because, as Coffey (1999, 36) discusses, I wanted "to acknowledge and critically [...] engage with the range of possibilities of position, place and identity" that I have with the data and the field.

Although the research is interpretive, the work is still a representation of what happens in dance practice. Great thought and care was taken to devise the interviews around what happens in practice, such as in rehearsal (i.e. dancing, talking about dancing, videoing dancing, watching oneself dancing on video), and to try to give voice to the processes of the often silent dancer (Green and Stinson 1999, 104).

The video is considered both a rehearsal and a methodological tool for the research. Video is used as a reflective tool in practice at times to attempt to see a representation of what the audience sees; to see one's own dancing from the audience's point of view. Thus, video is used here to interrogate ways in which dancers deal with being performers and performing for audiences.

This article presents ways that a contemporary dancer's process can be articulated in dialogue with Merleau-Ponty's concept of reversibility for the benefit of dance practitioners, educators, and others interested in reflecting on particular types of embodied expertise.

Intertwining

Merleau-Ponty (1968) proposes one idea of reversibility, intertwining, to discuss perception of one's body in the world.[4] He best illustrates his idea of intertwining with the example of two hands touching, more specifically, one touching one's own hand. In sum, he argues that when I touch my own right hand with my left, I both feel the left hand touching my right and yet at the same time I am the left hand which touches the right. He applies the same argument to seer and seen. Seer and seen have a reciprocal, intertwined, and circular relationship in the same way:

> Since the same body sees and touches, visible and tangible belong to the same world...he who sees cannot possess the visible unless he is possessed by it, unless he is of it, unless, by principle, according to what is required by the articulation of the look with the things, he is one of the visible, capable, by a singular reversal, of seeing them — he who is one of them. (Merleau-Ponty 1968, 134-35)

He argues that flesh intertwines the physical object which reflects, such as a mirror, and the eyes that see. "Flesh is inserted into the relation between the one who sees and the thing seen" (Kozel 2007, 35). Subject and object intertwine in these acts of seeing as touching and touching as seeing. "I am both subject and object through the act of seeing" (ibid., 2007, 36).

Not only is perception multi-sensorial, wherein seeing and touching have a constant interrelation, this is so because the body and the world come from the same place — the body "is made of the same flesh as the world" and "this flesh of my body is shared by the world, the world reflects it" (Merleau-Ponty 1968, 248). Macann (1993, 182) interprets this idea in more explicit spatial terms: "there is a tactile dimension to seeing and a visual dimension to touching". Thus Merleau-Ponty argues for a conceptual intertwining of the external space into internal space and vice versa. "I do not see [space] according to its exterior envelope; I live in it from inside; I am immersed in it" (Merleau-Ponty 1968, 248). One dimension is conceived of as 'internal', experiencing, and the other dimension as 'external', acting; the body ('flesh') he conceives of as intertwining the two dimensions. It is the same world, the same body, but different perspectives. Merleau-Ponty uses binary terms to try to explain a unification and, in part, tries to explain intertwining in terms of a spatial relation, as a kind of internalisation of the external, and vice versa.

The dancer's descriptions support the application of Merleau-Ponty's intertwining because at times she indicates that she tries to make the visible tangible and the tangible visible. Watching other dancers, watching the choreographer, and video-based self-reflection, are some of the ways the dancer indicates intertwining of the 'external' space, including the people in it, with her 'internalised' kinaesthetic and imaginative 'space'.

Watching other Dancers

When I ask the dancer about what helps her imagine how the movement might look from an external perspective, she says that seeing other dancers in rehearsal do the same movement helps her. She suggests with this description that she internalises the 'external other' dancers into her own imaginative projections.

> Dancer (D): …so you know I have seen five other people do it all day…so knowing what it looks like on them, but knowing that I look differently, because I am … well, you know, my particular physique; but also because I have a different intention here, or I know that I do that part differently, or maybe something like that; so it's sort

of like this overlay…it is like looking at someone else, but adding your own…sort of…if that makes sense…

She indicates by her description that she takes movement seen on other dancers, 'out there', into her own dancing experiences felt 'in here', and vice versa. For instance, she says, "this overlay…it's like looking at someone else but adding your own". She suggests she knows her own way of doing the movement, from kinaesthetically experiencing her "particular physique" and intentions, and that she then merges this knowing with the viewing of the other dancers. This then helps her re-imagine how she might look and feel doing the movement.

Watching the Choreographer

Likewise, the dancer says she tries to make the movement *feel* the same way as the choreographer *looks* doing it. Similar to the example above, the dancer suggests she takes visual information of the choreographer moving 'out there' and translates that into her kinaesthetic experience 'in here'; however, in this case she more directly states that she tries to imagine how the choreographer feels, and what she thinks he wants her to feel, while she does the movement. The dancer again suggests she "overlays" an imagined idea of the choreographer doing the phrase when she does the movement *and* watches herself do the movement on video. While watching the video recording, she says:

> D: it looks more like [the choreographer] when he is doing it, like, I can see that my flow is correct, if that makes sense, that my…um….he wants it where your leg goes out and then your head, you know, snakes away, so I was actually getting that, which was good, because it should have a lot of pull. Yeah, so, that was the image that I was going for, so, that was, like, 'oh that's correct'.
> Interviewer (I): So, when you say going 'for that image', is that [the choreographer's] image?
> D: Yeah.
> I: Ok, so, what you've seen [on the video] is sort of a matching of….
> D: How it's like, quote unquote, 'supposed to look'.

The dancer indicates that she occupies more than one 'place' at once when she internalises the 'externally perceived' movement and tries to *feel* the movement in the way that the choreographer *looks* doing it. She assesses whether she does it the way she kinaesthetically and imaginatively intended, the way it is 'supposed to look', when watching the video; thus she supports the argument that she has an imagined, 'internal', visual expectation of how the movement should look, based in part on her previous kinaesthetic experience, and in part on how the choreographer looks doing it from an external perspective.

Kinaesthetic Empathy

These two examples distinctly evoke the concept of kinaesthetic empathy which is important to further establish the idea of intertwining as a spatial relation. By kinaesthetic empathy I am referring to the idea which is "…the capacity to participate [via a type of resonance] with another's movement or another's sensory experience of movement…" (Sklar 1994, 16); a type of "virtual participation" with another's kinaesthetic experiences (Reynolds 2007, 14).[5]

In particular, I find Parviainen's (2002) discussion of kinaesthetic empathy, based on Edith Stein's (1970) work, relevant. Parviainen argues that a dancer has a 'body topography' and utilises this topography to understand implicitly that she has her own 'here' and the other dancer has his own 'here', 'over there', in relation to her 'here'. Thus, a dancer understands that another dancer has his own body topography just as she has her own body topography. Empathic projection, Parviainen argues, then allows the dancer to be moved to the body topography of the other dancer — the dancer does not literally move to the other dancer's position, but, via kinaesthetic empathy, shares a kinaesthetic terrain with the other dancer.

The dancer reiterates Parviainen's idea of a shared kinaesthetic terrain when she describes her relationship with the choreographer and the other dancers above, particularly when she says that to understand and explore how to do and feel the movement on her own body, she tries to see and feel the movement in a similar way as she imagines they do, yet still in her own way. For instance, when she states above that "it looks more like when he [the choreographer] is doing it, like, I can see that my flow is correct…" She suggests that she merges the understanding she has of her own body topography, doing and projecting the movement, with the body topography of the other dancers and the choreographer, and vice versa. She creates a kinaesthetic terrain between the 'in here' of her body topography with the (imagined) body topography of the others 'out there'. In addition, when she states above that "so you know I've seen five other people do it all day…so knowing what it looks like on them, but knowing that I look differently [because of my particular physique]…", the dancer indicates that she internalises, kinaesthetically and imaginatively, the 'external' projected movement of the other dancers and also internalises the external eye(s) of the choreographer and an imaginary audience.

Video Self-Reflection

Another way that intertwining came up is when the dancer watches her video self-images made during the interview. When the dancer does the phrase a second time, *after* watching the video, she suggests watching the video impacts on how she does the phrase the second time; in other words, the look of the movement on video affects her next kinaesthetic experience. For instance, in one part of the video, she saw her hips were not moving in a certain way that she wants them to, so, the next time she dances the phrase, she says she intentionally changes the movement of her hips according to what she saw on the video. In another instance, she says:

> D: [...] yeah so that section, I tried to go back to...so, the one where I fall and then drop, its right before I go to the floor at the end...trying to...
>
> I: Oh, is that when you fall on your knee and go into the floor bit?
>
> D: Mmhmm, right before that, I had noticed it looked awkward...and so I tried to kind of smooth that out and go back to whatever it originally was ...it was like "what's the movement there?", because that's why it looked so...it's because it's specific movement, but I have to make [it] clear...[long pause].....I don't know that I succeeded, I wanted to make it more clear, more clarity throughout the movement, but I don't think ...it's not there yet...

The dancer suggests that she directs her kinaesthetic attention while dancing to correct parts of the video image replaying in her memory and imagination, again suggesting internalisation of the external perspective. She indicates that the previous video image and previous rehearsal experiences fold into her next experience of that movement.

The dancer suggests in this description that she is kinaesthetically empathic with her video self-image as well, adapting Parviainen's (2002) idea above. Meaning, the dancer's description suggests the idea that, similar to her perception of 'other' dancers' dancing, she takes the 'other' self-image 'there', in the video, and translates that 'here' into her next lived kinaesthetic experience. The dancer indicates that she takes the body topography of the 'video self-reflected dancer', her 'virtual' body topography, if you will, and maps that into her kinaesthetic, lived, body topography. This is to consider, as dance scholar Susan Kozel (2007) suggests, the extent to which sharing the body through digital devices might allow dancers "to construct collaboratively new physical states or states of conscious awareness" (ibid., 306) and that "through technologies our relations with ourselves shift (our movement, our perceptions, our thought processes) [...]" (ibid., 215). And as dance scholar Dee Reynolds further articulates that:

> Kinesthetic empathy, where spectators identify with the mover and themselves experience virtual movement sensations, is often associated with a logic of 'sameness' and reduction of difference (e.g. Foster, 1999), but virtual participation in the movement of another can also have a de-centering effect, accentuating the 'otherness' of self and the tension between exteriority and interiority. (Reynolds 2007, 14)

In other words, the video self-reflection provides the dancer with an external perspective of her dancing and provides a perspective which is *similar* to how she views other dancers' dancing. She re-interprets the movement according to what she sees of the 'video self-reflected dancer' in a similar way to how she re-interprets the movement after seeing other dancers. In this way she indicates that, to an extent, she creates a kinaesthetic terrain across the 'in here' of her body topography and the 'virtual' body topography of the 'other' 'video self-reflected dancer' as well.

Body Schema and Body Image

Posing the dancer's experiences as intertwining, specifically in relation to kinaesthetic experience and video self-image, reconfigures current phenomenological distinctions between body image and body schema for the case of this dancer (Gallagher 2005). The dancer's examples suggest that body schema and body image intertwine in her experience, in the context of professional contemporary dance practice, which adds to the way these terms are conceptually distinguished according to non-dancer experience. Philosopher Shaun Gallagher, (2005) in his rich discussion of these phenomenological terms primarily in terms of cognitive science empirical research, acknowledges that body image and body schema "behaviorally [...] interact and are highly coordinated in the context of intentional action" (ibid., 24). He also points out that "a distinction [...] will not be adequate to explain all aspects of embodiment" (ibid., 24) and "complexities...will constrain [the concepts'] use" (ibid., 37). One of these he notes is the dancer,

...who practices long and hard to make deliberate movements proficient so that movement is finally accomplished by the body without conscious reflection [the dancer] uses a consciousness of bodily movement to train body-schematic performance. (Gallagher 2005, 35)

It is beyond the scope of this article to discuss these phenomenological concepts in detail as Gallagher does; however, interrogating them briefly helps flesh out the spatial intertwining argued for above in line with Merleau-Ponty's reversibility.[6]

Gallagher's provisional characterisation of body image and body schema, which he elaborates on in his text, is that body image "consists of a system of perceptions, attitudes, and beliefs pertaining to one's own body" (ibid., 24). Or, "more generally, about the image that a person has of their own body" (ibid., 17). That is, body image is related more to "having a perception of (or belief about) something" (ibid., 24), whereas body schema (or schemas) "is a system of sensory-motor capacities that function without awareness or the necessity of perceptual monitoring" (ibid., 24). Body schema is related to "having a capacity to move (or an ability to do something)" (ibid., 24).

Significant to my discussion is the way that body schema is conceptually conceived to interact with body image, according to the dancers' descriptions above. In other words, I want to address the potential frequency in which the dancer's body image, and the "perceptions, attitudes, and beliefs" (ibid., 24) and "image" (ibid., 17) she has of her own body intertwines with her body schema, and accomplishing movement "without awareness" (ibid., 24). The dancer's descriptions do not alone, as they are presented above, challenge a difference between consciously reflecting on the body as it is represented externally, as image, and automatic, habitual, and pre-reflective dance movement, as motor schema.[7] On the contrary, the descriptions above support the argument that the video self-images encourage the dancer to consciously reflect on how the movement is perceived as image, which then impacts on her conscious experience the next time she does the phrase. However, considering that this and similar types of experiences happen frequently in dance practice, it can be argued that the dancer will, over time, integrate her body image with her body schema in a way which is particular to the context of professional dance practice. Considering the specific performative contexts the dancer is frequently put in, such as rehearsals in which the dancer wants to make movement look a certain way, challenges the same kind of interaction between imagining how her body image appears from an external perspective and the motor capacity to accomplish the movement, at least in the way that this interaction of body schema and body image are conceptualised for non-dancers. In other words, becoming skilled as a dancer, often with specific choreographic intent, even in contemporary dance where external image is not emphasised as much as it is in ballet (Ravn 2009), includes many repeated experiences of seeing (or hearing via teacher or choreographer description) how movement appears, or should appear, at the same time as making certain movements habitual. Thus, repeated experiences of the kind of intertwining the dancer indicates above — of video self-images and her kinaesthetic experiences — make it difficult to disentangle conceptually the 'in here' of her body topography from the 'out there' of the body topographies of the 'other'. The dancer provides another way of conceptualising the interaction of body image and body schema for the context of professional Western theatre dance wherein performance, and projecting choreography to an audience, is a central part of the practice. It could be argued that, by the time the dancer becomes professional, she has made a great deal of imagined movement habitual so that though the kinaesthetic feeling of her movement is at the foreground of her attention as a professional, her kinaesthetic feeling of her movement has nevertheless uniquely developed in tandem with an imagined idea of how her body appears.

Chiasm

However, as much as there was an indication of intertwining, the dancer also suggests that there are moments when she is reminded of the separateness between 'external' visual perceptions and her 'internal' imaginative and kinaesthetic experiences. There are also moments when 'a gap' was expressed by the dancer; a gap between her kinaesthetic experience and memory *and* the video self-images. For instance, as she watches the video for the first time, she comments (ellipses represent length of pause while watching video):

> D: Everything leads from my belly and it shouldn't. .... uh......................
> not...well that was ok....it's all the transitions that aren't there ....that's better....................[laughs] [...] I'm not doing it correctly so I'm like "what am I doing?"......................oh that looks better actually than it feels, the end part [little laugh]...

So in this instance of watching the dancer indicates that some of the video 'matches' what she expects to see, e.g. "that's better", but also that there are other parts of the video that do not 'match' and throw open a gap between her previous experience and the video image, e.g. "I'm not doing it correctly so I'm [asking myself] 'what am I doing?'"

At the limits of reversibility, Merleau-Ponty (1968) argues, there is chiasm. Again, he parallels the problem of chiasm with "seeing-seeing oneself" and his touching-touched arguments.

> The untouchable (and also the invisible) for the same analysis can be repeated for vision: what stands in the way of my seeing myself is first a de facto invisible (my eyes invisible for me), but beyond this invisible (which lacuna is filled by the other and by my generality) a *de jure* invisible: I cannot see myself in movement, witness my own movement. (Merleau-Ponty 1968, 254)

It is for the same reason that I cannot 'truly' touch myself (because I am the touching at the same time as I feel the touch) that I also cannot 'truly' perceive my own movement because as I see myself moving I am the seen. A mirror, for instance, is an extension of my body so it cannot help me escape the relation I always have with my body either — the mirror mimics the fissure that I already experience in my body.

> The flesh is a *mirror phenomenon* and the mirror is an extension of my relation with my body...to see oneself, is to obtain such a specular extract of oneself. I.e. a fission of appearance and Being — a fission that already takes place in the touch (duality of the touching and the touched). (Merleau-Ponty 1968, 255-56)

Merleau-Ponty argues that the mirror is a reminder of the otherness that already exists in oneself and that "every perception is doubled with a counter-perception" (ibid., 264). The gap between seer and seen resides within the self, because the body-self is also an other to itself and the mirror (or video) only reminds me of this problem (Parviainen 1998, 64).

Merleau-Ponty thus suggests that the problem of chiasm, particularly in self-reflection, is that the dancer's eyes are in the very body which moves and is perceived; the dancer cannot see externally to her body, because that with which she sees — the eyes — are also part of the body which moves. The dancer will never be able to view the mirror or video image removed from the previous lived kinaesthetic experience and kinaesthetic memory will always colour her viewing; in any self-reflection she views, she is either experiencing at the same time (e.g. mirror), or has experienced that movement previously (e.g. video). "There is always an écart between moving and moved (visual) to the dancer her/himself"

(Parviainen 1998, 66). For a dance performer this can be difficult and frustrating, especially when she wants to be successful showing movement in a particular way.

The metaphor of a gap is particularly significant here because of its spatial reference. For example, these descriptions of a gap felt in experience by the dancer are similar to what one feels when encountering a literal gap (empty space) in the world, such as when walking along a smooth paved road and suddenly coming across a large hole in it, which is an empty space, but causes a kind of gap in the experience of walking and in the perception of 'smoothness' of the road. In the instances of chiasm, the dancer feels a gap thrown open between her kinaesthetic and imaginative memory of the dancing and how the movement appears visually. It is an experiential gap from the dancer's perspective.

Matched/Mismatched Intentionality

While Merleau-Ponty (1945; 1968) often writes about intentionality, particularly in *Phenomenology of Perception,* he does not write about chiasm related to intentionality at great length. Yet, a problem according to the dancer's descriptions, and what impacts on a momentary spatial and functional felt gap between the dancer's kinaesthetic experience and perceived video self-image, is a kind of 'mismatched intentionality'. Chiasm occurs when the dancer's kinaesthetic and imaginative intentions, according to the previous dance experience, are not seen on the video. By intentionality I am referring to the

> …generic term for the pointing-beyond-itself proper to consciousness…Intentionality [having] to do with the directedness or *of-*ness or aboutness of consciousness, i.e. with the fact that when one perceives or judges or feels or thinks, one's mental state is about or of something. (Gallagher and Zahavi 2008, 109)

In the case of the dancer, she indicates that, in the moments of dancing, she directs her dancing consciousness to project the movement in a certain way and chiasm is experienced when she does not perceive this intentional action, as expected, on video. After watching the video the first time, the dancer talks about her transitions not appearing as smooth as she thought they would:

> D: It was alright….[the video] kind of looked how I think I look, basically, but… it's all my transitions…it's like I do a movement and then there is like this fuddly-bit

and then I do another movement and it's not....it's not connected, it's not flowing…
the transition isn't actually starting the next movement…

Thus, chiasm, on occasion, relates to moments when what the dancer intends to
project, and feels and imagines she is projecting, is not matched on the video.

Time and Video Self-Images

Another issue is the differences in duration between perception of video and
mirror reflections. Merleau-Ponty only discusses a mirror, and yet with video
there is a difference *in time*. That is, video self-reflection occurs *after* doing and
experiencing the movement and so this problem of chiasm and mismatched
intentionality with video is distinct because the dancer is able to detach herself
from the dancing experience while watching the video (whereas with a mirror
she is dancing at the same time). The dancer has an additional lens of memory
and expectation in viewing from a still position. She primarily looks for movement which matches what she imagined and intended to project in the past. This
durational distance impacts on the type of disruptions the dancer describes. It
is a more analytical stance because she is passively watching the dancing after
doing it — she does not change the movement or shift her dancing right there
in the moment of watching as she does with the mirror. Video was not around
when Merleau-Ponty wrote his phenomenology which is a good reason why he
does not write about intentionality and chiasm in this way at great length.

Nevertheless, there is a similar shape to the dancer's video interactions and
Merleau-Ponty's ideas of chiasm, even though the latter are predominantly based
on interactions with mirrors. Indeed in one part of the interview the dancer vol-
unteers an experience she had with the mirror:

D: ...the other day [in ballet class] I looked [in the mirror] and I said to myself, "really? that's what my posture looks like?", you know it's one of those....

What is most striking, however, is that no matter how much intertwining the
dancer indicates in the descriptions above, especially with video self-images, this
is always counter-posed with moments of chiasm and the problem that she can
never bridge the spatial divide between feeling her dancing 'internally' and the
perspective she/he/they/it has/have watching, 'externally'.

Becoming

Returning to Merleau-Ponty's (1945) discussion of becoming, in *Phenomenology of Perception,* helps conceive of the dancer's above descriptions of intertwining as a response to chiasm. In other words, moments of chiasm help the dancer distance herself from herself, as well as the choreography, her technique, other dancers, and the video self-image, and re-imagine a new way of being, of dancing, and of being watched from an external perspective. Indeed the dancer suggests this in her own way at one point of the interview:

> D: I like using video to then say, "ok, so, here's what I'm doing", "here's what it feels like I'm doing" and then be able to look at it and say "oh that's still not right there"; to actually be able to see it from the outside perspective is good.

She suggests that her imaginative intertwinings are useful in her goal toward becoming the dancer she wants to become, or be, and projecting the choreography in the way that the choreographer asks and/or she wants to. Macann (1993) summarises this point of view of chiasm as, part of, processes of becoming well:

> But to experience oneself as cut off from the other is to hold open the possibility of a transcending of this isolation, an integration of my being with that of the other which, precisely because it is that of an other, permits me to transcend myself in my very being-with-the-other, to experience myself as something more than I am given to be by myself. (Macann 1993, 192)

Moments of chiasm, though disruptive and potentially troubling at times, can also be conceived as a necessary part of the rehearsal and/or training process of Western theatre dance practice. As Gail Weiss (1999) argues, Merleau-Ponty offers "the development of an intracorporeal spatiality [...] that provides a more positive and productive account of the formation of the body image...as an intersubjective [or intercorporeal] phenomenon that need not be grounded in deception" (ibid., 13). Experiences of chiasm, and gaps being thrown open between kinaesthetically experiencing the dancing 'in here' and imagining or viewing the dancing 'out there', might be conceived as productive toward the dancer imaging other ways to feel *and* do the movement and give the dancer a sense of agency in the choreographic process.

Conclusion

This article presents one contemporary dancer's descriptions about negotiating how movement feels kinaesthetically, 'internally', and how it might appear to others, 'externally', as a spatial relation. The dancer's descriptions indicate one part of Merleau-Ponty's concept of reversibility, which is an intertwining of her 'internal' kinaesthetic and imaginative experiences with 'external' other dancers and video self-images. The dancer's engagement with video self-images in particular add to current conceptions of body image and schema, according to non-dancer experience, and proposes how repeated experiences of intertwining might have long-term impact on the dancer's perceptions of her own movement. The dancer's descriptions also indicate the other side of reversibility, which is that as much as there is intertwining there are also moments of chiasm between kinaesthetic and imaginative experiences *and* video self-images. However, these moments of chiasm do not necessarily have to be conceived only as negative, but may also be conceived as a complex, yet necessary, part of the dancer's sense of becoming, and being, a professional contemporary dancer.

The article, more broadly, adds to a burgeoning discourse about dancers' multi-dimensional and multi-sensorial experiences in practice (Rouhiainen 2003; Kozel 2007; Potter 2008; Anttila 2007; Legrand and Ravn 2009; Ravn 2009). As such, it articulates a specific kind of embodied relation, expertise, and kinaesthetic intelligence, which might be applicable to the realm of embodiment addressed in other disciplines, such as cognitive science (Warburton 2011), or feminist and cultural studies. As Daly (1992) claims,

> Dance studies have much to offer ... precisely because the object of study is the body, that crucial site where culture and nature intersect. The dancing body provides a kind of living laboratory for examining the production of the body: its training, its image, its story, and its ways of creating the world around it. (Daly 1992, 257)

This article examines the living laboratory and productive practices of a professional contemporary dancer, more precisely what is conceived of as 'external and internal space' in certain cases of becoming, and being, a dancer.

ACKNOWLEDGEMENTS
I thank the dancer for her generous participation in the research and two anonymous reviewers and the editors for their invaluable feedback.

BIBLIOGRAPHY

Aalten, Anna. 2004. "'The Moment When it All Comes Together': Embodied Experiences in Ballet". *European Journal of Women's Studies* 11: 263-276.

Albright, Ann Cooper. 2011. "Situated Dancing: Notes from Three Decades in Contact with Phenomenology". *Dance Research Journal* 43(2): 7-18.

Anttila, Eeva. 2007. "Mind the Body: Unearthing the Affiliation between the Conscious Body and the Reflective Mind". In *Ways of Knowing in Dance and Art*, edited by Leena Rouhiainen 79-99. Helsinki, Finland: Acta Scenica 19, Theatre Academy.

Chiseri-Strater, Elizabeth, and Bonnie Stone Sunstein. 1997. *Field Working: Reading and Writing Research.* New Jersey: Prentice-Hall Inc.

Coffey, Amanda. 1999. *The Ethnographic Self: Fieldwork and the Representation of Identity.* London: Sage Publications.

Creswell, John W. 2007. *Qualitative Inquiry & Research Design: Choosing Among Five Approaches.* 2nd ed. Thousand Oaks, CA: Sage Publications Inc.

Crossley, Nick. 2001. *The social Body: Habit, Identity and Desire.* Thousand Oaks, CA.: Sage Publications Inc.

Csordas, Thomas J. 1993. "Somatic Modes of Attention". *Cultural Anthropology* 8(2): 135-156.

Daly, Ann. 1992. "Dance History and Feminist Theory: Reconsidering Isadora Duncan and the Male Gaze". In *Gender in Performance*, edited by L. Senelick, 239-259. Hanover, NH: Tufts University.

Ehrenberg, Shantel. 2012. "The Dancing Self/other: Kinaesthesia and Visual Self Reflection in Contemporary Dance" unpublished PhD, University of Manchester, Manchester, UK.

Gallagher, Shaun. 2005. *How the Body Shapes the Mind.* Oxford: Oxford University Press.

Gallagher, Shaun, and Zahavi, Dan. 2008. *The Phenomenological Mind: An introduction to philosophy of mind and cognitive science.* London and New York: Routledge.

Green, Jill, and Susan W. Stinson. 1999. "Postpositivist Research in Dance". In *Researching Dance*, edited by S. H. Fraleigh and P. Hanstein, 91-123. Pittsburgh: University of Pittsburgh Press.

Green, Jill. 2003. "Foucault and the Training of Docite Bodies in Dance Education". *The Journal of the Arts and Learning Special interest Group of the American Education Research Association* 19(1): 99-125.

Kozel, Susan. 2007. *Closer: performance, technologies, phenomenology.* Cambridge, MA: The MIT Press.

Kvale, Steiner, and Svend Brinkmann. 2009. *InterViews.* Thousand Oaks, CA: Sage Publications Inc.

Legrand, Dorothée. 2007. "Pre-Reflective Self-Consciousness: On Being Bodily in the World". *Janus Head, Special Issue: The Situated Body* 9(1): 493-519.

Legrand, Dorothée, and Ravn, Susanne. 2009. "Perceiving subjectivity in bodily movement: The case of dancers". *Phenomenology and Cognitive Science* 8: 389-408.

Macann, Christopher. 1993. *Four Phenomenological Philosophers*. London and New York: Routledge.

Mason, Jennifer. 2002. *Qualitative researching*. 2nd ed. Thousand Oaks, CA: Sage Publications Inc.

Mason, Jennifer, and Katherine Davies. 2009. "Coming to our senses? A critical approach to sensory methodology". NCRM Working Paper. Realities, Morgan Centre, Manchester, UK.

Merleau-Ponty, Maurice. 1945. *Phenomenology of Perception*. Translated by C. Smith. London and New York: Routledge.

Merleau-Ponty, Maurice. 1968. *The Visible and the Invisible*. Translated by A. Lingis. Edited by C. Lefort. Evanston: Northwestern University Press.

Novack, Cynthia J. 1990. *Sharing the Dance: Contact Improvisation and American Culture*. Madison: The University of Wisconsin Press.

Parviainen, Jaana. 1998. *Bodies Moving and Moved*. Tampere: Tampere University Press.

Parviainen, Jaana. 2002. "Kinaesthesia and Empathy as Knowing Act". Paper read at NOFOD Conference on Dance Knowledge and Cognitive Aspects of Dance, 10-13 January, at Trondheim.

Potter, Caroline. 2008. "Sense of Motion, Senses of Self: Becoming a Dancer". *Ethnos* 73(4): 444-465.

Purser, Aimie Christianne Elizabeth. 2008. "Exploring the embodied bases of being through Merleau-Ponty and dance: a conversation between philosophy and practice". Unpublished PhD, University of Nottingham, Nottingham, UK.

Ravn, Susanne. 2009. *Sensing Movement, Living Spaces: An investigation of movement based on the lived experience of 13 professional dancers*. Saarbrücken, Germany: VDM Verlag.

Ravn, Susanne. 2010. "Sensing weight in movement". *Journal of Dance & Somatic Practices* 2 (1): 21-34.

Reynolds, Dee. 2007. *Rhythmic Subjects*. Hampshire: Dance Books.

Reynolds, Dee, and Reason, Matthew, eds. 2012. *Kinesthetic Empathy in Creative and Cultural Practices*. Bristol & Chicago: Intellect. Original edition.

Rothfield, Philipa. 2005. "Differing Phenomenology and Dance". Topoi 24: 43-53.

Rouhiainen, Leena. 2003. *Living Transformative Lives: Finnish Freelance Dance Artists Brought into Dialogue with Merleau-Ponty's phenomenology*. Helsinki: Acta Scenica, Theatre Academy.

Sklar, Deidre. 1994. "Can bodylore be brought to its senses?". *The Journal of American Folklore* 107(423): 9-22.

Stein, Edith. 1970. *On the Problem of Empathy*. 2nd ed. The Hague: Martinus Nijhoff.

van Manen, Max. 1990. *Researching Lived Experience: Human science for an action sensitive pedagogy*. Edited by P. L. Smith, *SUNY Series in the Philosophy of Education*. Albany: State University of New York Press.

Warburton, Edward C. 2011. "Of Meanings and Movements: Re-Languaging Embodiment in Dance Phenomenology and Cognition". *Dance Research Journal* 43(2): 65-83.

Weiss, Gail. 1999. *Body Images: Embodiment as Intercorporeality*. New York and London: Routledge.

Zahavi, Dan. 2011. "Varieties of Reflection". *Journal of Consciousness Studies* 18(2): 9-19.

NOTES

1   There are a number of other multi-sensorial relationships that could be explored in dancer experience, but because of the complexity of these relations, only one is focused on here.

2a   It is beyond the scope of this aticle to sufficiently address the problem of 'the power of the visual' and how visual self-reflection might contribute to normative behaviour and self-surveillance, such as has been argued by Green (2003). Instead, I emphasis the lived experience described by the dancer in hopes to later more fully "test whether experience bears out genealogy" (Rothfield 2005, 51). See also Ehrenberg (2012, 168-184).

2b   About seventy-five pages of dialogue.

3   See also Aimee Purser's (2008) use of the metaphor of 'conversation' and Leena Rouhiainen's (2003) of 'dialogue' between contemporary dancers' described experiences in practice and Merleau-Ponty's phenomenology.

4   Although there is a great deal of controversy about Merleau-Ponty's (1968) ideas in the *Visible and Invisible*, in large part because it is an unfinished text (Rouhiainen 2003, 114), his ideas on reversibility, namely intertwining and chiasm, are useful as a springboard to think through the dancer's descriptions.

5   For more on the topic of kinaesthetic empathy, see Reynolds and Reason (2012).

6   For a more thorough phenomenological discussion of the problem of body image and body schema related to dance experience see Legrand (2007) and Ravn (2010).

7   By 'pre-reflective' I refer to experience which goes unnoticed, rather than being 'unconscious', following the position that pre-reflective experiences "are initially like nothing for us, and that they only enter the realm of phenomenality when subjected to a reflective process that allows us to become aware of them" (Zahavi 2011, 9).

AUTHORS' BIOGRAPHIES

Sarah Rubidge is professor of Choreography and New Media at the University of Chichester, UK. An artist-scholar specializing in choreographic installations, her work has been shown nationally and internationally. She is regularly invited to give keynote papers at international conferences and has published extensively since 1992, with several book chapters currently in print. Her most recent publications are "How Art matters" (2010) in *Athens Dialogues,* an interactive online Scholarly Journal published by Harvard University, and "Towards an Understanding of Choreography and Performativity in Interactive Installations" in *Contemporary Choreography: A Critical Reader* ed. J. Butterworth and L. Wildschut, Routledge (2009).

Lena Hammergren is professor of Dance and Theatre at the Department for Musicology and Performance Studies, Stockholm University, and the University of Dance and Circus, Sweden. Her research projects encompass dance historiography, and dance and cultural theory. Her latest publications include "The Power of Classification", in *Worlding Dance*, ed. S. L. Foster, Palgrave Macmillan (2009), and "Dance and Democracy in Norden", in *Dance and the Formation of Norden: Emergences and Struggles*, ed. K. Vedel, Tapir AP (2011). Since 2007, she is a member of the Board of Directors of the Society of Dance History Scholars.

Hanna Järvinen is a lecturer at the Performing Arts Research Centre of the Theatre Academy, Helsinki. As a cultural historian, she is particularly interested in the historical epistemology of dance and the pedagogy of dance history. She has published in e.g. *Dance Research*, *Dance Research Journal* and *The Senses and Society*.

Diane Oatley has a Masters in comparative literature from the University of Oslo, with an area of specialization in gender issues and expressions of the body in poetic language. Expressions of embodiment have been a consistent theme in her dance practice, research, and academic and literary publications. She is an independent scholar, writer and translator and has since 2005 lived between Oslo, Norway and Jerez de la Frontera in Andalucia, Spain where she is studying flamenco.

Susanne Ravn is associate professor at the Institute of Sports Science and Biomechanics at the University of Southern Denmark. Her research is based on an interdisciplinary combination of praxis, ethnography and phenomenology. She focuses on how dancers shape their bodies, senses and techniques differently and on the methodological challenges related to employing phenomenological thinking into ethnography. Among her recent publication are *Sensing Movement, Living Spaces,* VDM Verlag (2009) and 'How to explore dancers' sense experiences? A study of how multi-sited fieldwork and phenomenology can be combined' in *Qualitative Research in Sport, Exercise and Health* (2012). Ravn is chair of the Nordic Forum for Dance Research (NOFOD) board.

Camilla Damkjaer. After finishing her doctorial dissortation on Gilles Deleuze's philosophy and the choreography of Merce Cunningham, she has focused mostly on contemporary circus, working with studies of specific aspects of some of the circus disciplines as well as the changes that the art form has been and is still undergoing. She is currently working as a visiting senior lecturer at the Department of Musicology and Performance Studies, Stockholm University, and at the University of Dance and Circus, Stockholm.

Leena Rouhiainen is a dancer-choreographer and dance scholar, who has worked as a professional contemporary dance artist since 1990. She and her artistic collaborators have received several national awards for their artistic work in Finland. She completed her doctoral dissertation that addressed the problem of the freelance dance artist through a phenomenological perspective at the Theatre Academy Helsinki in 2003. Since then she has worked as a postdoctoral researcher and academy research fellow at the same institution. She was the head of the research project Challenging the Notion of Knowledge (2005 – 2007, Theatre Academy) and Intuition in Creative Processes (2008 – 2011, Aalto University, School of Arts, Design and Architecture). Now she is professor of artistic research at the Performing Arts Research Centre of the Theatre Academy Helsinki.

Paula Kramer is an outdoor dancer and practitioner-researcher, currently completing her PhD in Dance at Coventry University. Site-specific performance, awareness based improvisation, somatic practices and a postgraduate degree in political science all influence her research, practice and teaching. She studied intensively with Bettina Mainz (Berlin) and later completed the foundation year of the 'Walk of Life' training with Helen Poynor in the UK. Both practitioners are connected to the Amerta Movement and trained with Suprapto Suryodarmo. Paula was a member of the AHRC network project "Reflecting on Environmental Change through Site-Based Performance" (2010 – 2011) and is editorial assistant of the Journal of Dance and Somatic Practices.

Charlotte Svendler Nielsen, assistant professor and head of education studies at the Department of Exercise and Sport Sciences, research group *Body, Learning and Identity,* University of Copenhagen. MSc in Physical Education and Dance studies from the University of Brighton, UK. Has published articles in Danish, English and Spanish. Co-editor of a number of books and of the recently founded *Nordic Journal of Dance – practice, education and research.* Member of the executive board of Dance and the Child International (daCi) and chair of the scientific committee daCi/WDA Global Dance Summit 2012.

Shantel Ehrenberg received an Overseas Research Scholarship to conduct her PhD, *The Dancing Self/Other,* at the University of Manchester, UK. Her research focuses on dancer self-reflection via various technologies, such as mirrors, point-light displays, and video. Shantel earned her MFA at the University of California, Irvine, USA and her MSc at Trinity Laban, London, UK.